Coaching and
Mentoring at Work

Coaching and Mentoring at Work

Developing Effective Practice

Mary Connor and Julia Pokora

 Open University Press

Open University Press
McGraw-Hill Education
McGraw-Hill House
Shoppenhangers Road
Maidenhead
Berkshire
England
SL6 2QL

email: enquiries@openup.co.uk
world wide web: www.openup.co.uk

and Two Penn Plaza, New York, NY 10121-2289, USA

First published 2007

Reprinted 2007

A catalogue record of this book is available from the British Library

ISBN-10: 0335 221769 (pb) 0335 221777 (hb)
ISBN-13: 978 0 335 22176 9 (pb) 978 0 335 22177 6 (hb)

Library of Congress Cataloging-in-Publication Data
CIP data applied for

Typeset by RefineCatch Limited, Bungay, Suffolk
Printed and bound by Bell & Bain Ltd., Glasgow
www.bell-bain.demon.co.uk

The *McGraw·Hill* Companies

Contents

Authors and contributors

Dr Mary Connor

Mary is an independent consultant working as a coach, mentor, trainer and supervisor. Until recently she was a Principal Lecturer in Individual and Organization Development and Head of Programme for an MA in Leading Innovation and Change. For several years she has been involved in mentor development and research. She has an interest in ethical issues and is currently a member of the York Research Ethics Committee (NHS). She is also a member of the Research Governance Committee, in the Department of Health Sciences at the University of York.

Julia Pokora

Following an early career with BP and Exxon, Julia established an independent organization and management development consultancy, and at that time was an Associate with Ashridge Teamworking Services. She now has 20 years' consultancy experience and has worked with private and public sector organizations. Recently, she has focused on leadership development for teams and individuals, and on developing mentoring and coaching capability in the Health Service. She holds an MSc Occupational Psychology and a Graduate Diploma in Counselling.

Wendy Briner is Leadership Coach and Researcher at Ashridge Management College. From 1998, she was Director of Leadership Coaching for the Ashridge Leadership Process, introducing coaching as an integrated part of leadership development. Since then her main activities are designing, participating in and researching leadership coaching processes for the BBC, further education colleges, the World Health Organization and other private and public sector organizations.

Malcolm Hurrell is Vice-President of Human Resources at AstraZeneca UK. His experience spans both public and private sectors. He worked for several years in education and then moved into management development, working for Tioxide in the UK and then for three years establishing the new organization and operating plant in Malaysia. On his return to the UK he joined the pharmaceuticals industry where he has been an active practitioner of coaching and mentoring in business.

Shaun Lincoln is Programme Director of Coaching and Mentoring at the Centre for Excellence in Leadership (CEL). This has involved setting up a national network of CEL external coaches and mentors for the learning and skills sector and running internal coaching and mentoring programmes for senior management teams. He is an executive coach and human resource specialist with 15 years' international experience in leadership and management development, coaching and mentoring.

Dr Nancy Redfern is Specialty Dean Director at the Northern Postgraduate Medical and Dental Deanery, and Consultant Anaesthetist in Newcastle upon Tyne Foundation Trust. Since 1995, she has led the Northern Mentoring Programme for doctors, dentists, nurses and other healthcare professionals. As well as developing mentoring in her own trust she has worked with other deaneries, royal colleges and trusts in the UK, helping them to set up their own mentoring programmes and schemes.

Acknowledgements and permissions

We could not have written this book without the support of our immediate families, Bruce, Anna-Maria, Luke and Martina.

We thank all those who have contributed. Wendy Briner, Malcolm Hurrell, Shaun Lincoln and Dr Nancy Redfern generously shared their experiences and expertise. Dr Nuala Brice and Dr Pamela Hartshorne offered valuable perspectives from the outset. Terry Connor advised on graphics. Sue Covill and Alan Phillips commented on draft chapters, and Hilary Farrar helped with a case example.

Professor Gerard Egan's ideas continue to inspire developments in our thinking. Much of our coaching and mentoring work has evolved from the vision and opportunities provided by Dr Geraldine Bynoe and Helen Jones. Dr Nancy Redfern has been a powerful champion of mentoring networks and training, and she and Dr Marie Johnson are our valued associates in the Mentoring Development Group. We appreciate the enthusiasm and commitment of all the sponsors and facilitators with whom we work.

Finally, we thank our clients, and all those who have coached and mentored us, whether knowingly or otherwise. Learning with you, and from you, has informed and encouraged us in writing this book.

We are grateful to Thomson Learning for permission to reproduce Figures 1.1 and 1.2 from *Essentials of Skilled Helping* (ISE with Skilled Helping Around the World: Essential Thoughts on Diversity Booklet), *Managing Problems, Developing Opportunities*, 1st edition by Egan © 2006. Reprinted with permission of Wadsworth, a division of Thomson Learning: www.thomsonrights.com, fax 800 730 2215.

We are grateful also to the Chartered Institute of Personnel and Development (CIPD) and to Kate Hilpern, for permission to quote from *Coaching at Work*, Volume 1, Issue 2, January/February 2006: 42–5. The extract quoted is from an article 'Bringing Law to Order' written by Kate Hilpern.

Introduction

Why this book? Why now? For many years we have been involved in coaching and mentoring at work, both informally and in more structured settings. We have worked together, delivering training, for more than a decade. We could not find a book that addressed, practically, all of the aspects of coaching and mentoring at work that seemed important to us. Feedback from colleagues and participants was that they wanted a text which encapsulated the learning from training programmes and sustained them when they were on their own, back at work, trying to be effective coaches and mentors. So, we have written this book partly for them.

But we also wanted to have a voice. We noticed the ongoing debate about coaching versus mentoring, and in our everyday experience we found that these activities had much in common. Conversations with colleagues in both the public and private sector revealed that while terminology differs, there is considerable overlap in what many coaches and mentors actually do. So, this book seeks to identify the common ground, as well as to acknowledge the differences, and to explain the key principles that underpin both effective coaching and effective mentoring.

Another reason for writing this book was to answer some frequently-asked questions. Each chapter answers a specific question that might be asked by clients, coaches or mentors. We wanted to write a book that was accessible to busy people. A book that was full of practical examples and exercises, with ideas that could be used in everyday life and work.

Anyone who has tried to coach or mentor knows just how demanding the work can be. The notion that someone can be helped to help themselves, rather than being told or advised what to do, is a straightforward enough idea. It is not always easy to execute, and it is not commonplace. Spend a few minutes or hours listening to the conversations around you in the workplace, and you will see what we mean. Nevertheless, when we have experienced skilful coaching and mentoring from friends, colleagues and professionals, it has made a world of difference. So, we hope that this book will guide the reader in developing their skills and making a difference.

We are concerned about maintaining high standards in an emerging profession. The serendipity that has been prevalent in the provision of coaching and mentoring services is being rightly challenged by the current focus on competent, ethical and professional practice. In this book we aim to make the connection between ethical principles and everyday practice.

Both of us have benefited from wise mentors and coaches, some formal and some informal, some qualified and some not. We hope in this book to share something of their wisdom, which we have found to be more easily 'caught' than 'taught'. It is not easy to capture the essence of wisdom, but we experience a wholeness and a sense of deep integrity in those coaches and mentors who have, in brief moments as well as over many sessions, transformed aspects of our lives.

Finally, we wanted to write a book which could be read by those who were not sure whether they wanted a coach or mentor. Much is said about the partnership nature of coaching and mentoring, yet most of the literature and most training programmes focus on only half of that partnership! The book is written, therefore, for the other half, the 'clients', as well as for coaches and mentors.

The structure of the book

The book answers the questions asked by coaches, clients and mentors. It is aimed at anyone who is interested in coaching and mentoring in the workplace. You may be manager, professional, employee, HR specialist, trainer, consultant, student or full-time coach or mentor. We describe the key principles of effective coaching and mentoring at work, and illustrate these principles in practice. We apply a tried and tested framework to coaching and mentoring, with interactive examples illustrating skills, techniques and the development of the coaching or mentoring relationship.

Four contributors describe coaching and mentoring initiatives at work and we consider how a coaching and mentoring culture can be developed in organizations. We also address the important topics of coach and mentor training and ethical and professional issues.

Chapter 1 provides an overview of the similarities and differences between coaching and mentoring at work, and some well known coaching and mentoring frameworks. It proposes a definition of effective coaching and mentoring at work and outlines the nine key principles which underpin effective coaching and mentoring.

Chapters 2 and 3 focus on the individual coaching or mentoring relationship, looking at how the reader can become an effective coach or mentor (Chapter 2) or client (Chapter 3). These chapters contain, as well as illustrative examples, interactive exercises which involve you as a reader.

Chapter 4 looks at the advantages and disadvantages of using a framework, and describes in detail one framework, The Skilled Helper. Chapter 5 shows how the framework and key principles are applied. You are invited, as a reader, to become the coach in a case example, which illustrates the development of the learning relationship and shows how you might use the stages of the framework and the key skills. Interactive prompts involve you in using the framework and managing the relationship. Chapter 6 invites you to become the mentor in an interactive case example, and this case example focuses upon ethical and professional issues and questions for supervision or mentor support.

Chapter 7 presents some useful tools and techniques to support coaching and mentoring, with a discussion of their advantages and disadvantages.

Chapter 8 answers questions about training and development for coaches and mentors, giving you some ideas about what to look for in training programmes.

Chapter 9 focuses on ethical and professional issues and gives practical case examples for you to reflect upon. Ethical standards are linked with our own key principles for effective practice.

Chapter 10 uses case material from contributors who are actively involved in coaching or mentoring initiatives. They work in a variety of organizational settings. We reflect with them on their experiences and lessons learned, and draw together some key questions for assessing the coaching and mentoring culture in your organization.

Inevitably, constraints of time and space have meant that we have not been able to do justice to all coaching and mentoring topics. In particular, we are aware that team coaching, diversity and supervision are subjects which would each fill a book, and we would advise the reader to consult the bibliography (see p. 236) for additional material on all of these topics.

We hope that the book will be a source of encouragement and stimulation whether you are a client, a coach, a mentor, a sponsor or someone who may one day be one of these!

A note about examples used in the book

We have tried to make this book as practical and relevant as possible and so you will find that it is full of examples, many of which are interactive. Confidentiality in coaching and mentoring is key. For this reason, throughout the book we have constructed the examples rather than use client case material.

1 What is effective coaching and mentoring at work?

- Introduction
- Nine key principles for effective practice
- Coaching and mentoring: similarities and differences
- Coaching and mentoring: some approaches and frameworks
- Competence and professionalism
- Beyond competence: the wise coach or mentor
- Summary

Some client experiences

Jim: I was rambling on about my inability to cope with a work challenge. My coach said, 'We've worked together for quite a while now and I know that you are someone who can cope, actually, can do more than that, someone who can rise to the occasion.' I was stopped in my tracks. Here was someone who truly believed in me, more than I could believe in myself at that moment, someone who could see my strengths when I couldn't.

Eva: What I have appreciated about you as my mentor has been your professional acuity and care. It has sustained me in the middle of change. I have always felt stronger having spoken to you. I have known that while showing me kindness, you retain objectivity and your keen eye is ever vigilant! Your generosity of spirit and action has kept me afloat.

Alistair: As my coach, you're the one person I can rely on to tell me the truth about myself. You don't beat about the bush. You say it how it is. But I trust you to have my interests at heart. It has made me realize that it's OK to be straight with people, rather than bottling things up, and it has changed the way I manage at work. It's made a big improvement. I'm clearer with people and they with me, and the team is much stronger.

Sue: I was talking about the future, as I often did, and my mentor suddenly looked up and said, rather wistfully, 'You know, I'm wondering when you are going to get started on the future.'

Introduction

Our aim in writing this book is to capture the essence of coaching and mentoring, and to energize and equip the reader, whether as coach, mentor or client, and whether coaching or mentoring formally or informally.

Many managers and professionals offer coaching and mentoring within their organization or professional group. Even more of them use the skills in leading and managing individuals and teams. In addition, there are an increasing number of full-time coaches and mentors who are providing coaching and mentoring to people at work. This book is addressed to all these groups, and to those who are not yet actively involved in coaching and mentoring. It is for those who want to find out more about what is effective coaching and mentoring and who:

- are already coaching or mentoring;
- are seeking coaching or mentoring;
- want to become a coach or mentor;
- use coaching or mentoring skills or approaches at work;
- are participants on coaching or mentoring programmes or courses;
- are in coaching or mentoring networks;
- train or supervise coaches and mentors;
- want to establish or review the provision of coaching and mentoring in their organization or profession;
- are engaged in leadership, management or professional development.

Terminology can be problematic and so in this book we generally use the term 'client' to refer to the person with whom the coach or mentor is working. We acknowledge that in real life they may be called, for example, mentee or colleague.

There has been considerable debate in the literature about the differences and similarities between coaching and mentoring. It is evident that what is described in one organization as mentoring might be known in another as coaching. Recently, with acknowledgement that use of the terms varies widely, attention has turned to the common ground, and it is to this that our book is addressed.

What is this kind of helping, this kind of learning, which is not teaching or telling or advising or instructing? Whatever it is, it is certainly in demand, and the number of coaching and mentoring articles, journals, special interest groups and courses has risen, seemingly exponentially, in recent years.

Box 1.1 A definition of coaching and mentoring

Coaching and mentoring are learning relationships which help people to take charge of their own development, to release their potential and to achieve results which they value.

We argue that a learning relationship is central to both coaching and mentoring, which are more than just a set of activities or skills. Through the relationship, the client develops and changes, as, indeed, does the coach or mentor.

We see coaching and mentoring as complementary activities. Both help people to take charge of their own development. The coaching or mentoring relationship facilitates insight, learning and change. Through this relationship, potential is identified, possibilities become reality and tangible results are delivered. Coaching and mentoring help a person to see the present as a springboard to the future, and to be strategic about their own development. Whether the person seeks help with a specific work issue of current concern, or a longer-term career question, the coach or mentor will facilitate exploration, help in the formulation of goals and provide support while action is implemented.

Nine key principles for effective practice

Effective coaching and mentoring are underpinned by nine key principles (summarized in Figure 1.1). These principles, derived from our experience, have informed and guided our coaching and mentoring work. We introduce them here. In subsequent chapters, they are explored in greater depth and linked to case examples and interactive exercises.

1 The learning relationship is at the heart of change

The central principle is that learning and change occur through the relationship with a coach or mentor. Coaching and mentoring are not just an interaction, an event, an opportunity. Two people meet. They share knowledge, values, attitudes, skills and experience. They engage with one another, they relate to one another and if the coaching and mentoring is effective, they *connect* with one another. Dialogue is important in establishing and maintaining the connection. In a learning dialogue there is, on both sides, a willingness to share perspectives, to listen, to understand, to be open to new ideas and to take joint responsibility for the conversation and the outcomes.

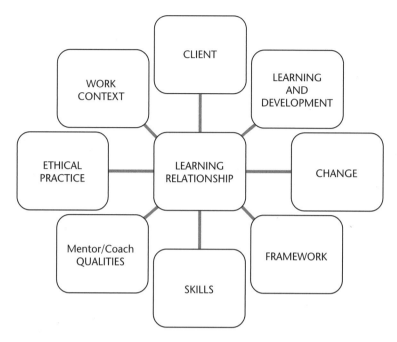

1   The LEARNING RELATIONSHIP is at the heart of change
2   The CONTEXT is work
3   The CLIENT sets the agenda and is resourceful
4   The COACH OR MENTOR facilitates LEARNING AND DEVELOPMENT
5   The OUTCOME is CHANGE
6   The FRAMEWORK for the change process provides movement and direction
7   The SKILLS develop insight, release potential and deliver results
8   The QUALITIES of the coach or mentor affirm, enable and sustain the client
9   ETHICAL PRACTICE safeguards and enhances coaching and mentoring

Figure 1.1   Nine key principles for effective practice

Dialogue sustains the connection and the relationship, and leads to learning and change. It follows, therefore, that the learning relationship is a partnership, and not an activity imposed by one person on another.

2 The context is work

This book is about coaching and mentoring at work. The focus is on the relationship with an individual client, although the principles apply also to team coaching. The client may want or need to improve their work performance in the short term, or they may be concerned with broader issues of personal, professional and career development. Short- and long-term issues are often interrelated. The effective coach or mentor values the client as a whole person within their work context. The focus of coaching and mentoring is the client's present and future experiences, problems, opportunities and development. The best results are produced when the focus is on developing strengths and resources, rather than on remedying deficits.

The effective coach or mentor knows enough about the work context to be able to facilitate exploration of issues and is aware that opportunities and resources in the workplace differ from person to person. Because effective coaching and mentoring release potential and deliver results, they can be enabling for those who have experienced being marginalized or disadvantaged at work.

Coaching and mentoring are not career patronage, neither are they counselling or therapy. The effective coach or mentor agrees with the client the boundaries of their coaching or mentoring work, and is aware of other resources and networks beyond these boundaries.

3 The client sets the agenda and is resourceful

Centre stage in the learning relationship is the client and their agenda. Being centre stage and being the focus of attention can be both challenging and empowering for the client. Some clients are reluctant, some are eager. Where a client is referred, there is an agenda with which the client may or may not agree. Some clients have clear goals, some only vague ideas. In all cases, the start point of the effective coach or mentor is to work with the client to help them figure out what they want. This process, the first step in facilitating the client's learning and development, may be relatively straightforward, or perhaps one of the most demanding parts of the coaching and mentoring relationship. However, unless the client chooses to be a partner in the learning relationship, and has a sense of purpose, the relationship cannot be successful.

Once the agenda is clear, the task of the coach or mentor is to help the client to identify and use the resources, both internal and external, that will enable them to change and develop. Affirming the client's resourcefulness, and communicating this affirmation to the client, is an important role. When the client seems to lack energy or focus, or bright ideas or direction, or creative alternatives, the coach or mentor can communicate hope and possibility, and work with the client to make these real. A coach or mentor can enable a client by believing in them at times when the client's self-belief falters.

4 The coach or mentor facilitates learning and development

The coach or mentor is a facilitator, not an instructor. They support and challenge the client to learn and to develop. The client learns by acquiring new awareness, insight, skills, ideas and knowledge. Development involves integrating their learning into the way they are. It is more important that a facilitator asks good questions than that they have 'right' answers. Good questions provoke new perspectives and change in the client.

The effective facilitator reviews the learning relationship and the learning process, and does not take these for granted. The client is asked about what they are learning and how they are learning it, and what might help their learning and development. The effective facilitator finds learning methods that suit the client. They help the client to clarify how they learn best, and how to make coaching or mentoring work for them.

Finally, the effective facilitator understands the importance of what happens between sessions. They know that coaching and mentoring sessions should be the catalyst for learning and action, not the substitute.

5 The outcome is change

Coaching and mentoring are about change. The client achieves something that they care about, that makes a positive difference in their working life or career. The real significance of change should be judged in relation to the client agenda and their goal. A change in attitude for one client may be just as important as a major job promotion for another. Insight and understanding are important in coaching and mentoring in so far as they lead to change. Of course, change is hard work. Change provokes resistance, a normal reaction to facing up to difficult issues. Resistance can be viewed as a sign that the coaching or mentoring dialogue is on track and that it is touching on important issues for the client. Effective coaches and mentors work with client resistance, rather than try to overcome it. They use resistance to help the client to clarify their values and their goals, and to explore what will help or hinder them in making changes.

6 The framework for the change process provides movement and direction

The coaching or mentoring journey is about change in relation to the client agenda. The framework provides a map for the journey, for both client and coach or mentor. It does not fully describe the landscape of the coaching or mentoring journey, but rather it provides reference points and a sense of direction. It can help if either party gets stuck or loses direction. The coaching or mentoring framework should be used with a light touch, or even set aside, if that is what would be most helpful for the client in their journey. It should not be used to constrain or limit exploration of the landscape.

7 The skills develop insight, release potential and deliver results

The effective coach or mentor uses skills which bring to life the coaching framework and enable the client to develop insight and release their potential. The effective coach or mentor is competent, using the skills in an integrated way within the learning relationship, not merely applying a set of competences. The skills communicate the coach or mentor belief in, and valuing of, the client. Wise and judicious use of the skills ensures a balance of support and challenge, of reflection and action. The effective coach or mentor has a repertoire of tools and techniques which they offer appropriately to the client to support their learning and development.

8 The qualities of the coach or mentor affirm, enable and sustain the client

The distinctive style, personality and values of the coach or mentor are prized by the client. This unique blend of attitudes, values, knowledge and experience can be shared as 'self'. Moreover, when the chemistry between coach or mentor and client really works, there is a sense of deep connection. The paradox of this connection is that it is not tangible and yet it is powerfully present and effective in bringing about client self-belief, hope, courage and action.

Effective coaches and mentors are not only smart, but also wise. They have the wisdom to make sound judgements on what they see, hear, and experience in the learning relationship. They communicate caring, valuing, respect and empathy. They model a way of being which is both human and professional. This is not deliberately 'taught' but is often 'caught'. Learning is not just 'from' the coach or mentor, but also 'with' and 'through' them. It is this third type of learning, 'through the coach or mentor' that is often overlooked. Yet it may be the most powerful learning of all! The client who experiences affirmation and positive challenge from a coach or mentor is likely to value themselves more. The more a client values themselves, the more they value others. This then impacts on both personal and professional relationships.

9 Ethical practice safeguards and enhances coaching and mentoring

The client is safeguarded if ethical principles inform and guide practice. Such principles might include: respect for client autonomy; faithfulness to promises made; acting in ways which are beneficial to the client; not doing harm; and acting fairly. When these principles are in operation there will be an openness and transparency in the coaching and mentoring relationship. This not only safeguards the interests of both parties, but also enhances the quality of their work together. Effective coaching and mentoring start with clear expectations, continue with a negotiated working agreement, include ongoing evaluation and finish with well-prepared endings. Ethical coaching and mentoring are informed by legal requirements and professional codes of practice. Working within agreed limits and boundaries helps the client to feel secure, for example in relation to issues of confidentiality or conflicts of interest.

Coaching and mentoring: similarities and differences

Our definition of coaching and mentoring is that:

> both coaching and mentoring are learning relationships which help people to take charge of their own development, to release their potential and to achieve results which they value.

In this book, we view coaching and mentoring as complementary. Both activities help people to take charge of their own development. The coaching or mentoring relationship facilitates insight, learning and change. Through this relationship, potential is identified, possibilities become reality and tangible results are delivered. The Chartered Institute of Personnel and Development (CIPD) notes the many similarities between coaching and mentoring, not least in the 'one-to-one relationship that provides an opportunity for individuals to reflect, learn and develop' (Jarvis 2004: 19). Both coach and mentor want to improve performance and deliver results, but the coach may be more hands-on in achieving specific skill development and change.

Some of the similarities between coaching and mentoring have been identified by Zeus and Skiffington (2000) (see Figure 1.2). Both activities base their assumptions on basic values and beliefs: that humans have the ability to change; that they make the best choices available to them; that coaching is not a quick fix: 'it is a journey where the process of learning is as important as the knowledge and skills gained' (p. xv). Zeus and Skiffington talk about coaching and mentoring as essentially a conversation where learning takes place through asking the right questions rather than providing answers. This leads to personal and professional transformation and reinventing oneself.

- Both require well-developed interpersonal skills
- Both require the ability to generate trust, support commitment, generate new actions through listening and speaking skills
- Both shorten the learning curve
- Both aim for the individual to improve his or her performance and be more productive
- Both encourage the individual to stretch, but can provide support if the person falters or gets out of his or her depth
- Both provide support without removing responsibility
- Both require a degree of organisational know-how
- Both focus on learning and development to enhance skills and competencies
- Both stimulate personal growth to develop new expertise
- Both can function as a career guide to review career goals and identify values, vision, and career strengths
- Both are role models

Figure 1.2   Similarities between coaching and mentoring

Source: Zeus and Skiffington (2000: 18)

If coaching and mentoring have much in common, then what are the differences?

Mentoring is often viewed as 'off-line help by one person to another in making significant transitions in knowledge, work or thinking' (Megginson *et al.* 2006: 4). The mentor may be someone more experienced or senior in the organization or profession, and often their services are offered, and taken up, voluntarily. Mentoring may be either short term or long term. It will usually involve personal, professional and career development. The mentor may be internal or external to the organization. Megginson *et al.* (2006) highlight two contrasting models of mentoring: sponsorship versus developmental. In sponsorship they note that the mentor actively champions the client with the primary motive of career or professional success. In developmental mentoring the mentor may be experienced but not necessarily more senior and the aim is to facilitate learning rather than provide answers. Parsloe and Wray (2000: 82) summarize mentoring as 'a process which supports learning and development, and thus performance improvements, either for an individual, team or business. Mentoring is usually understood as a special kind of relationship where objectivity, credibility, honesty, trustworthiness and confidentiality are critical'.

Within coaching the emphasis is changing. Experience is showing that the positive approach of helping clients to 'astound themselves' is far more beneficial than the type of managerial coaching which focused upon remedying performance deficits. Rogers (2004: 7) puts it this way: 'The coach works with clients to achieve speedy, increased and sustainable effectiveness in their lives and careers through focused learning. The coach's sole aim is to work with the client to achieve all of the client's potential – as defined by the client'.

Table 1.1   Differences between coaching and mentoring

Mentoring	Coaching
Ongoing relationship that can last for a long period of time	Relationship generally has a set duration
More informal and meetings can take place as and when the mentee needs some advice, guidance and support	Generally more structured in nature and meetings are scheduled on a regular basis
More long term and takes a broader view of the person	Short term (sometimes time-bounded) and focused on specific development areas/issues
Mentor is usually more experienced and qualified than the client. Often a senior person in the organization who can pass on knowledge, experience and open doors to otherwise out-of-reach opportunities	Coaching is generally not performed on the basis that the coach needs to have direct experience of their client's formal occupational role, unless the coaching is specific and skills-focused
Focus is on career and personal development	Focus is generally on development/issues at work
Agenda is set by the client, with the mentor providing support and guidance to prepare them for future roles	The agenda is focused on achieving specific, immediate goals
Mentoring revolves more around developing the mentee professionally	Coaching revolves more around specific development areas/issues

Coaching is increasingly being used by organizations to promote a learning culture, where leaders and managers are expected, as part of their role, to coach their own staff, who in turn learn coaching skills so that they can coach others. Coaching may be used as a tool for managing performance. Executive coaching is often provided externally and may be linked with leadership and management development programmes. The CIPD (Jarvis 2004: 19) has produced a useful summary of some differences between coaching and mentoring, as shown in Table 1.1.

We broadly agree with these distinctions although we are aware that, in real life, 'specific development issues' (coaching) and 'developing the client professionally' (mentoring) are often inextricably linked.

Several writers distinguish between the coach and mentor in terms of short- and long-term goals: 'A mentor is someone appointed or chosen to help another with the achievement of their long-term goals and career rather than immediate performance issues' (Downey 2003: 202). Downey portrays the effective coach as one who can turn potential into performance to achieve fulfilment and satisfaction at work. But this 'effective' coaching is not necessarily instruction; it is more like facilitation. He argues for a 'predominantly non-directive approach, an approach that evokes excellence, in which learning is intrinsic and satisfaction derives from the pursuit and achievement of meaningful goals' (p. 19).

Coaching and mentoring: some approaches and frameworks

There are several different approaches and frameworks used in coaching and mentoring. Most are useful with individuals and with teams. Some of these are derived from psychological approaches to motivation, learning, goal-setting and behaviour change. Those derived from Gestalt (Bluckert 2006), NLP (Vickers and Bavister 2005) and cognitive-behavioural approaches (Neenan and Dryden 2002) are examples of this. Some have developed from sports psychology, particularly in relation to understanding behaviour and performance (Bandura 1969). Recent approaches emphasize two elements. Firstly, the approach needs to be easily understood and used by busy leaders and managers who are expected to be internal coaches and mentors in organizations. Secondly, the focus should be on the talents and resources of the client and the possibilities in their work context, rather than on problems and deficiencies. Here are some frameworks which reflect these emphases.

The GROW model

Whitmore (2002: 173) writes about coaching for performance. His emphasis is GROWing people, performance and purpose. He argues that performance coaching is based on context, skills and sequence. He unpacks this framework thus:

- Context: awareness and responsibility
- Skills: effective questioning; active listening
- Sequence: Goals   What do you want?
            Reality   What is happening now?
            Options   What could you do?
            Will   What will you do?

This is a straightforward model starting with eliciting client wants and expectations and assuming that the client can articulate a goal or goals for a specific session or for several sessions. This is followed by reality checking, including others perspectives and auditing resources available to the client, to achieve the goal. This helps the client and coach to assess whether it is a workable goal. Options for change and action are then considered and finally commitment to the goal is examined. Downey (2003) has a useful diagram of the GROW model which includes an added first stage called 'topic', where the client says what it is that they want to talk about.

The Skilled Helper

This model of helping (Egan 2006) has been adapted for coaching and mentoring. It is a solution-focused framework for the coaching and mentoring process. There are three stages: What's going on? What solutions make sense for me? How do I get what I need and want? The aim is to help the client to identify valued outcomes and then to decide how to make them happen. The model is underpinned by core values of respect and genuine concern for the client. Basic communication skills are used to offer a balance of support and challenge throughout. The model is designed to be easily understood and used by the client, with the coach or mentor as facilitator of the learning and change process. We describe this framework in more detail in Chapter 4.

There are several features in common between Whitmore's GROW model and The Skilled Helper model (Egan 2006). Both approaches highlight the important relationship between wanting and acting. Both focus on articulating specific goals for change. Both test commitment to the goal. However, the differences are in the sequencing of events. In Egan's approach, for example, commitment is tested before options and action plans are drawn up. In both models it is important for the coach to be flexible and not to follow the model rigidly.

The Inner Game

Several writers on performance coaching and executive coaching base their ideas on the 'inner game'. Much of the thinking in performance coaching originated from ideas that worked in sports coaching, including the difference between the outer game of performance and the inner game of attitude and psychology. Gallwey (2000) states that the outer game of improved performance will only be possible if there are changes in the inner game of thinking and feeling. The power of positive thinking is at the heart of the inner game approach. Downey (2003:11) explains further. The important concept is:

potential minus interference is equal to performance

He explains that what prevents performance is the interference that comes between potential and achievement. He cites the following examples of interference that gets in the way and stops us focusing on the goal: fear, lack of confidence, the 'be perfect' driver, anger, boredom and frustration. The coach helps the client to identify interference and then to work with it to minimize its impact. This leads to 'relaxed concentration' which in turn leads to performance that flows. The relationship between this approach and sports coaching is obvious. We all recognize that 'flow' in excellent performance, whether it be tennis, playing the piano or producing an academic essay. This approach benefits from psychological understandings in relation to motivation, reinforcement, cognitive-behavioural understanding, rational-emotive behaviour and applied social psychology.

Non-directive approach

The non-directive approach has developed from research into the characteristics of effective helping relationships carried out in contexts such as health, therapy and education. In this approach, the coach or mentor is viewed as a facilitator of learning. The emphasis here is on providing the right conditions to enable the client to become their own coach. The conditions for effective facilitation are belief in the client and communication of genuine interest, respect and empathy. Some non-directive coaches and mentors do not use models and frameworks because they view these as not completely 'client-centred'.

In contrast, Downey is one writer who discusses using a non-directive approach with a model. He calls his approach non-directive coaching: 'Coaching is the art of facilitating the performance, learning and development of another' (2003: 21). He advocates the non-directive approach in relation to both the inner game and the GROW model. With regard to the GROW model he suggests adding the letter T. One axis of the letter T signifies expanding and one axis signifies focusing. He recommends the use of these two activities in relation to the GROW sequence. Both expanding and focusing would be done in a non-directive way. The method described next is another example of a non-directive approach.

Co-Active coaching

An interesting model which is different from those above is co-active coaching. It is based on four cornerstones which the coach uses to inform practice, rather than stages and steps to move through in sequence. This approach emphasizes client fulfilment, balance and process, and the way these contribute to success in work and life, and does not focus solely on work performance. The helping relationship is described as a designed alliance which requires listening, intuition, curiosity, action learning and self-management. The approach is non-directive. These are the four cornerstones (Whitworth *et al.* 1998: 3):

1 The client is creative, resourceful and whole.
2 Co-active coaching addresses the client's whole life.
3 The agenda comes from the client.
4 The relationship is a designed alliance.

When using this model the coach or mentor can focus all their attention on listening to the client and moving in whatever direction the client wants, rather than being distracted by having to check where they are in the pre-scribed steps or stages of other models. Experience and skill are needed to 'freewheel' in this way with the client.

Solution-focused coaching

This approach focuses on practicality and simplicity. It is positive and prag-matic (Jackson 2002). The methodology is based on: finding what works and doing more of it; finding what doesn't work and doing something different; finding and using resources; building on successes; and 'taking great care to simplify issues as far as possible, but no further' (www.thesolutionsfocus.com). The website gives six SIMPLE principles:

1 Solutions – not problems.
2 In-between, not individual – the action is in the interaction.
3 Make use of what's there – not what isn't.
4 Possibilities – from past, present and future.
5 Language – simply said.
6 Every case is different – beware ill-fitting theory.

The website also gives six solutions tools:

1 Platform – where are we starting from?
2 Future perfect – what if the problem went away overnight?
3 Scaling – where are we now?
4 Counters – whatever helps us forward.
5 Affirm – what's already going well?
6 Small actions – tiny steps that make the big difference.

Leaders and managers are finding this approach to be a straightforward way of helping colleagues to change and develop. It moves beyond looking at problems in the present situation to a focus on solutions which are within client resources.

Team coaching

While this book is primarily about the learning relationship between the individual client and the coach or mentor, in team coaching the client is the team. Team coaching is growing in popularity as a way of developing high-performing teams, which are often found to: have a high level of agreement about their common purpose; work closely together; be 'mutually accountable'; and value and respect individual differences (Katzenbach and Smith 1993). Team coaching helps to align individual, team and business goals.

Definitions of team coaching vary; however, many authors agree that task performance and team development are both important components of successful coaching. Therefore, a team coach might be expected to have an understanding of group dynamics (Bion 1961), group development (Tuckman 1965) and team roles (Belbin 2003), as well as an awareness of organization culture and its impact on team learning (Pokora and Briner 1999).

Team coaching may be used to: encourage more effective team-working in an existing group; accelerate the development of a newly-formed group into a working team; enhance the coaching skills of team leaders; and develop cross-boundary teams which address organization-wide issues. Barden (2006: 6) outlines how team coaching may be useful with a team which already works together:

> a team may be coached when it is no longer aligned with its purpose. That can occur when: the organisation has changed its focus and a key team is having difficulty in following suit. The team leader has – perhaps through individual coaching – become aware of the need for a new purpose and the team needs to revisit its key elements. When the team members are no longer acting towards a single purpose because of, for example, conflicting interests or systemic imperatives.

In practice, the team coach will often work with one or more management sponsors, as well as with the team, and may coach individual team members to enhance their participation in the team. Executive coaches may start work with an individual executive client and then be asked to coach the client's team. In this scenario, boundary issues and conflicts of interest need to be clarified.

The skill of the team coach includes: firstly, aligning team outcomes and achievements with business expectations and targets; secondly, maximizing the distinctive contributions of individuals to ensure high performance of the team as a whole. Although team coaching can be cost-effective and rewarding, it is not an easy option. It requires sensitivity, skill and adaptability on the part of the team coach who manages a variety of individual and organizational expectations and interests.

Competence and professionalism

This section will be of particular interest to those who are working full-time as coaches or mentors and to those who may be considering purchasing coaching or mentoring services.

Competence, capability and capacity

The effective coach or mentor not only possesses specific skills or competences, but is also reflective in their practice and aware of their ongoing learning and development needs.

The term 'competence' refers to the ability to perform to recognized standards. It implies successful performance against specific criteria: that, for example, a coach or mentor is 'fit for purpose'. While competence approaches have become popular in recent years, questions about their limitations have been raised, particularly in the context of management development. One of the issues highlighted by Burgoyne is 'whether performance can be divided into competencies and then re-integrated' (1990: 20), and the same question may be asked about coach and mentor competences. The undoubted usefulness of competence frameworks in coaching and mentoring must be weighed against the risks of reductionism through the adoption of a 'tick box' approach to professional competence. One way of addressing this concern is to ensure that accreditation processes assess capability and capacity as well as competences.

Fraser and Greenhalgh (2001: 799) note the focus on competence in traditional approaches to education and training and assert that 'in today's complex world we must educate not merely for competence but for capability (the ability to adapt to change, generate new knowledge and continuously improve performance)'. This is a challenge for coach and mentor training, and accreditation. Robust training and accreditation procedures should reflect not only competence at a given moment, but also capability, including the individual's willingness to monitor their own performance and development, and to be self-reflective. In addition to competences and capability there is the importance of developing the capacity of each coach or mentor. This will vary according to individual resources at any given time. Supervision and support, alongside continuing professional development, are the processes which enhance the ongoing capacity to learn, enabling the coach or mentor to maintain professional effectiveness:

> when competencies are assessed as observable behaviours or skills, successful performance depends on the capacity and capability of that coach or mentor to learn. This capacity develops continuously and so good accreditation procedures will require that the coach or mentor is not accredited on one occasion only, but that there will be evidence of ongoing learning and development in order for accreditation of professional registration to be valid.
>
> (Easterby-Smith *et al.* 1999: 150)

Competence frameworks

Some of the professional bodies concerned with coaching and mentoring have developed competence frameworks, and examples are listed below. Our nine key principles reflect these competences.

- The International Coaching Federation (ICF) has outlined four clusters of core competences: setting the foundation; co-creating the relationship; communicating effectively; facilitating learning and results (www.coachfederation.org).
- The European Mentoring and Coaching Council (EMCC) highlights eight areas of competence: process; domain-specific knowledge; expertise and focus; professionalism and building a practice; values and approach; communication; facilitating; and self. This list has been taken from a report of the EMCC Competency Research Project Phase Two Output, June 2005 (www.emccouncil.org).
- The Employment National Training Organization (ENTO) is developing a new occupational standards framework for coaching and mentoring. This will identify the key values and principles of practitioners, key purposes and key functions of coaching and mentoring at work. It will provide a basis for vocational qualifications for coaching and mentoring in the workplace and in the community (www.ento.co.uk).

Accreditation

There is currently considerable interest in the accreditation of both coach and mentor training programmes, and of individual coaches and mentors. This reflects a concern that those hiring or receiving coaching and mentoring services should know how to judge the competence and professionalism of the individual coach or mentor. In the UK, the CIPD has produced guidance (Jarvis 2004) for organizations wishing to develop coaching and mentoring and wishing to know what to look for when hiring coaches or mentors.

Some professional organizations offer accreditation: either for individual coaches and mentors, or for training programmes, or both. An example of training accreditation is the EMCC UK Quality Award for coach and mentor training, which has four award categories: Foundation; Intermediate; Practitioner; and Master. An example of individual accreditation is the ICF credentialing programme, with three designations: Associate Certified Coach; Professional Certified Coach; and Master Certified Coach. There are website addresses of some professional organizations in the Appendix.

Beyond competence: the wise coach or mentor

The wise coach or mentor is competent, but continuously strives to increase the capacity to learn: about themselves; about their clients; and about the organizations and contexts in which clients live and work. Every experience is viewed as a learning opportunity and this ensures continuous incremental improvement.

When we have experienced as clients the help of a 'wise' coach or mentor, what has made the difference? For one of us, it was like this:

> My mentor didn't yet have any formal qualification, but he was just a natural. So natural that I didn't even notice his skills, but they were certainly there. He wore his experience lightly, keeping himself in the background. But he was himself, he showed me that he cared, he gave me enough time to talk and think. He could be very challenging too, but he seemed to consider carefully when to be like this, watching me closely for my reactions. I was continually surprised at how well he seemed to know me. He would know just when to push and just when to hold back. I felt like I was moving along with my issues and targets and he seemed to intuitively understand when to say something and when to just stay quiet.

> I wanted to learn from him. I chose him because he knew how my organization worked and he knew the politics there. He shared his own experiences with me so that I felt I was with a real person and not just some 'professional front'. He gave me time. That was a big thing. I needed to make some changes at work, but wasn't ready at first. He never tried to move me too quickly into making those changes. There were moments when something would click. I may have suddenly

opened my eyes to something and we would share that eureka moment together, he would be as pleased as I was! There were other difficult moments when we seemed temporarily to be not connecting and he would take his time, give me time, and then ask if I would like to look at what was happening, together. This we would do and each time, although difficult, it brought our relationship to a new level of trust. The times when I sensed he had really understood, he didn't need to say anything, there was just a certain twinkle in his eye, a smile, a quizzical expression and in that moment I knew he was 'with' me.

So, what is this wisdom? Competences are tangible, wisdom less so. Wisdom seems to be about discerning what is needed at any one time and using sound judgement. To make such wise choices, the coach or mentor needs to be able to tune into the client on several levels at once. Such sensitivity, combined with caring, seems to give a special quality to the relationship. People talk about 'connecting', being 'in tune with one another', moving together 'in harmony'. These expressions attempt to capture the essence of being with a coach or mentor who is wise as well as competent, who trusts their instincts and intuition as much as their knowledge and skills, who knows when to hold back and do nothing, and when to move forward and actively engage, who uses all their senses to communicate a real belief in the worth and capacity of the client to achieve what they want and value.

Summary

In this chapter we have:

- Explored the similarities and differences between coaching and mentoring and reviewed how they are described in the literature.
- Proposed a definition of coaching and mentoring as learning relationships which help people to take charge of their own development, to release their potential and to achieve results which they value.
- Explored nine key principles which underpin effective coaching and mentoring.
- Introduced several coaching and mentoring frameworks which focus on developing client talents and resources.
- Described some approaches to defining and assessing coach and mentor effectiveness.

2 How can I be an effective coach or mentor?

- Introduction
- Why be a coach or mentor?
- Helping without telling
- Creating a working agreement
- Beginnings, middles and endings
- Building a learning relationship
- Using a framework
- Some core skills
- Knowing yourself
- Supervision, support and development
- Summary

Introduction

You may be wondering whether you want to be a coach or mentor. Perhaps you use coaching or mentoring skills at work, and are reflecting on your effectiveness as a leader and manager. Alternatively, you might be interested in finding out more about coaching or mentoring and how they might fit into your organization or profession. This chapter helps to answer these questions. It addresses, from the coach or mentor perspective, questions about roles and responsibilities, and about how coaching and mentoring work in practice. It focuses on individual coaching and mentoring.

In the chapter, the qualities and characteristics of effective coaching and mentoring are described. We explore how a learning relationship is established, sustained and concluded. We explain how those who offer coaching and mentoring can enhance their practice and continue their development.

The chapter includes practical exercises, checklists and activities, as well as case examples designed to illustrate key points.

Where you see this sign, there is an activity for you to complete or a question to consider. The questions are written assuming that you are already involved in coaching or mentoring. Even if you are not yet actively involved, you can reflect on what your answers might be. Sometimes, possible responses are provided, sometimes not.

Table 2.1 shows how each chapter section is linked to one of the key principles introduced in the previous chapter, so that you can see how principles relate to practice.

Table 2.1   Chapter sections and key principles

Section of chapter	Key principle
Why be a coach or mentor?	The context is work
Helping without telling	The client sets the agenda and is resourceful
Creating a working agreement	The coach or mentor facilitates learning and development
Beginnings, middles and endings	The outcome is change
Building a learning relationship	The learning relationship is at the heart of change
Using a framework	The framework for the change process provides movement and direction
Some core skills	The skills develop insight, release potential and deliver results
Knowing yourself	The qualities of the coach or mentor affirm, enable and sustain the client
Supervision, support and development	Ethical practice safeguards and enhances coaching and mentoring

Why be a coach or mentor?
Principle: the context is work

In the previous chapter we defined effective coaching and mentoring, and explored not only the differences but also the common ground and key principles. In both coaching and mentoring, one person is helping another with either short-term work issues or longer-term development. Their relationship, a learning relationship, is crucial in releasing potential and producing results. One person becomes a trusted and faithful guide for another on a journey of personal, professional and career development which may last for many weeks or months or for only one meeting. However, the objective is the same: to help someone to achieve change which they value. In this way, coaching or mentoring helps an individual to be strategic and proactive in their work and career.

While reading this description you may have recognized work you are already doing, or work in which you would like to be involved. Take a moment to reflect on your motivation by completing the following activity.

 Complete the following sentences.

- I'm interested in coaching/mentoring because . . .
- What I have to offer as a coach or mentor is . . .
- My experience of coaching or mentoring (whether formal or informal) is . . .
- Being strategic, in my view, means . . .
- Being proactive, in my view, means . . .
- How I help others to be strategic and proactive is . . .
- I value coaching/mentoring because . . .
- What I hope to achieve as a coach or mentor is . . .
- The benefits for those I coach or mentor are . . .
- The benefits to the organization/profession are . . .

What do your answers tell you about your motivation? What do you want to achieve though coaching or mentoring? Any surprises? Any questions raised?

A survey of mentoring research papers from the USA and Europe reported that benefits were not only for the client (40 per cent) and the business (33 per cent), but also for the mentor (27 per cent) (Garvey and Garrett-Harris in Megginson *et al.* 2006: 30).

Jo, an experienced mentor, and someone who is keen to continue her own development: I've helped several people to get clearer about their career direction, and to become more focused in their thinking. Now, I see them in the company being successful and fulfilled. I hope I've put something back into the organization and encouraged people. I know how important that is, and it wasn't around for me when I started out. I've also learned a lot about myself, for example, just because I'm more senior doesn't mean that I know what's best for someone. Mentoring has made me more aware of how I deal with people in general at work. It does take time and sometimes competes with other demands, but for me it is worth it.

Ryan, an HR advisor, who wants to become a coach: I enjoy working one-to-one with people, and I seem to be good at helping people develop their interpersonal skills, particularly influencing and negotiating. I think coaching may become a career for me. I'll need to invest in training and gain more experience. However, it's of increasing importance in my firm and I imagine that eventually I might head up a specialist coaching service within the organization.

Nita, a manager: Coaching is an integral part of my job, not a separate function. I'm responsible for developing my staff, and we have a very positive coaching culture here. I see myself as a resource for staff, and the benefits are tangible in terms of performance. What are the costs to me? Well, reminding myself that sometimes I need to bite my tongue and not rush in and fix things!

You can see from these examples that costs and benefits may be both tangible, for example, time or money, and intangible, for example, personal satisfaction.

  What are the benefits for you of coaching or mentoring? What are the costs?

The context of coaching and mentoring is personal, professional and career development. While coaching is often focused on the shorter term and performance, and mentoring on the longer term, in practice they may overlap. The checklist below will help you to identify any likely focus of your work.

  Look at the topics below. Which are you likely to be involved in when coaching or mentoring? With which are you most confident?

Typical mentoring topics
- Considering career choices
- Managing job transition
- Managing career
- Professional networking
- Organization politics

Typical coaching topics
- Developing people skills
- Managing conflict
- Developing as a leader
- Handling pressure
- Improving performance

While the boundary between coaching and mentoring may overlap, it is useful to understand what both coaching and mentoring are *not*. In this book we distinguish them from *patronage* and from *therapy*.

In patronage, a senior person nurtures the career advancement of a more junior colleague. The patron may act as sponsor for the individual and may use their own professional networks to aid the person's career or development.

In therapy, a qualified professional helps to resolve difficulties which may be long-standing, personal and not necessarily work-related. In coaching and mentoring the focus is the individual at work, and while this may encompass personal issues, coaches and mentors do not work in depth in the same way as therapists might. Table 2.2 describes some of the ways in which coaching and mentoring differ from patronage and from therapy.

Table 2.2   Patronage, coaching and mentoring, and therapy

Patronage	Coaching and Mentoring	Therapy
Career advancement	Problems and opportunities	Personal problems and difficulties
Career-related	Work- or career-related	Issues may be deeply personal/ unrelated to work
Patron unlikely to be trained	Coach/mentor uses skills and framework	Therapist is qualified practitioner
Boundaries less important – may be intentional overlap	Coach/mentor agrees boundaries	Therapist operates strict boundaries
May be same profession/ field	Coach/mentor may be internal or external	Therapist is outside organization
Patron opens doors	Emphasis is on learning and development	Therapist helps to resolve problems
Patron is senior	Coach/mentor may be senior/colleague/junior or independent	Therapist is impartial and independent
Patron may not expect feedback on relationship	Feedback is part of learn- ing relationship	Amount/use of feedback dependent on therapeutic approach

Emil, a mentor: I've been a mentor for several years for fellow professionals, helping them think through career and work issues. Of course, I have a good network and sometimes that's helpful, but my role isn't to smooth their career paths. In fact, over the years one or two have left the firm, and that's been right for them, they've moved on to new pastures. Occasionally someone brings something more difficult that I'm not skilled to deal with and we talk about how they might get help elsewhere, for example a relationship issue or a health problem.

Angela, a coach, has recently made the transition from counselling to coaching, and she reads a list of coaching competences. One item on the list refers to paying attention to the client's agenda, rather than what the coach thinks the agenda should be. Angela is an excellent listener and she is respectful and pays close attention to what her clients say. However, she has been wondering whether she sometimes steers her coaching clients, in her words, 'to get to the bottom of things' rather than 'to get on with things'. She says, 'Maybe I'm more interested in insight than action plans!' She decides that in future she will pay particular attention to this, and ask clients what they will focus on in each session, and what outcomes they want.

 In what ways are coaching or mentoring in your context different from patronage or therapy? Are there any topics that might arise which you think are outside of the scope of coaching or mentoring?

Helping without telling

Principle: the client sets the agenda and is resourceful

Coaching and mentoring are different from the kind of helping which many of us offer in everyday working life, when we give advice to people who benefit from our expertise. Expertise is at the heart of many jobs and professional roles. The expert helper, by and large, knows more about the topic under discussion than the person being helped.

Coaching and mentoring are different and equally valuable ways of helping. As a coach or mentor, although we may have experience and expertise, our primary role is to help the client to find for *themselves* resourceful ways forward in dealing with issues facing them. The coach or mentor helps the client to explore their own experience and resources. In this way, the client gains insight and generates their own solutions. These are more likely to be successful than solutions proposed by a coach or mentor. Table 2.3 illustrates the differences between expert and coach or mentor.

Table 2.3 Some differences between coach or mentor, and expert

Expert	Coach or mentor
Emphasis on knowledge	Emphasis on process
Expert insight is key	Helping skills are key
Provides direction	Provides a 'map'
Puzzle-solver	Facilitator/enabler
Gathers/analyses information	Enables information-gathering
Facts and logic	Facts, logic and feelings
Diagnoses the problem	Explores the problem
Problem can be solved	Problem can be managed
Definition of problem is objective	Definition of problem is subjective
Expert knowledge important	Client insight important

Coaching and mentoring focus on the way in which a situation is a problem or an opportunity *for the person experiencing it.* Here are some examples of client questions. These might arise in an everyday work conversation, for example between a manager and an employee, or in a more formal coaching or mentoring session.

- How can I develop my career?
- Is this job offer right for me?
- How can I manage a difficult colleague?
- How can I be more assertive at work?
- What's the best way to deal with this demanding customer?
- I'm concerned that the project won't be finished on time – what should I do?

The right 'answers' or ways forward with these dilemmas depend to a large extent on the person asking them. There is no single correct answer. These are examples of what Revans (1983), writing about action learning, called 'problems'. He uses the word 'problem' to describe an issue which can be dealt with in different ways by different people. He sees 'problems' as different from 'puzzles', which have one best or 'right' answer. Expert advice is important, and even vital, in finding the right answer to a puzzle, for example a complicated medical diagnosis. Problems, however, require a different approach, and coaching and mentoring can be more appropriate than expert advice. Of course, expert knowledge can play a part in coaching or mentoring; however, the role of the coach or mentor is primarily that of a facilitator or enabler, rather than a puzzle-solver.

Jack is an interpersonal skills coach for senior executives. He works with clients to help them clarify their skill development needs at work, and the factors which are both helping and hindering their development. He is familiar with research on effective communication, and can share this information with clients. Jack works with each client to identify the areas where the client is willing and able to try out new skills.

Ruhani, a social worker, uses a coaching approach to develop the trainees who work in her unit. She is highly experienced, and has realized over the years that 'if I just tell them the answer, or do it for them, then they don't really learn. I have to get alongside my staff, to ask them good questions which challenge and develop them, and of course I'm there as a safety net if they need it.'

So, coaches and mentors seek to enable and empower, rather than to offer expert answers or advice. The next exercise will help you to reflect on how much expert helping you do at work.

 How much expert helping do you do at work?

To what extent are the following usually true, or not?
In what ways are coaching or mentoring different from your usual helping role?

- I know more about the subject than the person I'm helping
- People seek out my knowledge and experience
- I know what facts or information are relevant to solving things
- I ask questions to gather relevant information
- I can usually give people the right answer or some options
- I gather facts and evidence
- I sort irrelevant from relevant information
- I generate options for people
- I propose solutions for people

Finally in this section, Shaun Lincoln (Sulaiman 2006) suggests an activity for those considering becoming mentors: 'Test yourself. Can you listen for more than ten minutes without giving advice? If you can't you might want to hesitate.' We would add here that, after hesitating, you might seek some training or development to enhance your skills!

Creating a working agreement

Principle: the coach or mentor facilitates learning and development

A clear working agreement is the foundation of a productive learning relationship. It describes how the coach or mentor and client will work together, and so gets their relationship off to a good start. Importantly, it frees up both parties to focus their energy and attention on learning and development, rather than being distracted by unresolved questions or concerns. The coach or mentor models transparency by being open about what they can offer, and what they cannot, and how they want to work. This builds trust in the relationship and creates the climate for learning. The working agreement is an opportunity to:

- agree with the client how you will work together;
- clarify any uncertainties;
- find out what they expect and want;
- answer their questions;
- deal with contractual issues.

Many people use coaching and mentoring skills in their management role at work. When the skills are used within a managerial or professional role, a formal agreement may be unnecessary because the learning relationship is already established. However, where coaching or mentoring is an off-line activity, whether the coach or mentor is internal or external, a more explicit agreement is useful.

> **Robert, a mentor in local government:** At the start of mentoring I ask the client quite a few 'what if' questions: What if we talk about something that can't be kept confidential? What if you don't turn up for a session? What if we think mentoring isn't proving useful? By asking these questions, I involve them in reaching an agreement, rather than imposing it.

> **Meg, a board-level coach:** Over the years I've learned that it's helpful to be clear about the things, not many, which are non-negotiable. For example, sessions always take place away from the client's office, to free them up from job demands, and always during working hours, so that they see coaching as part of their real work. On the other hand, it is important to find out about, and be responsive to, how the client learns best, and be flexible about what will help them.

Below is a list of items which might be included in a working agreement for coaching or mentoring. Work through the list and note your response to each item. Would you include all these items in a working agreement? Would you add any? Which do you view as negotiable? Non-negotiable?

Practical
- ☐ Pre-coaching or mentoring introductory session
- ☐ Location – where will you meet?
- ☐ Frequency – how often will you meet? Minimum/maximum number of sessions
- ☐ Length of session – what would you prefer? Agree to?
- ☐ Payment – how much? Payment procedure?
- ☐ Cancellation – policy for missed session? What if the client is late?

Working relationship
- ☐ Preferred ways of working together
- ☐ Tools and techniques you might use
- ☐ Your values and the learning relationship
- ☐ Balance of support and challenge you will offer
- ☐ Feedback – 360-degree, other?
- ☐ How client learns best
- ☐ Framework or model you use
- ☐ Your expectations – work outside of sessions

Professional
- ☐ Your qualifications
- ☐ Your experience/references
- ☐ Your responsibilities: legal, to the sponsor, to your profession or organization
- ☐ Any possible conflicts of interest?
- ☐ Note-taking – who takes? Who keeps? For how long?
- ☐ Supervision – your arrangements

Ethical
- ☐ An explicit working agreement
- ☐ Built-in ongoing review
- ☐ Confidentiality: extent and limits
- ☐ Clear role boundaries
- ☐ Ending session

Beginnings, middles and endings

Principle: the outcome is change

The coaching or mentoring relationship helps the client to achieve successful change. At each stage; beginning, middle and end, the coach or mentor works to support and enable client change. To do this, they create a safe and effective partnership, maintain productive ways of working and manage the ending. So, at each stage of the relationship, beginning, middle and end, the focus is different. The change of focus seems to apply, interestingly enough, regardless of whether the coaching or mentoring relationship extends over one session or over many months or even years. Below is an introduction to some important issues in each stage.

Managing the beginning

The coach or mentor aims to establish a productive learning relationship. Some aspects of getting started are illustrated by the case example of Harry (below), a coach who is getting started with a potential client.

Fully attending. The coach or mentor pays attention to both the non-verbal and verbal messages from the client. They try to maintain a relaxed and attentive posture, including appropriate eye contact, facial expression, tone of voice and leaning towards the client but not invading their body space. The coach or mentor clears their mind of other distractions, so that they can be receptive and open to the client. *Listening is not the same as hearing.* To communicate what they have heard, the coach or mentor reflects and paraphrases, clarifies and summarizes. All this is done tentatively, giving the client the space to correct any misunderstanding. In the following example, Harry picks up verbal and non-verbal cues from his potential client, and summarizes what he has heard her say.

> **Harry meets with a potential client**, who is very keen to have some coaching, saying that Harry has been highly recommended by her colleagues. The client's busy schedule means that she wants coaching meetings in the early evening, as she would find it difficult to take time out of the day. Harry notices that the client is not very relaxed – she frequently looks at her watch and checks her mobile phone. Harry says that he understands that she will find it difficult to make time, but that he offers sessions only between 9 and 5. The client says she is very keen to work with Harry and would be prepared to pay extra. He explains that he is unable to do this, and reflects tentatively that

perhaps finding time in the day might help her to prioritize coaching. However, he also offers the names of two coaches who offer more flexible hours.

Clarifying boundaries. The coach or mentor is clear about the working arrangements and what they can offer the clients. They also say what they are unable to offer. Harry has been clear about his boundaries, demonstrating genuineness, but also being respectful to the client by offering alternatives. She agrees to work with him.

> Harry's client manages to clear her diary and they meet for an exploratory session in working hours. By the end of the session Harry has helped her to prioritize her aims for coaching. These are: to improve her presentation skills and her time management. They agree that these two issues are probably related. They have also discussed how coaching can help her to achieve these aims, and what she wants from her coach.

Focusing and prioritizing. The coach or mentor helps the client to clarify and prioritize their aims, to focus their effort and attention and to increase the chance of successful outcomes. In the exploratory session, Harry has helped the client to focus on two issues.

Clarifying the working arrangements. This may include the framework and learning processes that might be used. Expectations and limitations are discussed, helping to establish trust and reduce uncertainties on both sides. In addition, the beginning of coaching or mentoring is the appropriate time to agree any contractual arrangements. The session continues, and Harry clarifies arrangements with his client, and is responsive to agreeing a schedule which is realistic for her.

> Harry explains how he works as a coach, and the framework he uses. He believes that it is important to agree goals and action plans at the end of each session, and review these at the start of the next, and he checks whether this way of working will suit his client. He suggests that they meet fortnightly, within working hours, but she is concerned that her busy schedule will result in her missing some appointments, so they agree to meet every three weeks, within working hours, initially for three months.

So, by fully attending to the client's expectations, by clarifying boundaries and working arrangements and by focusing and prioritizing aims, a learning relationship has been successfully established. The list in Box 2.1 contains useful reminders for coaches and mentors, and summarizes the important aspects of managing the beginning.

Box 2.1 Managing the beginning: some questions for coaches and mentors

---

- Am I able to give the client my full attention?
- Have we both been involved, as far as possible, in the decision to work together?
- Is this the right kind of help for the client at this time?
- Are we clear about the client's priorities for coaching or mentoring?
- Have we talked about limits of confidentiality? Possible conflicts of interest?
- Have I described the framework I use? My professional background and experience?
- Have we talked about how the client learns best?
- Have we agreed time/place/note-keeping/financial arrangements?
- We have begun to establish a working relationship? How can I tell?
- Am I concerned about anything? Any unresolved issues that might benefit from supervision or support?
- Have I created the opportunity for the client to express any concerns or questions?

Managing the middle

Having established the working relationship, the coach or mentor will help the client to:

- *Reflect on the work they are doing*, both during sessions and between sessions, and learn from experience. Reflective space creates opportunities for learning that are so often missing in a busy working life.
- *Develop insight both about their situation and about themselves.* The coach or mentor enables the client to be realistic about their context, and works with them to identify what will help and hinder them in achieving goals.
- *Challenge themselves, identify resources and develop their potential.* The coach or mentor helps the client to challenge self-imposed limitations, and self-limiting beliefs and attitudes. The client is supported in developing both internal and external resources which can help them achieve their goals.
- *Identify achievable change goals.* Goals vary in nature. Some may be visible, for example achieving a performance goal; others may be harder to see, for example sustaining a change in attitude. The value of a goal is the extent to which it helps the client to achieve the changes they want.

- *Plan and implement actions which help to achieve goals.* The coaching - r mentoring conversation is an important catalyst, but the proof of the pudding, so to speak, is in the changes that the client makes back at work. The coach or mentor helps the client to make realistic plans which they can implement.
- *Notice, celebrate and reinforce their successes.* The coach or mentor can support and energize the client by highlighting and acknowledging what they have achieved.

John was a highly successful events organizer, until a health problem meant that he could no longer drive, which was essential in his career. He described himself as 'washed up' and 'fit for nothing'. He needed a coach to help him identify and exploit the talents and resources that he had, rather than focus on his limitations. He was able to generate ideas about alternative career options. Together they planned how he might explore these options, and the coach helped him to get started on the plans. Experiencing some successes increased John's confidence and enthusiasm, and the coach supported him through some setbacks. Although it took time, John was able to find a fulfilling alternative career.

Box 2.2 contains some useful questions for managing the middle.

Box 2.2 Managing the middle: some questions for coaches and mentors

- What has the client done as a result of our initial session/s? What has helped or hindered them?
- Has the client identified change goals? Made any action plans? Tried to implement these?
- Have I drawn the client's attention to what they have achieved, and any successes?
- Am I using the appropriate balance of support and challenge?
- Have we talked about how we are working together? What is helping or hindering?
- How would I describe our working relationship? How would the client describe it?
- Am I using all my resources to help the client – for example knowledge, skills, experience, networks?

Managing the ending

In this phase, the coach or mentor helps the client to bring the relationship and the work to a conclusion. If the session is a one-off, the effective coach or mentor will ensure there is time at the end to address the relevant items from the list in Box 2.3. As a rough guide, in a two-hour session, 10–15 minutes might be set aside for this. Where a longer relationship is coming to an end, preparation for ending may take place over several sessions and will probably form a significant part of the final session.

Box 2.3 Managing the ending: some questions for coaches and mentors

- Are we clear about why we are ending, and when?
- Have we both been involved, as far as possible, in the decision to end?
- Is the client ready for the ending? If not, what can I do to help them?
- Have we acknowledged what the client has achieved?
- Have we reviewed how we have worked together?
- Have we discussed any work still to do? Considered how the client might take this forward?
- Have we discussed how the client will move on?
- Have we agreed what will be done with any notes?
- Has the client had the chance to make a good ending for themselves?
- Would I benefit from supervision or support?

Building a learning relationship

Principle: the learning relationship is at the heart of change

Client perception of the quality of the learning relationship is a significant factor in determining the success of coaching or mentoring. When their view of the relationship is positive, then coaching or mentoring is more likely to be effective. What is the learning relationship? Potentially it has three elements, and the client may:

- learn *from* the coach or mentor, from their experiences;
- learn *with* them, acquiring particular skills and abilities;
- learn *through* them, from the way they are, sometimes called their 'way of being'.

Some of the more intangible qualities of the relationship are not easy to capture in words, even though we may try when, for example, we discuss the working agreement. Carl Rogers, writing about helping relationships, described how, in striving to be trustworthy, he sought to fulfil the 'outer conditions of trustworthiness' (1961: 50), for example being punctual, maintaining confidences, being consistent. Over time, he realized that it was equally important to be 'dependably real' or congruent, a quality often described nowadays as genuineness. While it would be difficult to write 'genuineness' into a working agreement, it is undoubtedly vital in successful helping.

Genuineness involves being aware of our own feelings and being able to use them to connect in a real way with the client, rather than hiding behind a façade or professional veneer. Genuineness does not mean blurting out everything we are thinking or feeling. It does mean being aware of ourselves and our reactions and being willing to engage with the person, to be fully part of the learning partnership. The more we can be fully present and genuine in the relationship, the more likely is the client to be freed up to do likewise.

In the following example we see that genuineness may be challenging for the client, and the coach or mentor must ensure that any challenge is appropriately supportive. Notice how in the example the coach is not judgemental. They simply state the impact of the client's words on them as listener.

> My coach interrupted me and said, 'I know that this is really important to you, but you're giving me so much detail that I'm having difficulty in following you. Is all this detail helping you?' I was taken aback. Was it helping me? No, and it wasn't helping him either! I'd just assumed that it was useful and I realized I do that at work too. I flood people with data before asking them what they want. Although it was a bit of a jolt, it was powerful learning for me when he didn't pretend to be interested. Maybe that's what people at work do, they just pretend to be interested.

Respect means accepting and affirming the person as they are. As coach or mentor we may not agree with or like all aspects of the client's behaviour or views, but we aim to suspend our judgement and evaluation because these are not helpful. Demonstrating respect can be difficult when the other person makes decisions that we would not choose, as the following example illustrates. However, at times like these it can be most powerful.

> Eventually, I ended up telling my mentor that, despite everything the firm had done for me, I still thought that this wasn't the right career for me. I know people find that hard to hear. They see my success and think that I'm being ungrateful or self-indulgent, but he

was different. He listened very quietly and attentively. I guess I was expecting disapproval, but there wasn't any. I know he sees things differently, but he respects my view, and that means a lot.

The third important attitude identified by Rogers is *empathy*, which is different from sympathy. Rogers described how communicating empathy involved more than trying to understand 'about' someone in a detached way. When we communicate empathy, we try to appreciate how it is to be another person, to walk in their shoes, to experience their life as they experience it.

Empathy is a powerful tool in coaching and mentoring because it communicates to another person that we have understood, or at least tried to understand, their unique experience, rather than imposing our view or making assumptions.

 A colleague is talking. Below are two potential responses. One is empathic, one is sympathetic. How are they different? Which is the empathic response?

> *Colleague:* Fred is being impossible. We're jointly accountable for this project, but he's constantly passing the buck. He turns up late to meetings, hands all the tough decisions to me, and when the pressure is on, he goes off sick, whatever that means.
> *Response A:* He sounds terrible! I don't know how you cope!
> *Response B:* You're finding it tough – it seems as though he's not pulling his weight.

Response B is the more empathic response because it reflects the colleague's experience as seen by them. Notice that it implies neither agreement nor disagreement, but tries to communicate *understanding*. Response B is likely to be more productive in helping the colleague to address the problem, because it offers support but stays focused on the colleague.

Response A is more sympathetic because it implies *agreement* with the colleague. It is likely to lead to a conversation with the colleague about Fred, but not necessarily about what the colleague can do to change the situation. The risk with a sympathetic response is that we end up agreeing or colluding with a person, but not helping them to move forward in managing the problem.

In effective coaching and mentoring, the coach or mentor communicates empathy, respect and genuineness to the client. Sometimes this happens quite naturally. Sometimes it may be more difficult. This may be because a client is different from the coach or mentor, for example in culture, upbringing, beliefs or values. However, in effective coaching and mentoring, the client is acknowledged and valued as they are, and the challenge for the coach or mentor is to seek constantly to understand issues in the way that the client experiences them. Communicating this willingness to understand will help to build the learning relationship, which is at the heart of change.

Using a framework

Principle: the framework for the change process provides movement and direction

A model or framework can, when used sensitively, contribute significantly to effective helping. There are many views on which framework or model is best for coaching and mentoring, but there is agreement that it is important for the coach or mentor to be clear about their approach. This is recommended in the CIPD guide *Coaching and Buying Coaching Services* (Jarvis 2004), which cautions, at the same time, against those who seem inflexible in their approach.

One framework, the Egan Skilled Helper model, is described in detail in Chapter 4. Others are outlined in Chapter 1, and these include:

- the GROW model;
- the inner game;
- non-directive coaching;
- co-active coaching;
- solution-focused coaching.

 Box 2.4 lists some benefits of using a framework. Which are important to you? Are there any that you might wish to add?

Box 2.4 Possible benefits of using a framework

- Communicates the values and assumptions of the coach or mentor
- Demonstrates a professional approach by grounding practice in theory
- Demonstrates transparency by clarifying underlying approach
- Shares responsibility through discussion of the framework
- Creates hope by using a proven framework
- Provides a reference point for deciding what work needs to be done
- Encourages change by providing a map with direction
- Focuses on key issues
- Empowers the client if the framework is transferable to other contexts
- Helps to guide purposeful coaching and mentoring conversations

---

Lucy, an executive coach: My clients are interested in the coaching framework I use. I explain it to them and I think this reassures them that they are not being 'psyched out'. In fact, it's a framework which, after a time, they find they can use by themselves. I think that part of my coaching role is to offer useful tools and techniques which clients can try out in everyday work situations, and I say that right at the beginning.

 Use these questions to help select the right framework for you.
- What frameworks do you know about?
- Which have you used?
- Have you had training in a framework?
- What evidence exists to support the effectiveness of the framework?
- What has helped you personally in your development?
- What is congruent with your beliefs and values?
- What is relevant to your context?
- Which do other coaches and mentors recommend?
- Which would empower clients?

A cautionary note: a framework is only as good as the person using it. It is a useful guide, rather than a template. It should be used to help, rather than to unnecessarily constrain the coach, mentor or client. At the beginning of Chapter 4 the disadvantages as well as advantages of frameworks are discussed in more detail.

Some core skills

Principle: the skills develop insight, release potential and deliver results

Active listening

Core skills enable the coach or mentor to communicate the values of regard, genuineness and empathy. The skills bring to life the coaching or mentoring framework, and create a dialogue which is intentional and leads to change. In our experience of training coaches and mentors, the single most useful skill, which underpins all others, is that of active listening.

Figure 2.1 shows how active listening differs from diagnostic listening. When the coach or mentor listens diagnostically, they are trying to sift and sort information, to analyse what is relevant or irrelevant, trying to find a solution. This kind of listening can be useful when solving a puzzle, in the kind of expert helping described earlier. For example, a doctor might ask a patient if a pain is stabbing or diffuse, whether it is worse before or after eating. The doctor is eliminating potential causes, narrowing the search for solutions and using a decision tree. In this way the doctor filters out irrelevant data and narrows options according to a diagnostic pathway.

However, when the coach or mentor uses this kind of listening, it can be less than useful, because it puts them in the driving seat to steer the

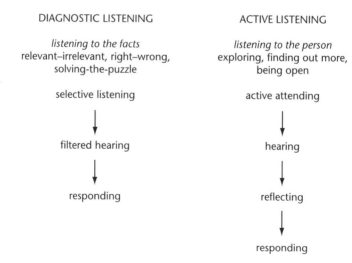

Figure 2.1 Diagnostic versus active listening
Source: Phillips and Pokora (2004)

conversation and generate their 'solutions'. When they listen diagnostically, they inevitably end up leading the client. The coach or mentor then asks closed questions to get information to 'solve' things, and they slip into the role of expert helping.

In contrast, when they use active listening, they add value by helping the client to expand their understanding of the problem or opportunity so that *the client* can manage it better. When the coach or mentor listens actively, they are open to all information and are free to follow rather than lead the client. In effect, they are holding up a mirror saying, 'This is what I see/hear. Is that right? Is that how it is for you?' When they listen actively with a 'credulous attitude' (Kelly 1963: 174) they are trying to take in all information, verbal and non-verbal, factual and emotional, with the aim of trying to understand from the client's perspective.

For many people, it takes considerable effort to stop diagnostic listening and to start active listening. The temptation to treat problems as if they were puzzles and to try to 'solve' them can be almost overwhelming!

When the coach or mentor listens skilfully, the experience may be like this:

> Imagine someone listening, not only to your words, but also to what's behind them – who even listens to the spaces between the words. Someone in tune with the nuances of your voice, your emotion, your energy – who is intent on receiving everything you communicate. Someone who listens to the very best in you, even when you can't hear it in yourself.
>
> (Whitworth *et al.* 1998: xviii)

The following example shows how active listening skills can be used, and how they are different from diagnostic listening. Jane is trying to help a newly-promoted manager who comes to her with a problem.

> **A manager describes the problems he faces in establishing an effective team**: I feel as if I've been parachuted into a war zone. The department is divided, with factions sniping at each other, and so much unproductive conflict. We have a major project deadline in four months, and it is vital that we start pulling together and stop wasting time and energy. Communication is breaking down – for example, at our weekly meeting, people become 'unavailable' at the last minute. I've inherited this situation – a hornets' nest – and I think part of the reason I was promoted was that the board believed that I could sort it out. I suppose I should be encouraged by their faith in me, but . . .

Jane is trying to help. She is listening diagnostically and here are some of her responses:

- How many people are there in your department?
- Have you thought about involving the HR function?
- Could you try a team-building day?
- What's the major project about?

These questions arise from diagnostic listening, and are easy to recognize. They usually help the person asking the question more than they help the person answering it! They include:

- suggestions framed as questions;
- questions to which the person with the problem already knows the answer;
- closed questions, which invite a one-word (often 'yes' or 'no') answer.

Below are some active listening skills, key in effective coaching and -entoring.

✓ paraphrasing the story: *'if I've understood . . .'*;
✓ prompting by echoing key words or phrases, with a question mark;
✓ creating space by counting to three (silently!) before responding;
✓ summarizing the key parts of the overall message.

 If Jane uses active listening, what responses might she make? Try to generate some responses by using the skills of paraphrasing, prompting and summarizing. Some possible responses are given in the next section.

Challenging: goals/blindspots/action

While support is an important part of the coach or mentor role, clients want and need challenge. The goals of challenge are derived from the key principles of effective coaching and mentoring. When clients are challenged, and encouraged to challenge themselves, they learn how to:

- develop insight;
- release their potential;
- focus on change goals;
- implement action;
- achieve results;
- become more strategic and proactive.

Think of a time when you were faced with a difficult issue, a problem. What were any helpful challenges that you received? Any unhelpful ones? What made the difference? What are the characteristics of a skilful challenge, i.e. one that you can accept and act on?

Continuing with the previous example, these are some examples of how Jane might use active listening to help the manager to challenge himself:

- *Paraphrasing:* If I've understood you right, it feels like a war zone, and you've been parachuted in to sort it out, and fast.
- *Prompting:* War zone? *Should* be encouraged?
- *Summarizing:* You're finding this a pretty tough situation to handle. You're new; external expectations are high; and the team seems to be in self-destruct mode.

Active listening acts as a mirror, so that clients they can see and hear themselves more clearly.

When Jane uses active listening, the manager is helped to challenge himself. He notices that:

- He resents being 'parachuted in', even if he is supposed to be encouraged
- The metaphor of war is a strong one and he asks himself if things are really that bad
- He wonders if all the team are in 'self-destruct mode'; maybe he is overlooking some potential allies

When the coach or mentor uses active listening skills, they encourage the client to self-challenge. They build trust, by demonstrating that they are trying to understand how the client sees things. Challenge is potentially strong medicine, and the coach or mentor earns the right to challenge by demonstrating the core qualities of respect, empathy and genuineness.

Box 2.5 contains a list of challenges that might be used in coaching and mentoring. Imagine that you are Jane. Read down the list and identify some challenges which might help the manager. How might you phrase the challenge? Here is an example: *I don't know if I'm on track here, but I'm wondering whether you think that it's an impossible task?'*

Box 2.5 Areas for challenge in coaching and mentoring

- *Feelings:* what are the client's feelings in the situation? The client may focus on what they are thinking, or what's been happening.
- *Others' perspectives:* how do other people see the situation? How do they see the client? The client may focus only on their viewpoint.
- *Evidence:* are there any facts to support/contradict the client's thoughts or feelings? The client may over-interpret or generalize or lack evidence.
- *Blindspots:* is there anything the client might have overlooked?
- *Ownership:* in what way is the situation a problem or an opportunity for the client? The client may focus on other people rather than themselves.
- *Patterns:* has the client 'been there before'? Do they recognize a pattern in their life?
- *Goals:* is the client clear about what they want instead of what they've got? The client may find it easier to say what they don't want.
- *Action:* is the client willing and able to do something to move towards their goals? The client may find it easier to talk rather than to act.
- *The 'here and now':* is something happening in the session which mirrors how the client describes things at work? Or something that contradicts it?

 Look again at the list. Which of these challenges have you used in coaching or mentoring? Which do you find easiest? Which might be more difficult for you?

Knowing yourself

Principle: the qualities of the coach or mentor affirm, enable and sustain the client

The skilled coach or mentor understands their own strengths and style, and how these can benefit clients. Clutterbuck's 'twelve habits of the toxic mentor' (www.coachingnetwork.org.uk) warns quite rightly of the danger of expecting to be a complete role model in every way, but nonetheless, in our experience, successful coaches and mentors are often seen as role models in *some* way by their clients. They have a quality or characteristic which others admire, aspire to or see as lacking in their own development. As discussed earlier in the chapter, the client may want to 'learn with' the coach or mentor, understanding their experience as a successful person, 'learn from' them, acquiring particular skills and abilities, and 'learn through' them, from their 'way of being' in the sessions.

Box 2.6 contains a list of qualities. Which are most characteristic of you? In what ways might you be a role model for others?

Box 2.6 Some qualities of a coach or mentor

- *Supportive:* a confidential non-judgemental listener
- *Sounding board:* good at bouncing around ideas
- *Challenging:* able to challenge constructively
- *Networker:* skilled at identifying and knowing how to develop connections
- *Respected:* commands attention of others
- *Assertive:* able to state wants and needs without being aggressive
- *Open:* receptive to new ideas and ways of thinking
- *Transparent:* communicates their values and 'walks the talk'
- *Creative:* able to think laterally and 'outside of the box'
- *Visible:* known in the organization/professional community
- *Interpersonally skilled:* at negotiating, conflict resolution
- *Strategic:* able to take the long-term view
- *Kind:* sensitive to others and shows care for them
- *Genuine:* being themselves, not hiding behind a professional façade
- *Just:* treats people fairly and equally, is not prejudiced or partial

---

In addition to differing qualities, we each have different helping styles. Table 2.4 shows some contrasting styles. All of these are potentially useful in coaching or mentoring.

 From the list in Table 2.4 select the five words that best describe you, and the five that are least like you. What does that tell you about your style? What are its strengths? Any debits? You might ask someone who knows you well to complete the exercise and compare the two descriptions.

A third way of gaining insight into your style and helping qualities is with the use of professionally-administered psychometric instruments, such as the Myers-Briggs Type Indicator® questionnaire (MBTI® questionnaire).[1] This may help you to appreciate how you prefer to work with others. Reflecting on your

---

[1] MBTI and Myers-Briggs Type Indicator® are registered trade marks of the Myers-Briggs Type Indicator Trust.

Table 2.4 Some helping styles

Task-focused	Broad-ranging
Easy going	Organized
Leading	Following
Listening	Talking
Agreeing	Arguing
Supporting	Challenging
Detached	Involved
Energized	Relaxed
Realistic	Imaginative
Planned	Spontaneous
Questioning	Accepting
Theoretical	Practical
Thinker	Doer
Hope for the best	Plan for the worst
Easy to read	Not easy to read
Immediate	Considered
Evaluative	Non-judgemental
Exciting	Safe

style can help you to understand your coaching and mentoring strengths, and your areas for development, as in this example:

> **Alex** prefers thinking about possibilities and the future, sometimes at the expense of noticing what's going on in the present. One of his coaching strengths is helping someone to consider possibilities, ways forward and 'what if' scenarios. However, he knows he must be careful not to rush ahead too quickly. He works hard to pay attention to understand how things are for the client at present.

Supervision, support and development

Principle: ethical practice safeguards and enhances coaching and mentoring

Supervision and support

Working as a coach or mentor can be stimulating, challenging and demanding. Supervision and support provide a confidential context for the coach or mentor to discuss their work and any problems associated with it. Importantly, the coach or mentor is the focus of the conversation, not the client.

What is supervision? Below are some examples.

A **coach uses** his regular supervision sessions to discuss concerns about the way he is working with his client, who is having a difficult time at work. The coach is worried that the client may become reliant on him, and wonders whether as coach he is inadvertently encouraging this. The supervisor helps the coach to examine what he is doing in coaching sessions and they identify that he often steps in to make suggestions when the client seems stuck. They explore other ways in which the coach might help the client which would encourage the client to be more proactive in their life, rather than rely on the coach.

A **coach says:** I see my supervisor on a regular basis but infrequently. It has been important to know she is there if a difficulty arises. Once or twice I've had concerns about whether I'd dealt with a situation in the best way, or what to do for the best, and knowing my supervisor was just a phone call away was very reassuring.

A **mentor says:** I'm quite new to mentoring and I use regular supervision to help me reflect on how I'm working. It's helped boost my confidence and develop my skills. My supervisor has also been helpful in keeping me up to date with new developments.

The Association of Professional Executive Coaching and Supervision (APECS) refers to supervision as 'the relationship between the coach and a qualified person who is not in any managerial relationship with the coach wherein the coaching work with particular clients may be discussed in strict confidence with the purpose of enhancing the quality of the coaching work and of ensuring client safety' (www.apecs.org).

The Association for Coaching (AC) notes that while supervision is a formal arrangement for maintaining adequate standards of coaching provision, 'it is also a supportive process. Supervision has sometimes been called "Super Vision" as a way of demonstrating that it is not restrictive or prescriptive but rather a process for increasing creativity' (www.associationforcoaching.com).

Both these definitions draw attention to the formal nature of supervision, as a planned purposeful activity and something more than a casual chat.

The EMCC *Guidelines on Supervision* (2004) lists 12 criteria recommended for choosing a supervisor. Box 2.7 lists some questions, derived from the EMCC criteria and adapted. Some of these questions may be more important to you than others, and this may give you some clues for finding the right supervisor for you.

Hannah works as a coach and mentor: I've known my supervisor for a long time. She taught on a coaching programme I attended, so I

Box 2.7 Questions for choosing a supervisor

- Has the person been a coach or mentor or client?
- What coaching/mentoring framework do they use? Is this compatible with yours?
- Have they been supervised?
- How much/what type of experience do they have as a supervisor?
- Are they available for supervision at times/frequency to suit you?
- Have they been trained in supervision?
- What framework do they use for supervision?
- Do they communicate respect, empathy and genuineness to you?
- Can they be impartial as your supervisor (i.e. no conflicting roles)?
- Do they possess the qualities/skills which you are seeking in a supervisor?
- Do they subscribe to a code of ethics or belong to a professional body?
- Do they understand the context in which you work?

---

knew we both used the same coaching framework. I didn't think about asking which supervision framework she used. However, there was something about her quality of listening and attending that really impressed me even though she didn't know too much about the context in which I work. She just seemed like the right person. And she is!

The importance of supervision is well recognized in many helping professions, so much so that it is mandatory in some. In coaching and mentoring, the EMCC *Code of Ethics* requires that all members have regular supervision and the APECS *Ethical Guidelines* refer to ongoing and regular supervision. In practice, the definition of 'regular' varies according to the nature and amount of coaching or mentoring work undertaken.

In addition to individual supervision, or as an alternative, it is possible to have co-supervision and group supervision. Terminology can be confusing, because the term 'supervision' is not used everywhere. Co-supervision and group supervision may be referred to as coach or mentor support. However, they potentially offer the same benefits, helping mentors and coaches to work safely and effectively, to avoid burn-out, to refer appropriately, and to continue to develop skills and self-awareness.

Supervision has been described as fulfilling several roles: normative, formative, restorative and perspective (Inskipp and Proctor 1989; Bond 1993). Applying these headings to coaching and mentoring, supervision may:

- help the coach or mentor to work safely, ethically and legally (normative)

- help the coach or mentor to learn and develop skills and understanding (formative)
- support the coach or mentor in dealing with the demands and stresses of the role (restorative)
- help the coach or mentor to maintain an overview of their work, and connections with other ways of helping (perspective).

 Box 2.8 provides a list of some of the benefits of supervision and support for the coach or mentor. How do they apply to you? Are some more important than others?

Box 2.8 Possible benefits of supervision and support
<ul><li>Anticipating problems and avoiding/minimizing them</li><li>Working as effectively as possible</li><li>Responding to clients who are challenging</li><li>Developing skills and confidence</li><li>Getting support</li><li>Maintaining perspective</li><li>Staying connected with other approaches</li><li>Maintaining boundaries and working ethically</li><li>Developing self-insight</li><li>Working fairly and valuing diversity</li><li>Challenging assumptions about self and others</li></ul>

For more information on supervision, you may wish to refer to the guidelines produced by some of the professional bodies listed in the Appendix.

Development

Development is at the heart of coaching and mentoring work, and coaches and mentors should practise what they preach! The safe and effective coach or mentor is reflective, monitors their own competence and pays attention to developing their capability. These qualities can be thought of as self-supervision (Hawkins and Shohet 2000).

Reflective practice is important, particularly if you are not a full-time coach or mentor, but do use coaching or mentoring skills in your job. If this is the case for you, then formal supervision may not be relevant or appropriate. However, taking the time for reflection on the experience of using the skills, for example in an action learning set or a co-mentoring or co-coaching arrangement, may well be useful.

The list in Box 2.9, adapted from Connor (1994), identifies some ways to promote your ongoing development.

 Read the list in Box 2.9. In what ways are you currently developing? What could you do to enhance your development?

Box 2.9 Developing coaching or mentoring capability: a checklist

- *Training:* what coaching or mentoring training have you attended? What future training would be useful to enhance your capabilities?
- *Supervision:* do you have a supervisor? How regularly do you see them? Are you making the most of supervision?
- *Writing, research and publicizing:* are you creating or using opportunities to write about you work? To tell others? To lead or become involved in research?
- *Professional organizations:* are you a member of a coaching or mentoring organization? Of the section of your own professional body which relates to coaching or mentoring? Could you start up an interest group?
- *Conferences:* do you attend conferences, as speaker or delegate? Do you network to keep abreast of current ideas and new developments?
- *Being a client:* do you take time to get one-to-one support for yourself when needed?
- *Reflective practice:* are you part of a coach or mentor support group? An action learning set? Could you start one?

Development can take many forms. Unlike the other examples in this book, this experience is taken directly from real life and Gordon has given permission for his name to be used.

> **Gordon is a doctor who attended a mentor development programme.** He enjoyed the programme, started mentoring, and a year later attended a follow-up day, where he met other mentors and heard about mentoring schemes. He influenced key stakeholders to fund mentor training, mostly, but not exclusively, for hospital consultants in the hospital where he worked. He helped out on these courses as a facilitator, and also on courses in a nearby region, as well as continuing to act as a mentor in his own locality. At the same time he had started an MBA, and undertook research into doctors' attitudes to

mentoring. He was able to use the research to influence his hospital to endorse a mentoring scheme. Further mentoring training programmes were run and a group of trained mentors was established. These mentors, including Gordon, formed a support group, where they could practise skills and techniques and keep up to date. He was asked to speak at a national conference, and share his experience with others who were interested in finding out more about how to set up mentoring schemes. In a broader context, within the geographical region where he worked, Gordon supported mentoring for helping clients to develop career opportunities and also for supporting those in difficulty at work.

Summary

In this chapter we have:

- Shown how the key principles of effective coaching and mentoring can help to answer the questions frequently asked by coaches and mentors.
- Offered interactive prompts to enable you to clarify your motivation for coaching or mentoring, and to assess your coaching or mentoring qualities, approach and skills.
- Illustrated with checklists and examples how the coach or mentor develops the learning relationship at each stage, and uses the core skills effectively.
- Helped you to consider how you would establish and use a working agreement, and select a coaching or mentoring framework.
- Stimulated thinking about how to get the best from support and supervision, how to choose a supervisor and how to continue to develop your coaching or mentoring capability.

3   How can I be an effective client?

- Introduction
- Getting the right coach or mentor
- Knowing yourself
- Having realistic expectations
- Negotiating a working agreement
- Thinking ahead and being strategic
- Being proactive
- Learning from support and challenge
- Using reflective space
- Developing your imagination
- Identifying your resources and working smart
- Setting goals and making action plans
- Developing skills, making changes and delivering results
- Summary

Introduction

The purpose of this chapter is to help you to get the most out of coaching and mentoring by knowing what you can do to be fully active in and between sessions. It should give you some insight into yourself, and into what the coach or mentor might expect of you. It also aims to inform you about what you can expect from your coach or mentor, and how to get it.

The chapter starts by helping you to clarify how to get the right coach or mentor for your particular needs and wants. Throughout the chapter we refer to you as 'client' whether you are involved in coaching or mentoring. You may be an individual client, working with one coach, or you may be part of a team that is being coached. You will see how your personality preferences and learning style can affect the working relationship with a coach or mentor. Examples from coaching and mentoring are used to show differences as well as similarities. The importance of developing a clear working agreement is explained. Ways in which you can be proactive and make the most of the reflective space in sessions are outlined. There are examples of developing imagination, identifying resources, using skills, formulating goals and implementing action plans.

 Wherever you see this symbol there is an invitation for you to reflect upon how you can make the most of coaching and mentoring.

Getting the right coach or mentor

Box 3.1 Do I need a coach or a mentor?

If you need help with an issue at work which is time-limited, short-term and fairly specific then you may wish to work with a coach. If your need is for someone who can help more generally with your professional or career development then you may want to seek a mentor. You need to be aware that coaching and mentoring are described differently by different people and therefore, when choosing, do take care to read how the coach or mentor describes what they do, to see if it fits your purpose.

So what do you want, a coach or a mentor? You may even want both, for different needs in your life. Coaching at work is often about performance. It can be individual or team coaching. You may be coached by your manager or leader, who may be both coach and assessor. In this case, you will need to negotiate the coaching agenda carefully, to ensure that it meets the expectations of both you and your manager. You may request 'off-line' coaching within the organization, or even externally. This is particularly useful if it is an issue which is broader than a specific performance issue, or where there may be problems of confidentiality or conflicts of interest between you and your manager (see Table 3.1).

Executive coaching is often external to the organization. You may be paying an external coach or mentor yourself, or your organization may pay for your coaching or mentoring. In the latter case, it will be important to clarify and agree the expectations of all parties, the boundaries of confidentiality and the lines of communication.

Table 3.1 Internal vs external coaching and mentoring

Internal	External
Advantages	*Advantages*
Easy to meet together	Can be totally objective
Knows the organization	Easy to maintain confidentiality
Can network for you	Clear boundary: you and work
Understands the politics	Likely to be uninterrupted
Has personal experience of obstacles	You may prepare more carefully
May know people you talk about	Conflict of interest less likely
May be able to access resources	Knows other networks
Disadvantages	*Disadvantages*
Sessions may be interrupted	May cost more
People will know	Travel takes time
Confidentiality may be harder	Need to explain about your work
Boundaries may be more difficult	The coach or mentor may not be monitored
You may be more casual and informal	the way an 'insider' is

When you have decided whether you want a coach or a mentor, internal to your organization or external, you will need to find the right person for you. For this, you need to know something about yourself. The literature on coaching and mentoring emphasizes that the chemistry between the client and the coach or mentor is significant. Knowing about your personality and the way you react to the support and challenge that will be given in coaching and mentoring will help you to make the most of the learning relationship.

Knowing yourself

What is it that you need and want in a coach or mentor? How do you learn best? What sort of person can help you most to gain insight, explore possibilities, set goals and deliver results?

 Think of a time when you were helped in the past with a work issue or with a career opportunity. What was it in you, and in the person helping you, that really made the difference?
Think of a time when someone tried to help but it didn't work. What was it about the way that person tried to help that didn't work? Was it something in them, or something in you, or both?

Here is the example of Tim who had to look around until he found the right mentor.

> **Tim recently joined an advertising agency** and was assigned an experienced senior colleague as his mentor. The mentor was generous with his time and in the way that he shared experiences of working in the agency, but Tim found that the sessions were dominated by the mentor advising him what to do. What Tim really needed was some reflective space where he could talk over some of the concerns and opportunities arising in his new job. When he tried to raise issues, the mentor adopted a well-intentioned but nevertheless unhelpful 'if I were you' approach. Fortunately, Tim has now met another colleague, trained as a mentor, who is willing to act informally as a sounding board. He helps Tim to explore the issues on his mind, and reach his own conclusions. Tim continues to see the more experienced senior colleague from time to time, but uses those sessions to get advice on more technical aspects of work.

 So, what sort of person are you: what do you know about your personality preferences; what makes you put your trust in other people to whom you turn for help; what makes you respect them; what makes you feel safe with them?

The lists in Table 3.2 will help you to pick out your own personality preferences and clarify what sort of coach or mentor is best for you. Try ticking items that apply to you in the column 'I see myself as'. *There are no right or wrong answers, just preferences.* You may want to tick one of each pair in a row, or both in the pair, or neither may apply to you.

When you have done this, go to the column headed 'I want a coach or mentor who is' and repeat the exercise. You may find that you want someone like you, or that you would value someone who differs from you. If you have completed any psychometric questionnaires or inventories they may give you additional information about your preferences.

Clients learn about themselves through dialogue with their coach or mentor. When this is effective it will increase your insight into issues, problems and opportunities. It will increase your motivation to make the changes that are really wanted and the actions that will deliver results. The effective coach or mentor understands how to help you to motivate yourself and to believe in yourself. In order for you to make the most of this learning *you need to be aware of how you like to learn.*

Do you know anything about your preferred ways of learning? There is a learning styles questionnaire (Honey and Mumford 2006) which suggests

Table 3.2   Personality preferences when choosing a coach or mentor

I see myself as		I want a coach or mentor who is	
Reserved	Outgoing	Reserved	Outgoing
Objective	Subjective	Objective	Subjective
Sensitive	Robust	Sensitive	Robust
Challenging	Supportive	Challenging	Supportive
Involved	Detached	Involved	Detached
Cool	Warm	Cool	Warm
Active	Reflective	Active	Reflective
Intuitive	Evidence-based	Intuitive	Evidence-based
Practical	Conceptual	Practical	Conceptual
Problem-solver	Listener	Problem-solver	Listener
Controlling	Adaptable	Controlling	Adaptable
Humorous	Serious	Humorous	Serious
Imaginative	Realistic	Imaginative	Realistic
Empathic	Sympathetic	Empathic	Sympathetic
Directive	Non-directive	Directive	Non-directive
Open	Closed	Open	Closed
Fair	Just	Fair	Just
Spontaneous	Considered	Spontaneous	Considered
Transparent	Opaque	Transparent	Opaque

that each of us has preferences for learning. For example, when we started to write this book we talked about how we would approach the task of writing. For one of us, it was a case of sitting in front of the computer and starting to write. For the other, it was a case of going to read other books on the subject before feeling able to start. Kolb and Fry (1975) suggested that there are four main approaches to learning: reflection, theorizing, pragmatism and action. People should be able to move between these styles and this is called the learning cycle. The descriptions below will help you to identify how you learn best and what type of coaching and mentoring will suit your learning style.

 Put these in your order of preference:

- Applying ideas in practice
- Observing and reflecting
- Experiencing and doing
- Thinking and conceptualizing

So, what will you want from your coach or mentor: exploration, discussion, practical targets, skill development or action?

Figures 3.1 and 3.2 show how different learning styles are used at different stages of the learning cycle, and will help you to establish which are your most and least preferred styles. When thinking about how we learn it is useful to remember that we do not learn from experience, but from reflection upon that experience.

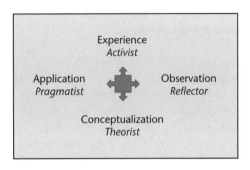

Figure 3.1   The learning cycle and learning styles
Source: Adapted from Honey and Mumford (1992)

PRAGMATIST	REFLECTOR
Keen to put ideas to the test	Careful and methodical
Loves practical activities	Doesn't jump to conclusions
May focus on task more than people	Doesn't like to be pushed into responses
Wants practical tips to use in real life	May appear unassertive
Needs time to practise and experiment	Needs time to think and consider options
ACTIVIST	THEORIST
Likes change	Likes logic and reason
Ready to experiment	Literal not lateral
Wants action	Asks challenging questions
Responds quickly	May not rate intuition
Likes fun	Prefers certainty and objectivity

Figure 3.2   Characteristics of the styles

When you are working with your coach or mentor there is an opportunity to move through these different ways of working and learning as you go through the process. However, you may find that if your coach or mentor has a different learning style from you it could affect your working relationship, the difference may be creative, or it may result in you feeling that you are not being understood or helped. So, there are two guidelines here. Firstly, know your own preferences. Secondly, talk openly with your coach or mentor about their preferences and talk about what you need from one another. Then make sure that you can review on a regular basis how well you work together.

Having realistic expectations

Coaching and mentoring are not the answer to all our problems. The coach or mentor is a *facilitator* but not a *fixer*. You may seek help with an issue, a problem or an opportunity and you probably have the resources within yourself to manage that. But for whatever reason you may become stuck and unable to access those resources, and so seek some coaching or mentoring. The process will help you to become unstuck, it will release your own potential to achieve the desired results. It will work only if the relationship between helper and helped is balanced, with each person taking responsibility. This can be difficult to manage if coaching has been imposed on you. But even if it is imposed, you can still choose how to make the most of it. The coach or mentor is responsible for managing the process and for providing specific skills within a framework of ethical practice. The client is responsible for setting the agenda and for taking action as a result of the coaching or mentoring.

Much of the really important work in coaching and mentoring takes place between sessions when you are either reflecting upon the previous session, acting as a result of it, or preparing for the next session. In order to be an effective client you will be proactive, not reactive. You will gradually become your own coach or mentor as you learn the skills and frameworks that have worked for you in the sessions.

> **Helen works in marketing**. She was sent for coaching by her line manager because of problems with team relationships during project work. She turned up expecting her coach to have all the answers. She was disappointed. The coach tried to get her to look at the problem from the perspective of the team as well as from her own point of view. But Helen was not ready to do this because she felt defensive at being 'told' that she needed some coaching. She attended two sessions but then went back to the manager and said that it had been a waste of time.

This example is not uncommon. Readiness for coaching and mentoring is important. If it has been suggested by others it does not always work. But in the next case example it did.

Tony is a manager. He had never heard of coaching when his boss suggested that a coach might help him to deal with his difficulties in meeting deadlines at work. Although Tony didn't understand what coaching was, he asked around and thought he would give it a try. He was recommended a coach who was outside his department but within the same organization. He arranged an introductory meeting where he negotiated how they might work together. By the time he arrived for his first proper session he had a clear idea of what to expect of himself and of his coach. They met on four occasions. This first session was mainly Tony talking and the coach listening as he revealed a lifelong problem with procrastination. They agreed some goals about charting his current tasks and prioritizing them. In the second session the coach presented some approaches that others had used successfully and Tony was able to evaluate which of these might fit for him. He then tried some out before the next session.

The third session was a debriefing of the action taken, with the coach helping Tony to formulate some specific, realistic goals and action plans. In the final session they evaluated the progress and talked about ending their working arrangement. Tony realized that he had a lifelong pattern of procrastination to change and that this would take time but he now had the confidence and skills to keep working at it.

In these two examples, both were referred for coaching but Tony was realistic, proactive and successful whereas Helen was passive and expected a magic wand instead of a coach!

Negotiating a working agreement

You have decided that you would like to start some coaching or mentoring. What next? You can find someone through personal recommendation or through coaching and mentoring networks and organizations. Before approaching someone, think through these aspects of a working agreement:

Working relationship
- ❑ What outcomes do you want?
- ❑ Expectations of sessions and work between sessions?
- ❑ Preferred ways of working together?
- ❑ What do you want and need in terms of respect, trust, empathy?
- ❑ What do you want and need in order to learn, change, release potential and deliver results?

Practical

☐ Introductory session to decide if you can both work well together.
☐ Location – where would you meet?
☐ Frequency – how often would you like to meet? Number of sessions?
☐ Length of session – ideal for you, and realistic.
☐ Payment procedures – pay yourself or payment by your sponsor/organization?

Professional

☐ Qualifications of the coach or mentor?
☐ Experience and reputation of the coach or mentor?
☐ Responsibilities: legal, to the sponsor, to your profession or organization?
☐ Supervision, support, continuing professional development of coach or mentor?
☐ Recording and note-taking. Who takes? Who keeps? When destroyed?

Ethical

☐ Negotiated, and signed, working agreement?
☐ Built-in ongoing review?
☐ Confidentiality – extent and limits?
☐ Clear role boundaries?
☐ Possible conflicts of interest?

You will find useful information about all of these in Chapter 2 and in Chapter 9 which will tell you what to expect in terms of good ethical practice.

Thinking ahead and being strategic

'Being strategic' means thinking ahead about your own working or professional life. It may mean developing a vision of what you want to be in one year, two years, five years and ten years from now. Having a coach or mentor helps to keep your focus on the now and on the future. It is the responsibility of the coach or mentor to help the client to keep scanning the horizon, rather than getting bogged down in the activity of everyday working life.

Do you have a plan for your future?
Have you a vision of where you would like to be in 5 years time?
Have you worked with someone to clarify your values and goals?
The most successful companies and organizations are constantly addressing these questions. The most successful people do it too, often accompanied by a coach or mentor.

To get the most out of coaching and mentoring it needs to be part of your overall strategy for personal and professional development. In this way, you will become the leader in your own life, rather than allowing your work to lead you. Clients who prepare for coaching or mentoring sessions by reviewing what has happened between sessions will maximize the benefits of the reflective space with the coach or mentor.

> **David has had a mentor for three years**. He is a prison governor. He wanted a mentor because he found the pressures of work at times overwhelming. There is constant change and never-ending targets to be met. As governor he did not want to confide in anyone within the prison and so he joined an Action Learning Set which provides the opportunity to work one-on-one with a mentor. Meetings are every three months. He sets the agenda for the meeting and his mentor uses the framework outlined in Chapter 4. He ensures that only half of the two-hour mentoring session is spent on issues which need to be resolved immediately. The other hour is spent in exploring longer-range issues, what his ideal future would be and how he might achieve that in practice.

Being proactive

As a client, it helps if you set the agenda for your coaching or mentoring sessions and allow your coach or mentor to facilitate that agenda. If you need coaching for a specific issue or problem you will probably want your coach to be quite active in the process. Examples of this include helping you to role-play a particular scenario that has been problematic or practising a specific skill such as assertiveness. Decide what you want before you meet with your coach or mentor and then discuss how the session will address what you want. Make sure that the sort of working arrangement you have allows for constant evaluation of the process and of the dynamic in the working relationship, perhaps by spending the final few minutes of each session with client and coach or mentor saying what they feel has been achieved, what helped and what hindered. You can then agree targets for the next meeting, and for your time between sessions. Here are some examples of ways in which clients have been proactive.

> **Sarah, an administrator in a telecoms company**, always arrived for her coaching session with a written list of things she wanted help with, and she prioritized them.

> **Bill, a sales manager in an oil company**, would think of a couple of situations at work where he wanted help and then he would use the

learning from dealing with these in order to inform his judgement and skill in other areas. So, when he left the session and got into his car he always talked into a Dictaphone to summarize the session before driving off. He wanted to capture the learning before he got swamped with the next round of sales.

Pat, a paramedic, kept a reflective journal. She would arrive in the session and open the journal and pick from it some incident that had been especially significant.

Martin worked in computers. He liked to bring written reports and documents to reflect upon and he always wrote a summary of the sessions in bullet-point form, bringing this with him next time, to review any action taken.

Christine was a conference organizer and she valued just having space. She did not want to work from documents or reports, she had enough of those at work. But she always gave herself 30 minutes of quiet time to prepare for her mentoring session, before setting off from work to travel to her mentor.

 What would you do to be proactive? Try to think of 3 ways that would work for you.

Consider: your time; your usual ways of reflecting; how you learn; how you might prepare for a session; how you would act between sessions.

Learning from support and challenge

Any effective learning relationship will have an appropriate balance of support and challenge. If you read the previous chapter you will know what the coach and mentor does in order to provide this potent mix in a way that empowers rather than overwhelms or overprotects. Everyone is different in the amount of support or of challenge that they want and need. Our needs vary at different points in our working life. Consider the example of Isaac.

Isaac has emigrated and is settling into a new job in engineering. Mentoring was recommended to all newly-recruited staff from overseas and Isaac was pleased to be offered this support. When he started to see his mentor he was feeling very isolated, having left his family to come for work in a new country. Although he had been a high-flyer at home, he suddenly felt very much like the new worker on the block. He had a very understanding mentor who just gave him the space to talk about his feelings and who offered warm support. Isaac was relieved. He wanted no more than this at first. Others were giving him the technical help he needed.

He met with his mentor on a monthly basis at first and after three months he said that he felt very supported and would now welcome some advice about whether to pursue a research opportunity which could take his career to the next stage. His mentor became more active and he helped Isaac to challenge himself about what he might achieve. This stage of mentoring was very powerful, but unnerving at times. Isaac said that he benefited greatly from this. He would have resisted too much challenge without support, and yet with too much support and not enough challenge he would not have stretched himself to the next stage of his career.

 What would you like in terms of support and challenge?

Do you want to be continually challenged or do you want the sort of support that will enable you to challenge yourself?
How will you ask for this?
What will you do if your coach or mentor gets the balance wrong?

Using reflective space

One of the most often reported benefits of coaching and mentoring is the opportunity in busy working lives to take stock, in the reflective space provided by the coach or mentor. At first, this may make you feel uncomfortable because while your coach or mentor provides the silence you will search for thoughts, feelings and insights into the experiences that you have brought for discussion. You may try to avoid doing this because it is challenging and uncomfortable even though it is very productive and helpful. A good coach or mentor will never expect you to talk about things that you do not wish to share. They will help you to decide what you really want to explore.

Some clients break the silence by changing the subject or using humour to distract their coach or mentor. However, if you can allow yourself to be psychologically 'held' by the attentive listening of your coach or mentor, then you will allow your inner voice to speak to you. Things which have been pushed down into your subconscious by the frenetic activity of everyday living can then slowly come up to the surface. You learn to listen to yourself. In terms of general health, this is known to be very beneficial. It induces relaxation. You breathe more slowly and deeply, your pulse rate slows and you can then give voice to your wants, your needs, your problems, your issues, your opportunities and your dreams. Some people do this for ten minutes every morning as a way of focusing on the day. If you are not used to doing this, then it may be worth trying to do it at some point in each day as part of becoming your own coach and mentor. You will then make more efficient use of the reflective space when you are with your coach or mentor. It is not just the time set aside that makes space 'reflective' it is the *quality of the session*.

 If you were to use a coach or mentor, how would you want to make most use of the time for reflection?

What do you already do in your life that is similar to this?
What difficulties might there be for you in working in this way?
What qualities and interventions would you want in your coach or mentor to help you? (For example, not having too much silence while you think about things, or asking your coach or mentor not to interrupt if you are thinking about something.)

Your coach or mentor will use skills of non-verbal and verbal communication to support you in your thinking and exploration. They will reflect back to you what you say, they will question and prompt and clarify, challenge and summarize. They will help you to explore fully your 'story' of the issues, problems or opportunities that you wish to discuss and they will help you to prioritize the ones which need more immediate attention. You can then focus upon these in order to draw up wish-lists of possible ways forward. In order to benefit from this part of the process you need to trust yourself and your coach or mentor. You also need to be open and straightforward so that your working relationship is one in which both of you take responsibility for the outcome. Undue dependency or indeed independence is not desirable. *Interdependence* and *mutuality* bring results.

> **Rosaleen, a PR consultant**, invariably arrived for her coaching session apologizing for being late yet again. She would sit down quite out of breath and would explain that she had not had time to think about what she wanted to talk about today. The topics of conversation had

not been prioritized by her, and she tended to ramble. However, the skills of the coach in questioning, prompting and summarizing helped her to become aware of the most important issue which needed change. She needed to be more strategic in terms of marketing herself. The coach helped her to define specific goals and to make realistic plans for action. She could never have done this for herself because of her tendency to live for the moment and be always rushing from place to place. Having prearranged coaching sessions forced her to stop and reflect. It was this that brought change. Within six months of the first coaching session she had implemented her marketing strategy and the work was coming in at a steady pace.

Developing your imagination

Clients often want to see a coach or mentor because they are feeling a bit stuck. They may lack the imagination to discover possibilities for moving forward. Their potential is being stifled. The most effective clients are willing to engage in approaches and exercises which develop the imagination, the 'what if' scenarios. Some people are born with a preference for imagination and intuition but others find this more difficult. All can benefit from mentors and coaches who help to 'think out of the box' or to 'engage in blue-skies thinking'.

> **Chan was a financial manager.** He had been in his current job for several years and was well respected and well established. He applied for an exciting new opportunity in another region. He was offered the job but if he moved he would miss all that he had so carefully built up. He was given a week to decide whether he wanted the job and he went round in circles weighing up all the costs and benefits of going or staying. He could not decide. Then he turned to a mentor for help. She knew his current job and she said (rather directively) 'You can take that job now or you can stay here and die slowly.' She was inviting him to use his imagination. The picture he painted in his head left him in no doubt that he should accept the job. He did. It was the best move of his life. The job he left was gradually eroded after a series of painful reorganizations. Was he glad he had gone!
>
> **Greg had just qualified as a teacher.** He went for one session to a mentor. He was about to take up his first teaching post but was not really sure that this was the career for him. He wanted the mentor to help him to clarify his career ambitions. The other option he was considering was catering, because he had contacts in the restaurant

business. After listening to his story and his doubts about teaching, his mentor asked him to close his eyes, try to breathe slowly and deeply and to relax. He was to tell the mentor when he felt relaxed. This he did. The mentor then asked him to imagine himself in five years' time in a classroom in a school where he might have been teaching for the past five years. The mentor said, 'Tell me when you have a picture and describe to me what you see.' Greg said, 'I see an old man, bending over a desk, marking books.' The mentor helped Greg to fill in some details in the picture: what the old man was wearing; what he was thinking and feeling; what the pupils were doing. When the picture was complete the mentor carefully asked Greg to bring himself back to this room and then to open his eyes again. He reminded Greg that he was back in the office and that he was Greg, a newly-qualified teacher.

The mentor noted how young and energetic he appeared now and how different from the picture he painted of himself after five years of teaching. He asked Greg what he thought of the picture of himself that he had painted. He said, 'I'm horrified to think that could be me!' They then did the same exercise looking at the possible Greg five years down the line working in a restaurant. A completely different picture emerged, of a vibrant, ambitious young man who was going places. Insight dawned. Greg decided to take up his teaching post, but to leave after the probationary year and pursue his career in catering. In only one mentoring session, with skilful use of his own imagination, a career decision was made.

You will notice how powerful imagination can be! It is important that such exercises are used safely. It is also important to feel safe with your coach or mentor. One way is to check that they work ethically, in the ways outlined in Chapter 9. Brainstorming or thought-showering techniques are used to generate as many possible ideas as you can in the shortest possible time. These techniques are useful in coaching and mentoring. To be of most use you might need to practise using them on yourself. For example, 'If I won the lottery'. They work best if the client is relaxed, is focusing on what might be rather than what is, is not hindered by 'but' or 'ought' but focuses on 'want'. If you are a 'yes, but' sort of person you will benefit greatly from learning how to change it to 'yes, if'!

 Do you have a good imagination?

Do you find it easy to imagine what might be, rather than just what is?

Do you tend to say 'yes, but' rather than 'yes, if'?
Which of these do you voice more: your 'wants' or your 'oughts'?
How would you like to be helped to use your imagination more as a way of picturing your ideal future?

Identifying resources and working smart

Coaching and mentoring are about releasing potential and delivering results. In order to do this you need to identify your resources. Easier said than done! The process of coaching or mentoring will help you to become more aware of underused or unused resources. Some of these will be in yourself, and some will be in the people you live and work with. Some resources will be organizational or structural ones.

 Think about the personal resources you would bring to coaching or mentoring. For example: energy, passion, motivation, courage, stamina, persistence, resourcefulness, skills, knowledge, experience.

Now think of the resources that you could call upon in people around you. For example: their time, their know-how, their networks, their experience. Finally, reflect upon the resources in your place of work: the context, the structures and the processes. Don't forget that time is a resource that is often underused or misused!

If you can identify and exploit resources, within yourself and in others, you will work smart and become more effective. Hopefully, you will open up many more possibilities by engaging the help, knowledge and skills of others at work and at home, and therefore you will not be alone in achieving your objectives.

When Marian first started seeing her coach it was because she wanted to become more visible with senior managers in the supermarket chain where she had worked for ten years. She had watched male contemporaries leapfrog over her in the promotion stakes. What was she doing wrong? She wanted her coach to tell her what was stopping her from getting promoted.

The coaching provided her with the opportunity to challenge herself about unused resources. She began to realize that she was not being proactive about getting promotion. She had not been using the skills and resources on herself that she used so well when developing projects for the supermarket. She remembered times when she had made herself more visible in a previous job. At that time she had networked with senior leaders in the organization; she had found ways of showcasing her work at committee level; she published in a national retailing publication and she regularly went to her immediate superiors to inform them about ideas for innovative projects which she volunteered to lead.

As a result of the coaching she tried out some of these ideas again and brainstormed other strategies with her coach. The coach gave her some reading material on assertiveness and they practised together some presentation skills which she then tried out for real at work. She identified some trusted colleagues and asked for feedback on her new, more visible style. She then took the feedback to a coaching session and, after reviewing with her coach she modified what she had been doing and had another go. At last, she was positively impacting upon her future instead of being overwhelmed by day-to-day matters at work.

Setting goals and making action plans

Goals and action plans are part of the intentional activity that is coaching and mentoring. Some performance coaches expect clients to articulate the goal for each session, before the session begins. The work is then focused upon achieving that specific goal. In mentoring, where the focus is broader, there may not be such a specific focus for each session. However, it is always useful to clarify for oneself, 'What do I expect to get out of this session?' and 'How am I going to make sure I get it?' You will find examples of goal-setting and action planning in Chapter 4. We advise that you also think about having a goal or goals, as well as action plans, to take away from the session. These can relate to changes you want: in thinking, in feeling or in acting.

A goal is best expressed as a specific outcome, not a vague statement of intent. You may go away from a coaching or mentoring session saying that 'I want a better work–life balance' but that, as a specific goal, would be 'in order to achieve a better balance I will leave work at a pre-planned time each day and I will spend one hour with my children each evening before they go to bed'. A specific goal is SMART: specific, measurable, appropriate, relevant and in a timeframe. Goals help to make changes and changes help to deliver results. Your coach or mentor will help you to formulate realistic and meaningful goals that are in keeping with your values. They will also help you to develop the skills you need in order to act more effectively.

Developing skills, making changes and delivering results

This chapter started by considering what to expect of coaching and mentoring. It then focused on how you could put your own personality, preferences and resources into making it work. The outcome of the coaching or mentoring will hopefully be change, small change or life-changing change. You will probably learn new skills and new ways of thinking, feeling and acting. These will enable you to turn your wish-lists and dreams into reality. The skills will deliver results for you. In order to learn these skills you will need to be open to learning, you will need to practise and get feedback, and you will need to monitor your progress – and all this in partnership with your coach or mentor.

Summary

In this chapter we have:

- Helped clients to understand how to be proactive in order to get the most out of coaching and mentoring.
- Provided self-assessment questions to increase awareness of what you, as a client, want and need.
- Stimulated thinking about how to get the best fit between client and coach or mentor in terms of personality preferences, expectation, limits, knowledge, experience, resources and work context.
- Given an example of what an effective working agreement might contain and indicated how to discuss this with a new coach or mentor.
- Used several case examples of issues which may arise for clients, giving the opportunity to reflect on what to do in similar situations.

4   What is a useful framework?

Introduction

In this chapter we present one framework in detail. We begin by evaluating the advantages and disadvantages of using frameworks in coaching and mentoring. An overview of The Skilled Helper is then given, followed by a detailed explanation of how to use each of the three stages. The Skilled Helper is used worldwide, and has been developed over the past 30 years by Professor Gerard Egan (2006). Over the past decade we have trained coaches and mentors who consistently tell us that the framework is robust and enabling. They find that the framework and skills are easily transferable to other professional, leadership, management and work roles. In this chapter we discuss their experiences, as well as our own, to identify tips and issues when working with clients in each of the three stages.

In the two chapters that follow, we work through an example of using The Skilled Helper in coaching (Chapter 5) and an example of using it in mentoring (Chapter 6). You may even find it useful to look at one of these examples before reading this chapter.

Why have a framework?

Coaching and mentoring are intentional helping activities. Listening is not enough. Time is precious. Coaching and mentoring cost money. In our working lives we operate from frameworks and models all the time, often in the form of policies, procedures and protocols, for example those used for appraisals or for presenting a business case. We carry these around in our heads and refer to them as necessary. We also use our personal and professional judgement to decide when a particular framework does not serve our purpose and then we turn to something else that helps us to achieve our objectives.

In coaching and mentoring we are helping people to articulate and achieve their objectives. We are guiding them. We facilitate. We enable learning about self and about opportunity. We motivate for change. We encourage action that delivers results. The professional associations and bodies for coaching and mentoring are concerned about regulating these activities, to ensure that coaches and mentors are properly equipped and fit for purpose. Using tried and tested frameworks that enhance the experience and achievement of the client is one way of ensuring quality. There are several frameworks used by coaches and mentors and we have explained some of these in Chapter 1.

Advantages and disadvantages

Frameworks are of value only if they are client-centred, not model-centred. The message is: start with wherever the client is, and let the framework follow the client, using only the parts of the framework that are appropriate. A framework can guide the coach or mentor when mapping out an intentional process for helping the client to gain insight, decide upon goals and develop strategies for action. However, the map is not the territory (Korzybski 1994). The client decides on what is needed and wanted, and any framework needs to be adapted to the unique requirements of the client. We pinpoint other advantages of using a framework in the next section. Here are some disadvantages:

- focus on skills and process instead of fully tuning in to the client
- relationship may be affected by too close adherence to framework
- client issue may not fit with the framework in use
- client may not like the framework chosen by the coach or mentor

- distinctive style of the coach or mentor may be cramped by the framework
- coach or mentor may overlook valuable hunches and intuition
- coach or mentor may not stay with the significance of the moment
- important leads may not be followed up because they do not fit the framework
- the coach or mentor may be too conscious of where they are in the framework, rather than going with the flow, and following the client.

Why use The Skilled Helper as a framework?

Coaching and mentoring provide the opportunity to change and develop through working in a learning relationship with a coach or mentor. Movement often starts with a client feeling stuck with an issue or opportunity and through the process of coaching or mentoring they become more hopeful about possibilities, and they develop the courage to act, to make changes and to deliver results. The Skilled Helper offers a well-grounded, practical framework for coaching and mentoring sessions. Like all frameworks, it is not 'one size fits all' and must be tailored to the individual requirements of each client.

We have valued the fact that The Skilled Helper has been updated and refined over 30 years, with constant feedback from users. It is informed by humanistic, cognitive and behavioural approaches to the understanding of the person, applying these to knowledge from social psychology about people in contexts and systems. The result is a pragmatic approach, which turns theory into practical application. The advantages of using The Skilled Helper framework are:

- clients readily understand it and can easily use it
- users find it robust and enabling
- developed and refined over 30 years, now published in eighth edition
- Professor Egan consults to organizations worldwide
- an integrative model
- emphasis on change, leading to valued outcomes
- applicable across cultures
- applicable for a variety of helping situations
- positive and systematic
- a framework that can be shared with the client
- a framework that can be used by the client between sessions
- maps the process of coaching or mentoring sessions
- utilizes skills of support and challenge to achieve change

- coaches, mentors and clients find the skills transferable to life and work.

Using the framework within a learning relationship

The three stages of the framework are shown in Figure 4.1. Egan states that there are two goals of helping and the three-stage model is designed to achieve these goals. The first goal is to help clients to manage their problems more effectively and to develop unused resources and missed opportunities more fully. The second goal is to help clients to become better at helping themselves (Egan 2002).

The Skilled Helper is used within a coaching or mentoring relationship characterized by respect, genuineness and empathy. This respect ensures that the framework, used well, always starts with where the client is. It focuses upon how the client is at the present moment and how the client would like to be. In that sense, coaching and mentoring are intentional activities. This practical framework may appear to be rational and linear because it is presented in stages, but it is intended to be used flexibly according to the needs of the client. Egan has often stated that the model is for the client, not the client for the model. Underlying the helping process are basic communication skills which enhance the effectiveness of the coach or mentor. Consciously developed listening, responding and challenging skills are important

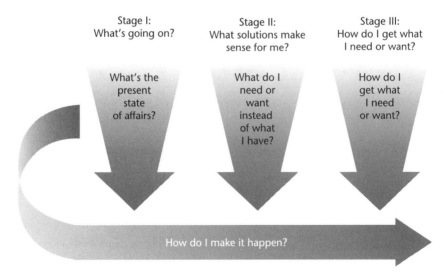

Figure 4.1   The Skilled Helper: three stages
Source: Egan (2006: 12)

throughout the process with the effective coach or mentor trying to maintain the right balance of support and challenge throughout.

How do the stages of The Skilled Helper achieve change?

The interactive stages and steps of The Skilled Helper model are shown in Figure 4.2. In order for the client to be able to change, the coach or mentor must communicate genuine interest, respect and empathy. Coaching or mentoring will then develop into an effective working alliance. Reviewing the working alliance openly and honestly through frequent evaluation can be a direct source of learning and change. The three stages of The Skilled Helper model are designed to move the client forward towards change and action. Each of the three main stages has three steps.

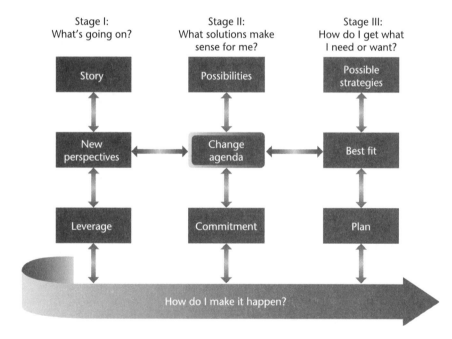

Figure 4.2 The Skilled Helper model showing interactive stages and steps
Source: Egan (2006: 18)

The first stage

The first stage helps the client to clarify the key issues calling for change. The three steps which work towards this exploration are: the telling of the story; the development of new perspectives; and the focusing upon issues where there will be the leverage to make a difference. This first stage helps the client to elaborate on an issue, a concern or an opportunity making sure that all aspects have been fully explored. The skills of the coach or mentor are used to help move from an overall 'story' to focusing and prioritizing something to work on. That then leads to the next stage which focuses upon options and goals.

The second stage

The second stage helps the client to identify what they need and want, that is, solutions that make sense for them. In the first step, the client is encouraged to engage creatively in imagining the possibilities of a better future. The psychological importance of this key stage is significant because by identifying 'wants' and not 'oughts' the client is more likely to develop the hope that will stimulate motivation to achieve stated goals. In the second step the client turns the wants and possibilities into a specific SMART goal. In fact, goal-setting is at the heart of this model for change. Egan calls this the 'change agenda'. The third step in this stage helps the client to test their own commitment to change and explore whether specific goals are realistic and valued. The hope for change can now develop into the courage to change. This leads into the third and final stage of the model, which deals with 'How do I achieve my goal?'

The third stage

The third stage helps clients to discover how to get what they need and want by developing strategies for action. In the first step, the stated goal gets tested through brainstorming all the possible strategies for action; then, in the second step, the client decides which of these is the best fit for their particular resources. Force field analysis can be used to examine the helpful and unhelpful factors which could influence the implementation of the action plan. The third step in this final stage is formulating and implementing an action plan.

Underlying all stages is the challenge of constant incremental change on the part of the client. Egan reminds us that talking about change is not the same as doing it. The coach or mentor can ensure that action permeates the helping process. Action does not always mean 'doing'. It can also, very profitably, entail thinking and reflecting. Work between sessions can help to achieve this sense of continuous growth and development.

We will now go through each stage of The Skilled Helper process in detail, highlighting the tasks of the coach or mentor at each stage. We will use a case example, Steve, to track through the main parts of each stage.

Stage 1: What's going on?

Steve's issue: 'Work seems to be dominating my life'

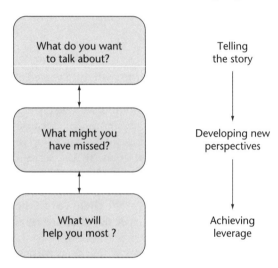

Figure 4.3   Key questions in Stage 1
Source: Adapted from Egan (2006: 168)

The client usually comes to see a coach or mentor because they feel stuck about a problem, issue or opportunity. So, the coach or mentor gives the person space to talk about what is going on. In this first stage of the process, rapport will be developed through the support that is offered while the client 'tells their story'. Attending, listening, paraphrasing, reflecting feelings, summarizing, probing and clarifying are skills that will be needed throughout this process. In addition, empathic challenge will be essential in order to identify areas that have been overlooked or avoided. These areas could be inaccuracies or deficiencies in perception of the problem situation, or underused resources and opportunities. New perspectives are developed from this exploration. Finally, in the first stage, the coach or mentor uses the skills of focusing, prioritizing and searching for the leverage that will enable the client to identify what would help them most. This process culminates in identifying something to work on that will make a difference. Once this is identified the client can move on.

Telling the story

The first stage of the coaching and mentoring process is used whenever a client comes to talk about an issue, problem or opportunity that they want to work on. So, it may be at the first visit, or it may be at any point in longer-term work where an issue needs to be explored, that action can be decided upon and taken. There are three steps at this stage of coaching or mentoring (see Figure 4.3). Each step will now be presented in detail.

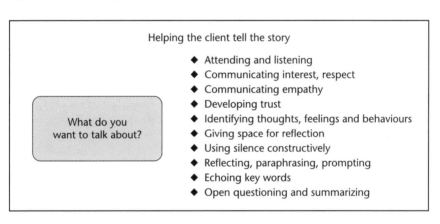

Figure 4.4   Stage 1 Step 1

The coach or mentor is first and foremost trying to build rapport to help the client tell their story (see Figure 4.4). At this stage the client needs space in order to reflect on what it is they want to say. Skills of support and challenge are used to help the client open up all aspects of the issue that are relevant. Basic listening skills are essential here. What is needed is attentive listening rather than diagnostic listening. Attentive listening includes observation of non-verbal communication as well as listening to the words used.

✓ *Note non-verbal communication:* eye contact, facial expression, posture, smiling or frowning, voice tone.
✓ *Note any discrepancy* between non-verbal signs and words spoken.
✓ *Listen carefully* to thoughts, feelings and actions.

✓   *Use silence*, when appropriate, to encourage talking.
✓   *Reflect back* succinctly and tentatively what has been said by the client so that they will hear what has been said more clearly.
✓   *Summarize and paraphrase* to let the client know you have understood.
✓   *Use open questions and probes* to clarify, challenge or check understanding. Such questions will include 'how' and 'in what way' and 'tell me more about'.
✓   *Repeat key words* from the client with a non-verbal question mark: 'angry?'; 'stressed?'; 'excited?'

These skills will help the client to relax and open up. They will also communicate interest, concern and empathy. These qualities in helpers are known to influence rapport between helper and helped (Rogers 1961). Once the client has perceived these qualities in the coach or mentor, then trust develops. Trust makes challenge possible and more likely to be effective. Throughout the relationship the coach or mentor is trying to establish the right balance of support and challenge. Too much support may provide comfort, but no change. Too much challenge may provoke, but may produce resistance rather than change. Challenge has the power to really make a difference, but if too strong, or too early, it may be rejected. If the coach or mentor challenges with empathy and with the intention of facilitating self-challenge in the client then there is the likelihood that the right balance of support and challenge will be achieved.

Developing new perspectives

The coach or mentor uses all the skills listed above to help the client to elaborate all parts of their story. In order to move forward it is important to check that no significant perspective had been overlooked. This is the second step in Stage 1 (see Figure 4.5).

This second step in Stage 1 gives something of a reality check on the story and a review of the possible resources that could be used by the client to move it all forward. Blindspots are explored and the client is encouraged to notice self-defeating patterns of thinking, feeling and acting. The coach or mentor helps the client to identify strengths and strategies which have worked well in the past and which could be applied now in the current situation.

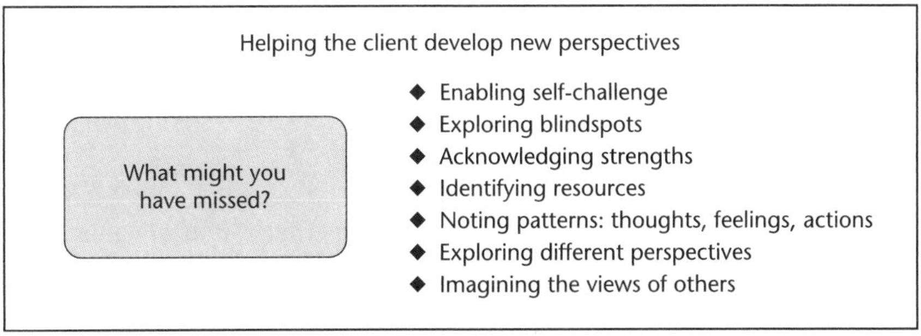

Helping the client develop new perspectives

What might you have missed?

- ◆ Enabling self-challenge
- ◆ Exploring blindspots
- ◆ Acknowledging strengths
- ◆ Identifying resources
- ◆ Noting patterns: thoughts, feelings, actions
- ◆ Exploring different perspectives
- ◆ Imagining the views of others

Figure 4.5   Stage 1 Step 2

One technique that is useful at this stage is outlined by two coaches writing from a neuro-linguistic programming (NLP) background. Eaton and Johnson (2001) say that creative people use frames to look at things from different angles. Table 4.1 shows how problem perspectives, or limiting frames, can be changed to productive ones.

Table 4.1   Changing limiting frames to productive frames

Limiting Frame	Productive Frame
Everything seen as a problem	Everything seen as a learning opportunity
Focusing on one element of an issue	Focusing on the issue as a whole
Noticing only your own perspective	Noticing how events affect others
Focus is on points of disagreement	Focus is on resolving differences

Source: Eaton and Johnson (2001: 39)

The coach or mentor can use these frames to, for example, ask the client a question about 'the big picture' if the client seems to be bogged down with detail. This is one way of helping the client to develop new perspectives. Other ways are to get the client to imagine the situation from the point of view of another person. Role reversal exercises can be helpful here (see Chapter 7 for an example). These are some of the questions the coach or mentor could ask:

- ✓ Is there *anything* you think you may have *missed*?
- ✓ If X were here now, *what might they be saying*?
- ✓ *Imagine* you are six months on; how do you think things would be, at work and at home?
- ✓ When you have *faced opportunities like this before* what, and who, has helped you to make the decision? Could you use any of those resources now?

✓   Do you *recognize any patterns* of thoughts, feelings or actions here, that
    have occurred before in your life? Do you want to repeat them? Or
    change them?

✓   What personal and professional *strengths* do you have which you
    could bring to bear on this situation?

Egan (2006: 192) gives a useful list of things that clients are able to say
when they have been helped to develop new perspectives:

- Here's a new angle . . .
- Here's something I've not thought of . . .
- Here's something I've overlooked . . .
- To be completely honest . . .
- Here's one way I've been fooling myself . . .
- Here's an important piece of the puzzle . . .
- Here's the real story . . .
- Here's the complete story . . .
- Oh, now I see that . . .

Achieving leverage

The first step of Stage 1 helps the client to have a full picture of the issue or
opportunity: 'it is about putting all the pieces of the jigsaw out on the table'.
The second step ensures that 'none of the important pieces are missing'. The
third step is to decide 'which are the really important pieces'. These will lead to
the point of leverage (see Figure 4.6). The third step in Stage 1 enables the
client to focus and prioritize and to find where there is the energy to work on
part of the issue or opportunity.

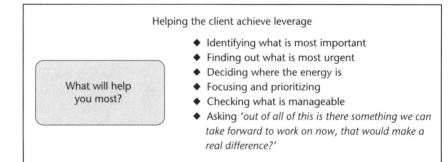

Helping the client achieve leverage

What will help
you most?

◆ Identifying what is most important
◆ Finding out what is most urgent
◆ Deciding where the energy is
◆ Focusing and prioritizing
◆ Checking what is manageable
◆ Asking *'out of all of this is there something we can
  take forward to work on now, that would make a
  real difference?'*

Figure 4.6   Stage 1 Step 3

Leverage is the part of the issue or opportunity, if worked on, would have the most impact. In order to arrive at this point of leverage the client needs to have:

✓   *summarized* all the parts of the story;
✓   *focused* on the most important aspects needing immediate attention;
✓   *prioritized* which part or parts to take forward.

Egan (2006: 193) gives some principles of leverage to help the client to decide which issues to choose to work on. We have adapted these:

1   If there is a crisis, help the client to manage the crisis.
2   Begin with the aspect that seems to be causing the most concern.
3   Begin with issues the client sees as important.
4   Begin with some manageable part of a larger situation.
5   Begin with a part that, if handled, will lead to some kind of general improvement.
6   Focus on a part of the issue for which the benefits outweigh the costs.

In our case example the client, Steve, has explained that work seems to be dominating his life. In Stage 1 he is helped to explore this issue, checking for anything that is missing in the story and then focusing and prioritizing on something out of that story that, if addressed, would take the issue forward.

At the start of Stage 1 Steve's issue was: 'Work seems to be dominating my life'
At the end of Stage 1 Steve's leverage statement: 'What I need to work on is getting a healthier balance back into my life'

Coach and mentor experiences of using Stage 1

They have noted these issues:

*   They need to remind themselves that diagnostic listening is not what is required in order to get the client to elaborate their story. Attentive listening, with few closed questions and plenty of reflecting, paraphrasing and summarizing, is most helpful in order to build rapport and enable the full story to be told.
*   They also often report that they have to safeguard against the tendency of thinking they need to know all the details of everything that led up to the situation presented by the client.

- They soon realize that questions are often asked to satisfy the curiosity of the coach or mentor, rather than to follow the story told by the client. They also experience that the session can degenerate into a question and answer interview, rather than 'telling the story'. This happens if the coach or mentor keeps using closed questions, rather than paraphrasing what has just been said, summarizing frequently or, when necessary, using open questions and prompts for clarification. A useful tip is to stay with recent and current events and keep focused on 'what is and what might be', rather than 'what was'.

- When trying to develop new perspectives careful judgement needs to be made about whether the story is complete, or whether it is worth checking for other information. If the client wants to move straight to leverage, then doing so might be appropriate if blindspots have already been addressed during the telling of the story. One of the main difficulties for the coach or mentor at this stage is to get the right balance between support and challenge. This is best done by being aware of the power of even the smallest challenges, such as echoing a key word like 'dominating?' Challenges may be like strong medicine. Sometimes the strongest medicine comes in small amounts!

Understanding how to achieve leverage can be difficult for some coaches and mentors. It can be helpful to remember that it is about focusing on the most meaningful parts of the story and then prioritizing. Some people find the following question useful for finding leverage: 'Out of everything that you have told me so far, is there one thing we could take forward to work on, that would make a real difference?'

Having read the issues experienced by other coaches ands mentors what do you think might be the issues or difficulties for you in Stage 1? Which of the steps would you find easiest and which would you need to work on: helping the client to tell the story; helping the client to develop new perspectives or helping the client to achieve leverage.

Box 4.1 At the end of Stage 1

The client will have:

✓ Explored the story
✓ Developed new perspectives
✓ Found a significant part to take forward

The coach or mentor will have:

✓ Attended to the client's non-verbal and verbal communication
✓ Listened actively
✓ Responded empathically using reflecting, paraphrasing and summarizing
✓ Repeated key words
✓ Used silence to provide reflective space
✓ Used open questions to clarify, challenge and check understanding
✓ Provided a balance of support and challenge
✓ Encouraged self-challenge in the client
✓ Stimulated the client to reframe of perspectives
✓ Enabled the client to focus, prioritize and find leverage
✓ Been a role model of facilitation for change

Stage 2: What solutions make sense for me?

Steve's leverage statement at the end of Stage 1 was: 'What I need to work on is getting a healthier balance back into my life'

The second stage moves the client from the stuckness which they may have experienced when they arrived for coaching or mentoring to the hope which arises from articulating their wants and needs. The client is invited to imagine possibilities and options, then to choose from them something which would be realistic to shape up into a specific goal. *After wanting and choosing, the client moves to committing to the goal.* Commitment moves the client from hope to courage, and from courage to action.

In order to begin work in the second stage the coach or mentor reminds the client of their chosen leverage point. This becomes the basis for brainstorming an ideal scenario in relation to the issue brought by the client. Steve has brought the issue that 'Work seems to be dominating my life'. After full discussion of all the aspects of this issue in Stage 1, he decides that the leverage point will be 'What I need to work on is to getting a healthier balance back into my life'.

If the coaching and mentoring has been done well, the client has removed their blinkers during the first stage and then in the second stage will explore all sorts of exciting possibilities 'in the ideal scenario'. This leads to *the choice of a wanted goal*. The choice of a wanted goal is very powerful in psychological terms. The driver for change is intrinsic, not extrinsic. The goal that is chosen as a result of this coaching or mentoring is more likely to be really wanted. It is therefore more likely to be acted upon. The final stage helps the client to follow the goal through to action and results (see Figure 4.7).

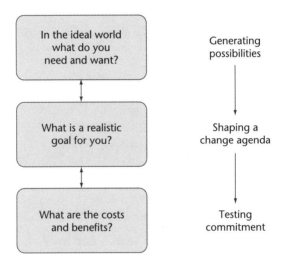

Figure 4.7   Key questions in Stage 2
Source: Adapted from Egan (2006)

Generating possibilities

Creativity and imagination help the client in the second stage to envisage their preferred scenario. The coach or mentor uses a variety of skills to encourage lateral thinking on the part of the client. These may include use of drawing, sculpting or writing. They may also include visualization or brainstorming (see Chapter 7). The idea is to open out possibilities, to encourage the client to, in a positive sense, 'think the unthinkable' so that within the seeds of a wild idea may be the germ of a realistic possibility. The skill of the mentor during the first part of Stage 2 is to keep accessing valued 'wants' and eliminating the effect of limiting 'oughts'.

In this step the coach or mentor is trying to encourage the client to produce as many ideas as possible in the shortest possible time (see Figure 4.8).

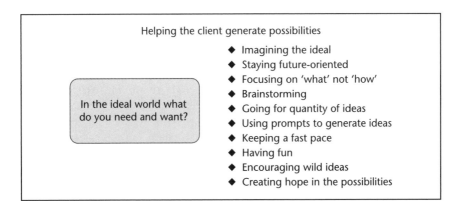

Helping the client generate possibilities

In the ideal world what do you need and want?

◆ Imagining the ideal
◆ Staying future-oriented
◆ Focusing on 'what' not 'how'
◆ Brainstorming
◆ Going for quantity of ideas
◆ Using prompts to generate ideas
◆ Keeping a fast pace
◆ Having fun
◆ Encouraging wild ideas
◆ Creating hope in the possibilities

Figure 4.8 Stage 2 Step 1

It is quantity rather than quality that is important. Here are some brainstorming prompts:

- What ideally do you want and need?
- In your ideal world . . .?
- Go on, be really wild and wacky.
- Who else is there . . . who is not there . . .?
- It is now X months into the future and you have achieved your ideal. Paint the picture for me . . . what have you got . . . what do you see . . .?

Some coaches or mentors find brainstorming difficult, and some clients do too. When listening to the story, during the first stage, it is possible to note whether the client finds it easy to imagine things in picture form, or do this through artwork. Two things are important, whichever format is preferred. Firstly, *the focus is future, not present.* Secondly, the focus is 'What do you want or need?' not 'How can you get it?' The 'how' question does not come until the final stage of the model.

Following that example, the coach or mentor wanting to generate possibilities would now ask Steve to imagine the ideal scenario in which there is a healthier balance in life. Steve would be encouraged to imagine a future time when this has actually been achieved and to say what would be in place that is not there now: what they might be doing, thinking and feeling that they are not doing, thinking or feeling now; what other people (partner, children, friends and colleagues) would be saying about the client in that ideal world; what work they would, ideally, be doing, and choosing not to do.

Shaping a change agenda

Having brainstormed as many 'wants' as possible the coach or mentor would then help the client to choose the most realistic and possible of these to take forward as a specific goal. The process moves from *wanting* to *choosing* (see Figure 4.9). The skills of choosing solutions, shaping these into workable goals and checking commitment to a desired goal are required to complete the second stage of the model. Methods such as a cost–benefit analysis can be used to check how painful the cost that is required to achieve the goal may be, and whether that cost can be outweighed by perceived benefits.

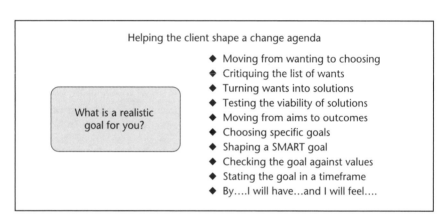

Figure 4.9 includes:

Helping the client shape a change agenda

What is a realistic goal for you?

- ◆ Moving from wanting to choosing
- ◆ Critiquing the list of wants
- ◆ Turning wants into solutions
- ◆ Testing the viability of solutions
- ◆ Moving from aims to outcomes
- ◆ Choosing specific goals
- ◆ Shaping a SMART goal
- ◆ Checking the goal against values
- ◆ Stating the goal in a timeframe
- ◆ By….I will have…and I will feel….

Figure 4.9 Stage 2 Step 2

Eaton and Johnson (2001) have drawn up a useful list of questions for coaches to elicit SMART goals (see Table 4.2).

Steve's leverage point was: 'What I need to work on is getting a healthier balance back into my life'
Working on this in Stage 2 leads to this SMART goal: 'By the beginning of next month I will be doing 30 minutes' exercise each evening after work. I will see my line manager within the next two weeks about delegating some of my work to another member of the team. I will feel healthier and I will be pleased that I have regained control of my life. I may also miss some of the work I have delegated!'

The coach or mentor would note here that although this fulfils the criteria of a SMART goal, the next step will be very important: testing commitment (see Figure 4.10). The client will need courage to sustain the exercise regime and may need help in delegating.

Table 4.2 Questions to elicit SMART goals

Elements of SMART	Useful questions
SPECIFIC Ensure everyone knows the aim	What will you be doing when you have achieved the goal? What do you want to do next?
MEASURED Define standards to work towards	How will you measure the achievement of the goal? What will you feel when the goal is reached?
ACHIEVABLE Ensure that the goal is realistic	What might hinder you as you progress towards the goal? What resources can you call upon?
RELEVANT Make sure the goal is worthwhile	What do you, and others, get out of this? Have other parties involved agreed to it?
TIMED Agree a timeframe	When will you achieve the goal? What will be your first step?

Source: Eaton and Johnson (2001: 31)

Here we see how a client moves from wanting to choosing. Out of all the possibilities listed in the brainstorm, the client chose two specific things to change: starting some regular exercise and consulting his line manager about delegating. It is a SMART goal because it is specific, he and his coach or mentor will know when it is achieved. The client thinks that it is realistic to see the line manager within two weeks and thinks that 30 minutes' exercise each day is manageable, sometimes by walking home from work and sometimes on the exercise bike at home.

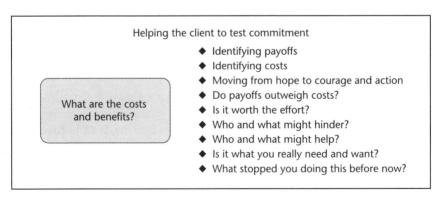

Helping the client to test commitment

What are the costs and benefits?

♦ Identifying payoffs
♦ Identifying costs
♦ Moving from hope to courage and action
♦ Do payoffs outweigh costs?
♦ Is it worth the effort?
♦ Who and what might hinder?
♦ Who and what might help?
♦ Is it what you really need and want?
♦ What stopped you doing this before now?

Figure 4.10 Stage 2 Step 3

Testing commitment

It is important to check how the client will feel if the goal is achieved. This client says that he will feel healthier and in control again. However, the loss that is felt from delegating work would need to be properly discussed. In the final step of this second stage the coach or mentor needs to ask: 'How committed are you to this as a goal?' If the client is not really committed then the chances are that it will not be achieved. The other key question is 'Does this goal meet your needs for a healthier balance in your life, and will it help to give you what you value most?'

The coach or mentor can help the client to do a cost–benefit analysis as a way of evaluating the factors that would affect commitment. There is a detailed explanation of how to use cost–benefit analysis in Chapter 7. Let us now revisit the example of Steve. Read again his SMART goal on page 88. In relation to this goal the cost–benefit analysis might be as shown in Table 4.3.

Table 4.3 Cost-benefit analysis

Benefits	Costs
Exercise will increase sense of well-being	I will need to be disciplined about doing the exercise and about prioritizing my work
Delegation will remove pressure	Delegation may bring other problems such as sense of loss and control
Partner and family will be pleased	Family will be disappointed if goal slips
I will regain control in my life and not feel overwhelmed	I will have to work smarter to make sure I leave work in time for exercise
My work will be more focused on the things I really want to do	I may need to spend more time training others to pick up the work

The client is helped here to identify both costs and benefits and in doing this becomes more aware of reasons why this goal has not been pursued before. Forewarned is forearmed! There will always be costs, but the client can learn how to manage these and not allow them to subvert the wanted goal. Becoming more conscious of the payoffs and rewards helps to strengthen resolve. This helps to increase the motivation to succeed and inspires the sort of courage which hopefully will propel the client to act and get results. Steve may decide that the benefits outweigh the costs but that regular review with the coach or mentor would be an important addition to the goal. This would ensure that the costs identified do not sabotage the efforts to change. Also, to provide the best chance of success, Steve may decide to enlist the support of his family, friends or colleagues, as well as the coach.

Once the client has been helped to commit to a specific goal the coaching or mentoring can move to the third and final stage. Up to this stage the focus has been on 'what': 'What is the present situation?' (Stage1), 'What ideally do you want and need in the future?' (Stage 2). Now that a goal has been articulated the client can move on to 'how': 'How can I help you to achieve that goal?'

Coach and mentor experiences of using Stage 2

Most of the experiences of using Stage 2 are liberating and energizing. The pace feels very different from Stage 1 in which there is a predominance of active listening, clarifying, supportive challenge and prioritizing. In Stage 2 the coach or mentor models to the client energy, imagination, creativity, hope and optimism. The client is helped to use the right side of the brain, to engage in lateral thinking and to give themselves permission to voice wild and wacky ideas which may contain seeds of reality when evaluated. Coaches and mentors have found that:

- Being completely clear about the leverage statement is the best introduction to generating possibilities.
- If brainstorming is used it can be useful to write down the ideas as they are spoken by the client and to check with the client whether they wish to write or whether they would like you to write while they speak. Either way, the brainstorm is theirs and should be given to them at the end of the session. Ideas should be written down verbatim and without judgement or discussion. In order to produce as many ideas as possible in the shortest time the coach or mentor encourages a fast pace.
- Some people find it difficult to use their imagination, whether they are helper or helped. It is important that these people are encouraged to keep going with the brainstorm because often the most significant ideas emerge near the end and if closure is too early this important information does not emerge. Another problem can be trying to encourage the client to express wild and wacky ideas. Perhaps the coach or mentor is a very grounded person who wishes to keep to what is realistic. However, often in the wild idea is the seed of reality. Developing wild ideas liberates the mind to access possibilities. It is often from one of these wild possibilities that new hope dawns which releases the energy to move forward.
- The second step of Stage 2 involves a critique of the generated

possibilities and it is important here to check with the client whether they prefer to tick off the brainstormed ideas one by one, or whether they want to scan the list and pick out a couple that seem most significant. Coaches and mentors need to stress that they are looking for ideas which are definitely wanted and which are not only probable but possible as well.

- The skill of setting the SMART goal is for the coach or mentor not necessarily to go through each bit of the SMART criteria painstakingly with the client, but to be listening carefully while the client is talking about the goal. If any areas of SMART have then been missed, the coach or mentor can prompt discussion about these. This should lead naturally into the final step of Stage 2: testing commitment.
- When looking at costs and benefits it is important not to overlook values and feelings.

At the end of Stage 2, some coaches or mentors think that the most important work is now done and that the client can do the 'action' bit for themselves. Not so! There is still important work to do in the final stage as we will see in the next section.

Box 4.2 At the end of Stage 2

The client will have:

✓ Brainstormed possibilities in relation to a leverage point
✓ Chosen a specific goal as the agenda for change
✓ Tested commitment to the goal

The coach or mentor will have:

✓ Encouraged visioning
✓ Used prompts to brainstorm
✓ Given permission to be wild and wacky
✓ Kept up a fast and fun pace
✓ Shaped up a SMART goal
✓ Identified important client values
✓ Used cost–benefit analysis to test commitment
✓ Checked how the client feels about accomplishing the goal

Stage 3: How do I get what I need and want?

Steve's goal is: By the beginning of next month I will be doing 30 minutes' exercise each evening after work. I will see my line manager within the next two weeks about delegating some of my work to another member of the team.

This is the final stage of the coaching or mentoring process in relation to any specific issue or opportunity. A specific and realistic goal has been checked to see if it is valued, and really wanted, by the client. Now is the time to see how it may be achieved. The coach or mentor helps the client to move from 'what' to 'how'.

The three steps in the final stage move from opening up the possibilities of a range of different strategies to evaluating which of these makes most sense for this particular client and then finally developing a plan of action; at this stage hope and courage are transferred into practical action. The coach or mentor will need to remain client-centred and not become directive in telling the client what to do. All the preparatory work of the first two stages will come to nothing if this stage is done too hurriedly. More haste less speed. Active listening and empathy now go alongside active planning for results.

When the action plan is agreed, the coach or mentor needs to discuss contingency plans in case the plan does not succeed. This is the responsibility of the coach or mentor. Because action takes place within a learning relationship, failure is viewed as a learning opportunity, not a disaster. Ethical coaches or mentors will ensure that the client can come back to report on action and results. At that point, the cyclical nature of this model becomes evident, as the client returns to 'tell their story'.

Possible strategies to achieve goals

The first step in this stage is to open up possible strategies for achieving the goal (see Figure 4.11). Egan reminds us that there are not just one or two ways, there are many possibilities. The aim is to help the client get in touch with as many possible strategies as can be thought of, whether they might work or not. Once more, at this stage, wild ideas are encouraged. This helps the client to 'think out of the box' in the hope that such thinking will release possibilities that might otherwise not have surfaced. The client can include strategies used by others even if they have not yet been used by the client. This helps to broaden the canvas. The coach or mentor uses prompts appropriately, while trying not to move into being directive by advising or telling the client what to do.

Prompts which help the client to explore may open up areas that are being

Figure 4.11 Key questions in Stage 3
Source: Adapted from Egan (2006: 245)

overlooked, for example: 'Are there any other strategies?' or 'Can you think of any strategies that others use which seem to work for them?' They cease to be helpful prompts and become advice or direction when they are like these: 'Why don't you . . .' or 'I found that doing it this way was very successful so why don't you try that?' The problem with these latter attempts at helping is that they start doing the work for the client, instead of the client searching for the answers. The possibility for learning is then reduced. If the client asks directly for your experiences then that would be the time to share them, with the proviso that 'this worked for me, but how do you think it would be for you?' The coach or mentor here is putting back to the client the responsibility to evaluate the shared experience and the process remains client-centred.

The coach or mentor now helps the client to review all the possible strategies which have been brainstormed (see Figure 4.12). They are invited to pick out ones which are most attractive and which most fit with their resources. This will increase the likelihood that the strategies will work for them.

For Steve's goal, the brainstorm of possible strategies might include:

- join a gym
- have a gym extension added on to the house
- hire a personal trainer to come to my home
- buy an exercise bike for home
- walk home from work instead of using the car
- leave office at 5.00 p.m. each day
- start working from home on two days each week

Helping the client brainstorm strategies

What strategies will help you get what you want?

- ◆ Restate the goal
- ◆ Brainstorm possibilities to achieve that goal
- ◆ Use prompts to help the client
- ◆ Prompts: people, places, times, strategies used previously, examples of others
- ◆ Encourage wild ideas
- ◆ Write down verbatim
- ◆ Keep going!
- ◆ Have fun!
- ◆ Fast and furious!
- ◆ Stay client-centred
- ◆ Summarize and reflect frequently for client to piggyback on ideas

Figure 4.12   Stage 3 Step 1

- meet with line manager in my office not his, so he can see work pressures
- be well prepared with statistics of hours worked
- give him plans for who and what to delegate
- rehearse this meeting with coach or mentor and feel confident
- plan beforehand what my 'walk away position' with manager will be

Best fit for resources

The next step of Stage 3 is to decide which of the brainstormed strategies would be best-fit for the client. It is important that the coach or mentor does not presume which strategies are most powerful or effective. You will notice that in the brainstorm example above, four strategies have been underlined because they have been chosen to achieve the goal. Two address the part that was to do with having 30 minutes exercise each day. The other two address the pressures at work. One includes a meeting with the manager whereas the other includes specific use of coaching or mentoring support. The coach or mentor would now use the ideas set out in Figure 4.13 to help Steve to develop these as workable strategies.

Techniques such as force field analysis or SWOT analysis can enable the client to become aware of what may hinder and what may help in achieving the goal. In SWOT analysis a four-box diagram is used to identify client strengths, weaknesses, opportunities and threats which could affect the successful outcome of a chosen strategy for action. In force field analysis the client identifies factors in self, others and the working, home and social contexts

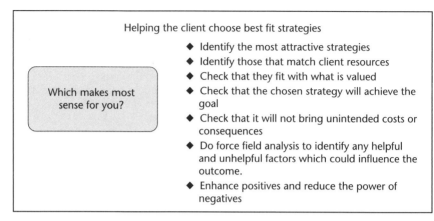

Helping the client choose best fit strategies

Which makes most sense for you?

◆ Identify the most attractive strategies
◆ Identify those that match client resources
◆ Check that they fit with what is valued
◆ Check that the chosen strategy will achieve the goal
◆ Check that it will not bring unintended costs or consequences
◆ Do force field analysis to identify any helpful and unhelpful factors which could influence the outcome.
◆ Enhance positives and reduce the power of negatives

Figure 4.13   Stage 3 Step 2

which could help or hinder. Having identified these the client can look at ways of minimizing the power of the unhelpful factors and maximizing the power of the helpful factors. There is a more detailed description of how to use force field analysis in Chapter 7.

In our example, Steve selected the goal of 30 minutes' exercise each day to address the problem of work dominating his life. He now looks at what will help and what will hinder his four chosen strategies to achieve that goal.

Force Field Analysis of Chosen Strategies

Goal: 30 minutes of exercise each evening after work

1 Walk home from work instead of using the car
2 Buy exercise bike
3 Meet with line manager
4 Rehearse this meeting with coach or mentor

GOAL

Enabling forces	Restraining forces
Want to feel healthier	May feel too tired to take exercise
Will buy exercise bike	Cost of bike
Walking makes me feel good	Cold, damp weather may stop me
Could refocus job	Not good at delegating
Capable of planning ahead	Line manager not pleased
My partner will encourage me	Promotion prospects could be affected

Figure 4.14   Force field analysis

Note in Fig. 4.14 that where the arrows are bold the coach or mentor will help Steve to give these factors special consideration. Having identified what might help or hinder, Steve is able to work out how to enhance the power of the helpful factors and decrease the power of the unhelpful factors. Finally, with all this information he is ready to execute a plan of action.

A manageable plan

In this final step of the model the client is helped to draw up an action plan in a timeframe. Critical path analysis (see Chapter 7) can be used to plot a sequence of actions and events chronologically. It is important that the realism of the intended actions is tested. Finally, contingency plans need to be discussed so that all will not fail if obstacles get in the way. Evaluation follows implementation and so the coach or mentor will ensure a follow-up session to review what succeeded, what failed, why, and what can be learned for the future (see Figure 4.15).

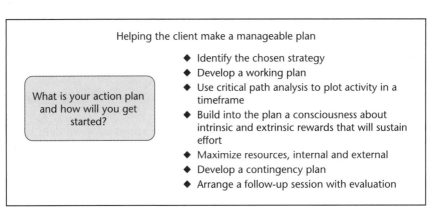

Helping the client make a manageable plan

What is your action plan and how will you get started?

◆ Identify the chosen strategy
◆ Develop a working plan
◆ Use critical path analysis to plot activity in a timeframe
◆ Build into the plan a consciousness about intrinsic and extrinsic rewards that will sustain effort
◆ Maximize resources, internal and external
◆ Develop a contingency plan
◆ Arrange a follow-up session with evaluation

Figure 4.15   Stage 3 Step 3

The coach or mentor will be aware of the way that inertia or entropy can prevent action from starting or prevent it being completed (Egan 2006). Inertia bedevils those who procrastinate. Entropy bedevils those who get started but 'fall apart' before completion. One of the responsibilities of the coach or mentor is to help the client to recognize whether either of these could come into play, and how to stop them.

The real test of whether the coaching or mentoring is successful is whether the client acts, makes changes and delivers the results that they want and need. So, specific and detailed action plans are important. At this stage some skill deficits may be apparent and may prevent successful action. The

---

Box 4.3 Planning for action: some questions to ask

- What's the timeframe for this action plan?
- What will you do first?
- What next?
- Who else is involved? How?
- What could stop this plan from succeeding?
- Who could stop this plan from succeeding?
- What will you do to lessen the chance of failure?
- When you have tried to do this sort of thing before, what has helped you most?
- Will that helpful factor work this time? What else could help?
- Who could help you most with this?
- Will inertia or entropy affect your plan? How will you avoid them?
- What will be the strongest motivator to ensure that you succeed?

---

coach or mentor will want to talk about these and help to develop whatever is needed.

In our work–life balance example the best-fit strategies included:

1   Walk home from work instead of using the car.
2   Buy an exercise bike.
3   Meet with line manager in my office so that he sees the work pressures.
4   Rehearse this meeting with coach or mentor and feel confident.

The action plan could be:

> **Steve's action plan:** 'I will start walking home from work three nights each week for the first month and then review that part of my plan. I will begin walking home from next Monday. In bad weather I will use the exercise bike instead. I will start arranging the meeting with my line manager, in my office, for three weeks' time. In the meantime I will have another session with you to rehearse the meeting. If I arrange that for two weeks from now, I will be able to come to the meeting having prepared what I think would be my position and what I think might be his.'

The contingency plan could be:

> **Steve's contingency plan:** 'If I find after the first week that I haven't kept to the exercise routine I will talk to my partner and ask for

support. Even if the walking home from work doesn't seem manageable I will commit to the bike instead. If I have problems with arranging the meeting with my line manager, or if I start getting very stressed before we are due to meet again, I will contact you, as you suggested.'

Coach and mentor experiences of using Stage 3

On the whole, Stage 3 seems fairly straightforward for coaches and mentors who have been used to problem management and problem-solving. This stage emphasizes that The Skilled Helper model is intentional and that action leading to valued outcomes is the overall aim. However, any part of that process can be used on its own, if that is what the client wants and needs.

- The main issues facing the coach or mentor are those involved in staying client-centred while in the active stage of action planning.
- The second step in Stage 3 can be done too hurriedly, indeed there can be a tendency to spend too little time in each part of this stage. In the first step, the brainstorm needs to be done in a detailed way, just as it was in the beginning of Stage 2 when possibilities in the ideal scenario were explored. In the second step, there needs to be a full critique of the brainstorm leading to a choice of strategies for action, not a quick romp through the list.
- Force field analysis, if done well, can identify important factors which will affect whether the action succeeds. Once more, it should not be hurried too much.
- The final step of putting the plan together needs attention to detail.

It can be very satisfying to complete the cycle of The Skilled Helper in this way and then there is a natural feedback into debriefing the results of the action in a future session. The effective coach or mentor will realize that work goes on not just in the sessions but, most importantly, between sessions as well. Everything that client and coach or mentor do together is just the preparation for where the real action takes place: in everyday life and work.

Box 4.4 At the end of stage 3

The client will have:

✓   Brainstormed several possible strategies for achieving the goal
✓   Decided which of these best fit values and resources
✓   Evaluated what may help or hinder the success of the chosen strategy
✓   Worked on a specific action plan
✓   Developed a contingency plan

The coach or mentor will have:

✓   Facilitated a brainstorm of strategies, using relevant prompts
✓   Evaluated possibilities to find best fit
✓   Used force field analysis, SWOT analysis or cost–benefit analysis
✓   Ensured that there is a specific action plan in a timeframe
✓   Supported the development of a contingency plan
✓   Checked with the client about how all this feels
✓   Provided the possibility of a session to evaluate action

Staying client-centred

As stated earlier, frameworks are of value only if they are client-centred, not model-centred. The message here is, start wherever the client is, and let the framework follow the client using only the parts of the framework that are appropriate within any coaching or mentoring session. It could be that only attending and listening is appropriate for a whole session because the client can use the reflective space to self-challenge and to decide upon action. It may be that all the client needs from the coach or mentor is some help with visioning the ideal future.

If the client has a clearly articulated goal they do not want to be dragged back through Stage 1 and Stage 2 simply in order to use a model or framework. The wise coach or mentor will listen carefully to the goal which is presented and will check that this is a SMART goal. If it is, then they can proceed to the next stage. However, if during the discussion about the goal it becomes apparent that it is not so clear or SMART after all, then the client will be ready to perhaps tell more of the story about why this was chosen as a goal. It may be that the goal was not chosen by the client, but by a line manager or close friend, partner or colleague. If so, it may be in the category of 'ought' not 'want'. Until it is wanted it is unlikely that the benefits will outweigh the costs and this is why action then fails. Of course, sometimes in organizations we are told what goals we will pursue, whether we like it or not, and in that case the coach or mentor has a more difficult job helping the client to find the part that is meaningful to them, within a larger goal which is not.

Evaluative skills are needed throughout the process, as the coach or mentor monitors carefully the progress of the client and encourages them to use the framework for action between sessions. At any point in the process the client can return to the first stage to 'tell the story' of how it has been between sessions. The skills of being able to go spontaneously with the flow of where the client is and apply the framework flexibly in the service of the client are perhaps the most advanced required of a coach or mentor. The Skilled Helper model is then used with integrity and wisdom, not mechanistically in the way a more inexperienced person may use it. It is used most effectively when it is known so well that it is in the background, with the client in the foreground. At this stage the coach or mentor has moved through the stage of 'conscious competence', to a level of proficiency that is characterized by 'unconscious competence'.

Links with the following chapters

In the next two chapters, case studies are presented: one of coaching and one of mentoring. You are invited to put yourself in the position of coach and mentor using The Skilled Helper framework to work with these clients, Anna and Paul.

The two case studies have been written to address different facets of coaching and mentoring. In Chapter 5, you are the coach for Anna. With Anna, you will focus upon using the skills and stages of The Skilled Helper framework. In Chapter 6, you are the mentor for Paul. With Paul, you will be reflecting upon ethical and professional issues in mentoring and upon issues you might take to supervision.

If you would like to know more about tools and techniques to use at different stages of The Skilled Helper model then turn to Chapter 7.

Summary

In this chapter we have:

- Discussed the advantages and disadvantages of using frameworks in coaching and mentoring.
- Presented one framework in detail: The Skilled Helper.
- Illustrated how the three stages of The Skilled Helper can be used to help clients to release potential and achieve results they value.

- Explained each stage and step in detail, giving examples of coach and mentor questions, prompts and interventions and using a case example to track client progress through the stages.
- Identified useful tips and cautions against possible pitfalls, by sharing the experiences of coaches and mentors who use this framework.

5 How can I use the framework in coaching?

- Introduction
- Using the framework: case example, Anna
- The first coaching session
- The second coaching session
- Summary

Introduction

This chapter demonstrates the way in which The Skilled Helper framework can be used in coaching. A case study, with commentary, forms the major part of the chapter, and it illustrates how the skills of effective coaching are used intentionally within The Skilled Helper framework. In the case study, coach and client work with the framework stage by stage, and you may wish to refer to Chapter 4 which describes the framework in detail.

The case study is designed to help you, as coach, to reflect on these questions:

- How do I use the skills of effective coaching with The Skilled Helper framework?
- How do the key principles help me to coach effectively?

You are the coach for Anna, a manager. The case study explores the development of your coaching relationship over two sessions. In each of the sessions, you work with her using all three stages of The Skilled Helper framework. The stages and steps of the framework are highlighted in the text as they are used in each session. At the end of each stage, there is a summary of how the framework and principles have been applied.

There are interactive prompts and questions for you, as well as explanations of how the framework and the principles of effective coaching and mentoring apply. At various points you are asked to:

- reflect on what is happening
- consider your response
- decide how you will help the client

 When you see this sign, there is a summary of how the principles of effective coaching and mentoring and The Skilled Helper framework are being used in practice.

Before you start coaching Anna, look again at Figure 1.1 on page 7 to remind yourself of the key principles. Then look again at Figure 4.2 on page 76 to remind yourself of the stages of The Skilled Helper framework.

Using the framework: case example, Anna

Anna has recently been promoted to her first managerial position in a financial services organization. She is bright and has no difficulty in grasping the technical aspects of complex assignments. Clients are impressed by her. The firm has recently conducted a 360-degree feedback exercise for all managers as part of a leadership development initiative. Feedback to Anna indicated that junior and support staff sometimes find her 'difficult'. Her boss has discussed the feedback with Anna, and as part of her personal development plan, talked about the options of either mentoring with a director, or more focused coaching support. Anna has opted for coaching. You are the HR specialist providing coaching services and you have met Anna and her boss. You have agreed to work with Anna, initially for four two-hour sessions, meeting monthly. You have also clarified the working agreement and discussed how you and Anna might use The Skilled Helper framework to structure and support coaching conversations.

The first coaching session

This is your first session, and you are wondering how things will go, and in particular, why Anna has chosen coaching rather than mentoring.

 What are your hopes and aims for this first meeting? Any concerns? If you need to refresh your memory, there is a section on 'beginnings' in Chapter 2 (page 33).

Stage 1: What's going on? The story – new perspectives – leverage

The story: At the first session, you ask Anna to describe how things are at work. Anna starts talking animatedly, and as you listen and paraphrase, she tells you how happy she was until the feedback exercise. Now, she says in a rather disgruntled manner, 'There is clearly a problem in the way people see me.'

 As coach, how might you respond? You could:

- Ask a question: how do they see you?
- Make a statement: yes, the feedback indicates that . . .
- Reflect her words in the form of a question: the way people see you?

You decide that the first two options run the risk of being too challenging at this early stage, so you choose the third.

Anna says, in a rather abrupt way, 'Well, they certainly don't like me.' She begins to talk about how surprised she was by the feedback and how she has always been 100 per cent successful in delivering on time and on budget, whatever it takes. Her job, she tells you, is extremely demanding and there isn't always time for 'handling everyone with kid gloves'.

 You say?

- I know the job's tough, but don't you think you're being a bit defensive?
- So it's tough delivering on time all the time, and it's been a surprise to hear it has ruffled a few feathers?
- I imagine anyone would be stressed in your role . . .

The first option lacks empathy, and the third is rather more sympathetic than empathic, so you choose the second.

New perspectives: Anna looks a little taken aback by your response, as if she was expecting more of a challenge, but slowly she relaxes and begins to tell you how hard it is to be a newly-appointed manager, being under scrutiny and anxious to do well. She talks about the constant pressure of deadlines, and how everything seems to rest on her shoulders. You notice that her demeanour has changed and the vivacious person has become quieter; the word that comes into your mind is 'smaller'.

 You say?

- Rest on your shoulders . . . that sounds like a burden . . . is it?
- How does it feel to be under such pressure?
- And if your staff were here now, and heard you talking, what would they be saying?
- In the past, how have you handled being under pressure?

All of these responses could be helpful, and you use them in turn as she elaborates the story, and tells you how, under pressure, she becomes rather bossy, both with herself and with others. She talks about the way her management style changes from 'how I try to be – calm and even tempered' into 'the gorgon'. As she says the words, she laughs at herself. You encourage Anna to tell you about 'the gorgon' and she paints a verbal picture that has you both smiling.

You sense that Anna is now more willing to reflect on her behaviour, and challenge herself, so you risk a challenge:

- If you worked for 'the gorgon' what would you do?

Anna says immediately, 'Oh, I'd quit or transfer as soon as possible!' She talks about how difficult she can be with staff, and in fact she is finding the new role much tougher than she anticipated and is even wondering whether this is the right job for her. She thinks that the technical aspects of work are much more satisfying than the people management aspects. This is why, she says, she chose to speak to you rather than a director, because 'I wanted to talk completely off-line.'

 You are wondering what to say next in order to summarize Anna's problems. Try to complete this sentence: 'Anna, the current situation seems to be a problem for you in several ways . . .'

Compare your answer with the suggestions below, all of which accurately describe ways in which the situation may be a problem for Anna. Did your answer include one or more of these points?

- The feedback has come as a surprise
- You are hurt by the feedback

- You are finding the new job harder than you expected
- You are wondering whether you are on the right career path
- You feel under constant pressure
- You are aware that your management style can be less than perfect!
- Perhaps you don't feel appreciated for always delivering on time?

Leverage: You are not sure what is most pressing or important for Anna, and you are also aware than you have only four coaching sessions. You are wondering whether her question 'Is this the right job for me?' is within your remit, and whether it might be more than you can deal with in four sessions.

 What do you say next? Which of the options below do you prefer?

- So, out of all of the things we've talked about, what seems the right bit for you to work on now?
- I wonder if you need to attend a stress a management workshop?
- Perhaps you need to sort out your career issues first.

You select the first option because it offers her the choice, whereas with the other two options you are making suggestions.

She says, 'Well, the career thing is a big issue, but maybe I need to see if I can get on top of this job first of all. That's what I want to work on, getting on top of this job and losing "the gorgon".'

At this point, you have reached the end of Stage 1, although not the end of the session.

 SESSION 1: USING STAGE 1 AND APPLYING THE PRINCIPLES

You have used each of the three steps of Stage 1 of The Skilled Helper framework. The framework has enabled you to work intentionally.

While both you and Anna knew at the outset about the problem, you've been able to explore in depth with Anna the ways in which it is a problem for her.

You've challenged her and enabled her to challenge herself in exploring new perspectives.

She has been supported in identifying something manageable to take forward.

You've worked hard to establish a safe, trusting relationship with Anna, who was quite 'prickly' to begin with. At one point you thought that she anticipated critical challenge from you, but when she received support and empathic challenge, she began to relax.

You noticed that a strength and resource she has is her willingness to laugh at herself, and you've been able to share humour together.

You've tried to ensure Anna has autonomy in choosing what to work on, and creating the coaching agenda. While you have steered the process, she has made the decisions about which issues to tackle.

You have helped Anna to focus on what she wants to work on, while at the same time acknowledging that she may want to explore broader issues. You wonder whether it might be more appropriate for her to be mentored by a director if she decides to explore these issues.

The coaching session continues.

Stage 2: What solutions make sense for me? Possibilities – change agenda – commitment

Possibilities: Anna has identified the leverage issue of getting on top of her job and losing 'the gorgon'. You suggest to her that, rather than working on *how* she can get on top of the job and lose the 'gorgon', which may seem like an obvious place to begin, you could start by imagining that she has achieved all that she wants and paint a picture of *what* would be happening in her ideal situation. You ask her to think forward in time, to describe what the ideal 'on top of the job and losing the gorgon' would be like for her. You've noticed that Anna uses visual imagery in the way she talks.

 What brainstorming prompts might you use? Try to add five to those below.

- So, imagine it's going really well. . . . describe your day . . .
- What are you doing?
- What are you thinking? Feeling?
- What have you stopped doing?
- Ideally, what are people saying about you? About your team?

There are more prompts in Chapters 4 and 7.

Anna's brainstorm list is several pages long, and you struggle to keep up with writing each item down verbatim, but you manage. You wonder how on earth she'll be able to sort through all the items, and so you ask her how she wants to select the important points. You suggest going through the list item by item, but Anna is highly intuitive and prefers to scan the list. She says that three things stand out for her:

- not losing my cool
- we're all one team, not just me the boss
- feeling calmer, happier

Change agenda: You hope that by identifying the important elements of what she *wants*, Anna can now *choose* a goal. The items that she has selected describe the direction she wants to travel in, her ideal. She now needs to choose something that she can achieve, a goal which will take her towards her ideal.

 Can you think of a question that you might ask to help Anna formulate a goal?

You ask, 'Anna, is there a goal emerging from this, something you can achieve, and want to achieve?' Anna says yes, her goal is that within three months her group will be functioning as a team, with her being part of the team and not, as she currently feels, apart from them. You ask her to phrase this as a SMART goal. Anna says, 'Within three months, the team will be working better with me, and I will feel more relaxed.'

 While this is useful first attempt at getting a goal statement, there are some difficulties with it. Can you spot them?

With your help, Anna refines the goal statement. She makes two important changes. Firstly, she focuses on achievements directly within her control, changing the goal from 'the team will' to 'I will'. Secondly, she tries to make the goal more specific and measurable. This is her revised goal statement:

> By the end of June, I will be acting calmly at work in all situations, and involving my team in responding to demands and deadlines, and I will feel happier.

If you wanted to review this goal against the SMART checklist in Chapter 4, what questions might you ask at this stage?

Commitment: Before you start working on how Anna can achieve this goal, you want to check that it is the right goal for her. You ask her about the advantages and disadvantages of achieving the goal, the costs and benefits, both for herself and others. (There is a detailed description of this technique in Chapter 7.) She thinks the advantages are pretty obvious: both she and the team would be happier and hopefully working more effectively. The disadvantages are less obvious; however, she notices that her goal is to *behave* calmly. She wonders if she will always feel calm. Maybe a disadvantage for her will be coping with how she feels and having to manage 'the gorgon'. She also wonders if all the work will get done, and whether standards will suffer.

 Paraphrase what you've heard, and check if this is the right goal for Anna.

Anna decides that the goal is fine, and now she wants to work on how she can achieve it. You have reached the end of Stage 2.

 SESSION 1: USING STAGE 2 AND APPLYING THE PRINCIPLES

Working through each of the steps of Stage 2 has enabled Anna to take one part of the problem which she can work on, and picture how that would be if things were much improved.

Anna found it easy to brainstorm. She was energized in this stage – it played to her strengths, and you mentally noted that brainstorming may be a useful technique to use again. You noticed how Anna's values became apparent as she described her ideal. While you weren't sure how you'd move from the creative ideal to the more practical goal, the process seemed to flow.

You found that being clear in your own mind about a format for a goal statement helped Anna to avoid the pitfall of setting a goal which wasn't really hers to achieve. The format challenged her to focus on what *she* could do. What you did was to steer the process, and with lots of reflecting and active listening, as well as using the framework, you helped her to move forward.

When you tested her commitment to the goal, she mentioned work standards. You remembered that something she'd talked about at the very beginning was getting the work done 'whatever it takes'. You wondered if this was important, whether you might have reflected this back to her. Maybe it would have been helpful to go back to Stage 1 and explore this? However, the moment passed and you mentally 'logged' it, and noted that perhaps it will crop up again.

Stage 3: How do I get what I need or want? Possible strategies – best fit – plan

Possible strategies: There are 30 minutes until the end of the session. You wonder what would be a good outcome from this session for Anna. You are rather concerned – you don't want to leave matters in mid-air, but neither do you want to force the pace.

 What might you say to Anna now?

You might say: 'Anna, I see we have 30 minutes left. You've identified a goal, now should we use the time to talk about how you might achieve it, or is there something else more useful that we could do?'

Anna tells you that she thinks that a lot has been achieved already. She has focused on something which is manageable, after initially feeling rather overwhelmed by the staff feedback. She says that in this last part of the session it would be useful to identify some actions for her to take between now and the next time you meet. You ask her to restate the goal, and then describe all the ways in which she might achieve it, including some wild and wacky ideas. She restates her goal: 'By the end of June, I will be acting calmly at work in all situations, and involving my team in responding to demands and deadlines, and I will feel happier.'

 What prompts might you use to help Anna to brainstorm all the different ways that she could achieve her goal?

In response to your prompts, here are some items from Anna's list:

101 ways to achieve my goal
- identify role models . . . other colleagues who stay calm . . . talk to them

- talk to my team more . . . involve them at the front end
- take more notice of my own behaviour . . . what do I do
- take five, take time out to think before I start rushing around issuing orders
- challenge deadlines . . . do I always have to respond instantly
- read a book. . . . find some techniques on how to manage stress
- join a relaxation class
- take a holiday, have a break

Best fit: You ask Anna which of these she wants to do, which would fit with her values and resources, and which have the fewest unwanted consequences. Anna says, 'That certainly rules out taking a holiday, because I'd have a mountain of work to return to!' You agree that it's important that she choose a strategy which doesn't add more stress at work and make the goal less likely to be achieved.

Anna decides that a good starting point would be to keep a record of her reactions in times of stress at work, and what actually happens when work pressures build. She says that this start point appeals to her. You prompt her to expand and she tells you that it's something that she can do every day, it's under her control, and she will generate her own data.

Plan: Anna has identified a strategy, and you are wondering what would help her to put it into action.

 What do you do next? What questions will help Anna firm up her actions? Help her to plan for contingencies? Help her to check that the actions will achieve her goal? There are some prompts in Chapter 4.

Anna commits herself to the following actions, which she writes down:

- At the end of each day, I will note down any incidents where I have been under pressure. I will use three columns: what I was thinking at the time, what I was feeling and what I actually did.
- When I notice myself about to go into 'gorgon mode', I will 'take five', by getting a coffee or going for a walk around the block or finding some other distraction.
- When we meet again in a month, I will bring my notes and discuss with you what has happened.

You have reached the end of Stage 3 and of the first session.

SESSION 1: USING STAGE 3 AND APPLYING THE PRINCIPLES

In Stage 3, you enabled Anna to identify manageable actions she could take before the next session. Anna was supported in choosing actions which would not increase her stress levels too much, but would be appropriately challenging for her. What she has chosen requires her to reflect and notice her own behaviour, thoughts and feelings.

You were aware that, as the session progressed, you were feeling under pressure. You remember that Anna's team have said they often feel under pressure, and indeed so does Anna. You wonder whether you might have shared this observation with Anna and asked to what extent are you both recreating in the coaching session what happens 'out there'.

However, you were pleased that, despite feeling concerned, you did offer choices to Anna about how to use the time.

You realize that you forgot to leave time at the end of the session to review with Anna how you have worked together, which would have been useful, especially since this was your first session. You make a mental note to ensure you leave time at the end of the next session, which takes place, as planned, a month later.

The second coaching session

Stage 1: What's going on?

 You are wondering how to start the second session. You consider saying:

- Hello Anna, how are things?
- Hello Anna, let's start by looking at how you got on with your action plans.

Which option do you prefer? Because . . .?

You decide that it's better not to make any assumptions about what's been happening, so you ask the more general question 'How are things?' Anna tells you that the past month has been 'an eye-opener' for her. As planned, she has kept notes, and has been surprised by what she found. Firstly, she noticed how often she gets stressed at work. Secondly, she noticed her feelings: annoyance at requests, anxiety about her team's ability (and her own ability) to respond, and impatience with others. As she has noticed this, she has tried to take time out and avoid venting her feelings on those around her.

 What do you notice about Anna's reaction to this data compared with her reaction to the 360-degree feedback? Why do you think that is? Reflect this to Anna, balancing support and challenge.

You say, 'You know Anna, when you talked about the staff feedback it was as though you didn't really want to believe it, maybe it was a bit difficult to take in. Today it's different – you are challenging yourself, and sounding quite energized.' Anna agrees, yes, this is her data and something she can work with. She says, 'I want to get on and make some changes. I can see now what I need to stop doing. I'm just not sure what to do instead!' It seems as if Anna is firing on all cylinders, so you match her pace. You say, 'OK, let's try this. Chose three behaviours you'd be happy to lose, three gorgon behaviours, and three you want to substitute.' She says, 'I want to stop issuing orders, taking charge and demanding. I want to start listening, involving others more but not [she laughs] lose control.'

At this point, you share with Anna some research about the skills of effective influencers, which describes specific skills that they use. In fact, they do a lot of active listening and involving others, and yet they are certainly not people who have lost control! She is interested in this, and says that she's keen to 'give it a go', to try out some of these skills and new behaviours, and see what happens.

You have reached the end of Stage 1, although not the end of the session.

 SESSION 2: USING STAGE 1 AND APPLYING THE PRINCIPLES

You trod cautiously at the beginning of the session. Anna is a client who has a lot of pressure at work and you didn't want to recreate that pressure in the coaching session.

You invited Anna to tell her story of what had happened since your first session. It was clear that in carrying out her action plans, she had generated some new perspectives for herself since last time.

Since she was enthusiastic, it seemed appropriate to offer some challenges and suggest some new perspectives in the session. You talked about the research on communication skills, and asked some focused questions. Your questions helped her to identify the leverage issue, which was 'developing new behaviours'.

> As she described these behaviours, she talked about how she wanted things to be in the future, and so she began to move in Stage 2, talking about the ideal and possibilities.

The session continues.

Stage 2: What solutions make sense for me?

 What do you do now? Which part of this stage will be most useful?

You say, 'Anna, remembering what we talked about last time, and putting that together with what you've said today, it sounds as though you have some ideas for a goal, and now you want to get going with it?' Anna agrees. She wants to ask her team for suggestions, not assume that ideas have to come from her, talk less and not always jump in first. Her goal is: 'By next time we meet, I will have spoken less and made fewer suggestions in our weekly meetings and elsewhere. Instead, I will ask for suggestions. I will feel pleased that I am doing this, and interested in whether I feel in control enough!'

You are at the end of Stage 2, and midway through the session.

 SESSION 2: USING STAGE 2 AND APPLYING THE PRINCIPLES

Given the work that you and Anna had done, your hunch was that you could quite quickly firm up a goal. Anna began to describe her ideal behaviour, and the goal, i.e. the change agenda, evolved from her description. It did not seem necessary to use an intentional brainstorming process, as you did in the first session.

You did not specifically ask Anna about the costs and benefits of achieving this goal, but you noticed that she was concerned about losing control, a potential cost of this goal. You have an idea about how to help her with this. However, you wonder whether you might have reflected this concern back to her, to give her the opportunity to talk more about it.

The session continues.

Stage 3: How do I get what I need or want?

An hour of your session remains. You suggest to Anna that one way of exploring possible actions would be to use the remainder of the time to practise some of the new behaviours. She could rehearse them, and notice how the words sound and how she feels as she says them, in particular how 'in control' she feels. You explain the process and some options: perhaps you could take the part of a team member responding to her, or perhaps she could play both parts, physically moving between two chairs as she does so. (There is a description of this technique, role-reversal, in Chapter 7.) Anna is enthusiastic to try this out and asks you to play the part of a team member. She tries out different scenarios and forms of words, and is quite heartened. 'When I hear myself, it doesn't sound like losing control at all, in fact it sounds better, more responsive, not just reactive.'

Anna writes down some specific actions she will try out between now and next time you meet. These are:

- I will do less telling and ask more questions
- When feeling anxious I will let my team know, not by being aggressive but rather by saying something like 'I'm concerned about'
- Under pressure, I will continue to 'take five' and give myself time to calm down
- I will read the article which you have recommended to me

You check with Anna whether all these actions are doable, and whether they fit with her goal.

 As coach, in what ways have you influenced this part of the session? What are the potential advantages and disadvantages of the way you've worked?

In the last part of the session, you suggest to Anna that you review together how you have worked over the two sessions, what has been achieved and what has been helpful or less helpful in the sessions.

 What questions might you ask Anna? Compare them with the checklist of questions in Chapter 2, page 36. How do you think the sessions have gone?

SESSION 2: USING STAGE 3 AND APPLYING THE PRINCIPLES

You have helped Anna to move from setting a goal to exploring different ways of achieving the goal, and finally to identifying specific actions that she will take.

You've focused on role-reversal as a way of exploring possible actions that might work for Anna and finding the ones that suit her best. You followed your hunch that working in this more immediate way, i.e. trying out some new behaviours rather than simply talking about them, would be useful for Anna. She seems to have enjoyed this different learning method, and it has built the rapport between you.

Anna has written some specific action plans which she is confident are achievable.

You got rather carried away with how well then session was going, and realized afterwards that you forgot to help Anna to plan for contingencies and what she might do if things didn't go according to plan.

However, you did remember to make time to review with Anna how you have worked together in this session and the previous one.

A learning relationship has been established. You have established trust, worked with Anna, and enabled her to gain new perspectives and set achievable goals for herself.

Postscript

In the remaining two coaching sessions, you continue this work. Anna builds her skills as she practises and refines the new behaviours. As her confidence grows, she plans an awayday with her team to look at how they are working together. She begins to try out skills with colleagues and with clients, so that she does less reacting and more clarifying what's wanted and needed. She finds she can even negotiate deadlines and reduce some of the pressure on her and her team.

The next chapter contains a mentoring case study. You are the mentor for Paul. As you work with him, you will have the opportunity to reflect on ethical and professional issues in mentoring, and on issues you might take to supervision.

Summary

In this chapter we have:

- Invited you to be the coach for a client, Anna, in a case example.
- Used interactive prompts and questions to help you to consider how you would work with Anna over two sessions.
- Described the stages and steps of The Skilled Helper framework and summarized how these occur in the case example.
- Highlighted how The Skilled Helper framework can support and guide the coaching conversation.
- Shown how the key principles help a coach to work effectively and to reflect on their practice.

6 How can I use the framework in mentoring?

- Introduction
- Case example: Paul
- Introductory session
- Session 1
- Session 2
- Summary

Introduction

This chapter demonstrates the way in which The Skilled Helper framework can be used in mentoring. The case study is designed to help you, as mentor, to reflect on these questions:

- How do the key principles of effective mentoring help me to reflect on a mentoring session?
- What are some of the ethical and professional issues that may arise in the mentoring relationship?
- What sorts of issues might I take to support and supervision?

You are the mentor. Paul has chosen you. You will have an introductory session with him and then two more sessions. There are interactive prompts and questions for you, as well as explanations of how the framework and the principles of effective coaching and mentoring apply. You will also be referred to other chapters in the book for more information, for example on a particular tool or technique. At various points you are asked to:

- reflect on what is happening
- consider your response
- decide how you will help the client

At the end of each session, when you see this symbol, it will indicate some issues that might be taken to mentor support or supervision.

Case example: Paul

Paul has recently been appointed as medical director in a large hospital. He is a respected doctor and works hard. He has attended a leadership development programme which included both coaching sessions and being part of an action learning set. This has helped build his skills and confidence in working with managers and chairing meetings. Paul has asked for some regular mentoring to support development in his new role. He has asked for you to be his mentor, because he sees you as a senior manager who is skilful in influencing and managing in the organization. These are areas where he thinks he still has much to learn. In particular, a challenge for Paul is representing the interests of doctors in the hospital while also reflecting management interests, since sometimes these seem to be in conflict.

Before you start mentoring Paul, refer back to Figure 1.1 on page 7 to remind yourself of the key principles. Then look again at Figure 4.2 on page 76 to remind yourself of the stages of The Skilled Helper framework. In mentoring, one person is helping another with either short-term issues or longer-term development. The relationship, a learning relationship, is crucial in helping the person to realize their potential and produce results. The mentor uses specific skills, frameworks and processes to develop insight and to promote change.

Introductory session

You are flattered that Paul has asked you to be his mentor. You are not so sure that you are the expert in managing and influencing that Paul thinks you are. You don't see yourself as a role model, but you realize that's what he sees in you! You do like to help people on their way and you have been pretty successful in your career.

 You are the mentor. What do you want to achieve in your first session with Paul?
Refer to Chapter 2 for an example of a working agreement. Are there any areas of the agreement that may be particularly important?
How will you decide if you can work together or not?

This is the first meeting with Paul. You explain that this is an introductory session. It is for each of you to find out if you can work together. You start by asking him in what way he thinks you may be able to help him as a mentor. This gives you valuable insight into his expectations. You are able to clarify what you can offer in terms of time, commitment, experience and knowledge. He says that he would like to have a mentor to whom he could turn from time to time to discuss his career and professional development. He would like to meet for a couple of sessions initially and then, if it seems to be working, perhaps once every two months. You agree to this. You suggest that you put time aside at the end of each session to review how you are working together. You give him a copy of the working agreement and allow him time to look over it and ask any questions. You explain the mentoring framework you use (The Skilled Helper), and offer him a diagram of it (see Figures 4.1 and 4.2 on pages 75 and 76).

Looking at the working agreement immediately raises the question of confidentiality, and Paul asks if everything in the sessions will be confidential.

Here are some responses. Which would you make? Or is there a better one?

- Oh, yes, definitely.
- I have some ideas about what the limits are. Would it be useful to talk about these?
- The sessions are completely in confidence unless there are legal or professional limits placed upon our confidentiality. We would both be bound by these. You can choose what you wish to disclose to me. If I was concerned about having to share some information with another person we would talk about it first, and I would help you, where possible, to take the initiative to disclose. How does that sound?

Another issue for clarification, because you work in the same organization, is about conflict of interest.

Paul: Can I just check? You're a senior manager in this hospital. If I criticize one of your colleagues would that be difficult for you? If I told you that one of my projects was failing, what then?

What other aspects of conflict of interest might there be?

Would the response below adequately answer Paul's question. If not, what do you suggest?

Mentor: When the mentoring system was set up we agreed that my first responsibility is to you, the client. So be assured that your interest comes first. If there is a problem I would be happy to help but I am not here as a mentor to get directly involved in managing it. I'm here to help you to do that!

Paul is pleased that you have approached this initial conversation in a straightforward way. He likes the fact that you have given him a working agreement for discussion, and offered a copy of the framework you will use together. This echoes the sort of transparency that he expects in his professional life. It makes him think that he can trust you.

You agree to work together for two sessions within the next month and then every two months. Each session will have a 15-minute review at the end. Sessions will take place in one of the bookable interview rooms, and each session will be for two hours. Paul is to set the agenda for each session and decide on relevant action between sessions.

 PRINCIPLES INTO PRACTICE: INTRODUCTORY SESSION

The context of the mentoring is Paul's development as a leader and his career. Your objective is to help him to be strategic and proactive.

The agenda is his and you facilitate the process.

You share with him a **framework** for change (The Skilled Helper) and he decides whether he wants to use it.

The outcome he wants is to become more skilful at managing and influencing the organization.

The learning relationship is crucial because he has stated that he wants to learn from you as someone he respects.

The qualities of respect, empathy, honesty and integrity help to build rapport and trust.

The skills which communicate these qualities are those of active listening, appropriate sharing and negotiating.

Ethical practice involves monitoring the possibility of a blurring of boundaries because of working in the same organization.

ISSUES FOR MENTOR SUPPORT OR SUPERVISION: INTRODUCTORY SESSION

What issues has this session raised for you in your work as a mentor?

Reflecting on this session, what are your areas of strength and areas for development in an introductory session?

How would you introduce and negotiate a working agreement and a framework?

What would you feel about a client's perception of you as a role model?

What might be potential ongoing issues around boundaries, confidentiality and conflict of interest in the relationship?

Session 1

You remember that Paul said he wanted a mentor to turn to from time to time to discuss his career and professional development. You start by asking him what he wants from mentoring that is different from what he got in coaching.

> *Paul:* The coaching was excellent. It helped me to understand my role and to develop some specific skills for handling situations that are new for me, like steering a difficult meeting. What I want now is to talk to someone who understands the complexities of leadership in the health service, and how to influence strategically and manage multiple interests. You seem to know how to do this. So, I suppose I'm saying I want to learn from you!

You say that you are happy to share your experiences wherever they seem relevant and that it sounds as though initially Paul wants to do quite a bit of exploration, rather than working towards specific goals. You remember the agreement that he would set the agenda for each session and so you ask him what he wants to work on today.

> *Paul:* I'd like to start in this session by asking you a couple of things about the way we work together – from the working agreement that you gave me. You talk about a learning partnership where you are responsible for facilitating my learning 'based on the objectives

agreed at the outset'. I have enough objectives in the day job! I was rather hoping I could use the sessions to think in a broad-ranging way about what's going on at the moment. Is that OK? It's just that sometimes I learn more by having the space to reflect and talk, rather than by having objectives.

You reply by saying that's fine, it is his time and you add:

Mentor: Would you like to start in that broad-ranging way now? If so, there is plenty of time for that. Or is there anything specific that you want to talk about in this session?

Paul says that there have been a couple of very difficult situations in his leadership role with colleagues. He would like to discuss these and he would also like to spend a little bit of time beginning to look at his career beyond his present job. Quite a tall order for a two-hour session!

 You are faced with a practical dilemma of how to facilitate the session in a way that allows Paul to be 'broad-ranging' and yet explore the two difficult situations with colleagues. You also need to allow time for the review at the end of the session. How would you decide what to do next?

You ask Paul how he would like to divide the time. You agree that you will spend the first 60 minutes talking about the difficult situations, the next 45 minutes on his career, and the final 15 minutes on review.

Paul starts to tell the story of his two 'difficult' colleagues. The first is a doctor, who is dismissive of management. He is highly regarded in his specialty, and much in demand at international conferences. He is often away and it falls increasingly to his colleagues to pick up his work. They are grumbling about this. Some managers are unhappy about his dismissive attitude. He is reluctant to comply with recently introduced protocols for appraisal and personal development plans. Paul, as medical director, has been asked to meet with this colleague and investigate.

After paraphrasing the story, you say, 'So you have been asked to meet with him?' and this repeating of key words helps Paul to continue.

Paul: Yes, and I'm dreading it. He's such a powerful personality! It will be quite an achievement if I get him to the meeting at all. But how to handle it? That's the difficulty. I don't want to end up with us shouting at one another. If I'm going to do this job successfully, I need to keep people like him 'on board'. That brings me to my next problem with the other colleague. I suppose the problems are related really! The other one is the finance director who keeps hounding me because there is an overspend on the medical budget. He wants to manage the overspend by cutting down on the doctors' study leave budget and conference attendance. This means that I will not be able to approve study leave applications and the consultants will see me not as their champion, but as the hard-arm of management. I feel as if I am between a rock and a hard place. This job is already making me feel exposed and isolated.

 Paul has fairly quickly presented two difficult situations. You want to keep the focus on Paul, rather than spending too much time talking about the other people involved.
Reflect back to Paul, what he seems to be thinking and feeling.

Mentor: Let me check that I understand. You're dreading the meeting with the doctor because he's such a powerful personality and you don't want to end up in a slanging match. On top of that you've also got a problem with the demands being made by the finance director. You're feeling 'between a rock and a hard place', exposed as well as isolated. You are caught between the pressures of the finance director and what your consultant colleagues want. Is that how it is?

Now that you have paraphrased what you have heard and checked your understanding with Paul he is encouraged to continue. He talks about how he enjoys a challenge and this is why he accepted the job. He knew that leading clinicians would be difficult, but he hadn't realized how exposed and isolated he might feel, so soon into the job.

Paul is still in the first stage of 'telling the story', but you can help him to clarify which part of the story he wishes to pursue in this session. Your summary has identified that his feelings of isolation and powerlessness are an important part of the problem for him. Now, focusing and prioritizing could identify a leverage point which would move Paul from the feelings of being stuck to an exploration of how things could be better.

Mentor: There is the difficult colleague, there is the finance director, and there are your feelings about the job. Which of these should we look at first?

Paul: I suppose that if I looked at how I react to these situations it would help. Have you any advice you could give me from your experience?

You know that Paul chose you as mentor partly because of your experience in the organization. You want to respond to his request for advice, but you also want to keep the focus on Paul and his experiences so that he learns what is useful to him.

 How would you respond?
How could you share your experience in a way that opens up discussion and invites Paul's ideas, rather than offering your solutions?

You start by sharing some experiences of similar situations, some where you were pleased with your reactions and some where you wished you had acted differently and you finish by saying: 'Those are examples of what worked for me. The same things may not work for you. Is there anything that seems useful to you in what I have shared?'

Having shared briefly some of your own experiences when in similar circumstances, you ask about Paul's reactions to his own difficult situations. You help him to challenge himself by developing new perspectives. You do this by asking him to reflect upon times in the past when he dealt with his own feelings of exposure and isolation, and what or who helped then. You help him to consider what resources might be available: friends, family, other clinicians and other medical directors in the wider network? Finally, you help him to get some insight into the perspectives of both the doctor and the finance director by asking, 'If they were here now, what would they be saying about you? About what they want from you?'

Time moves on, and you have spent 50 minutes on this topic. There is 10 minutes left to summarize this part of the session and pull it together. You are at the final step of the first stage of The Skilled Helper framework. You can help Paul to identify a point of leverage, something that would now help him move on with this issue. He says that the most pressing thing is to get more data about how to manage the meeting.

 Would you summarize what has been said, or would you ask Paul to summarize? What would you say in a concise but comprehensive summary?
How would you help him to find something to work on between now and the next session?

Paul decides that, in the next two weeks, he will make contact with the previous medical director to talk over how he managed situations like these. If that meeting goes well, he might even broach the feelings of exposure and isolation. He decides that he will postpone the meeting with the doctor until after the next mentoring session. At the next session he wants to look at specific strategies for not allowing himself to be intimidated in the meeting with his difficult colleague.

In the next 45 minutes of the session Paul talks about his career to date. He fills in some details for you and starts looking at where he might be going in the future. Unlike some medical directors, he does not want to stay in this job for the rest of his career. You don't wait too long before asking, 'Where do you see yourself in five years' time? In ten years' time?' These questions move him to focus on 'what might be' rather than 'what is'. He sees himself becoming more involved in medical leadership but not necessarily as a medical director. You ask Paul if he has completed any 360-degree feedback questionnaires. He has. You suggest that he bring them to the next meeting to see if they help to clarify his needs, wants and strengths.

 Finally, you review how you have worked together.

What might you include in the review of the session?
What do you think of the question below, as a starting-point?

You say: 'Could we finish by saying what it was like to work together today? What seemed to help or hinder? What did we appreciate and what would we like to be different next time?' The session concludes with both of you agreeing what Paul will do between now and next time. He writes down his action points. Finally, you check diaries for the date of the next session.

In this first session Paul has been helped to articulate his problems with colleagues and to develop insight into their perspectives as well as his own. He has identified resources in himself and in others, which may help him. He has also been helped to start exploring his ideal future, with regard to his career. There has been appropriate sharing of experience from you, the mentor, with regard to the politics of the organization.

PRINCIPLES INTO PRACTICE: SESSION 1

The **context** is twofold: firstly, Paul's role as a leader in dealing with colleagues, clinicians and managers; secondly, his career development.

The **mentoring objective** is to provide reflective space so that the story will unfold.

The mentor provides a balance of **support and challenge** so that new perspectives will develop and resources can be recognized and used.

The first stage of The Skilled Helper **framework** is used to explore the story, develop new perspectives and find a point of leverage.

The **outcome** Paul wants is to be able to manage himself when dealing with difficult colleagues and to start to look at career possibilities. He will network with a previous medical director to gain ideas about both of these.

The **learning relationship** is beginning to develop and the mentor uses active and empathic listening to develop trust and rapport but is then required by the client to share experiences in a facilitative way, rather than a directive way: sharing rather than telling.

The **qualities** that have been communicated are respect for Paul, genuine interest in his story and empathic understanding. He has been affirmed and sustained by this.

Ethical practice includes: responding honestly to a request for shared experience; keeping to the time boundary; allowing enough time to end the session safely; evaluation of the working relationship.

 ISSUES FOR MENTOR SUPPORT OR SUPERVISION: SESSION 1

Was it too ambitious to deal with career as well as leadership issues in one session?

Did you deal adequately with Paul's feelings of exposure and isolation?

How comfortable are you with Paul's expectations of you?

Should you have offered to network for Paul?

How can you work with him next time on specific strategies for not feeling intimidated?

How can you best use the 360-degree feedback next time?

Session 2

Paul returns for his second mentoring session, three weeks later, and you remember that he described how isolated he felt in his new role. You wonder how things are. You check the notes you made together:

1   Paul was to meet with the previous medical director to find out how he managed difficult colleagues.
2   He wanted help with specific strategies for dealing with his feelings of intimidation when he meets with his difficult colleague.
3   He was to bring to this session some questionnaire results that would inform future career plans.

 How do you start the session?

Which of these introductions might you choose and why?
Would you have a better introduction?

- Hello Paul. How are you today?
- Paul, I've looked at the notes we made last time. We listed three things, they were . . . Are these still what you want to talk about today?
- Paul, I am wondering what you want to get out of the session today.

Paul says that things have moved on since last time. He wants to spend the first half of the session looking at strategies and the second half looking at what the questionnaire results might say about his career, with some review time at the end of the session.

He tells you that he has met with the previous medical director. There has been a history of difficulty with both the doctor colleague and the finance director. The meeting made Paul realize that he wants to be more direct than his predecessor. It also confirmed that Paul's feelings of exposure and isolation did seem to come with the job, and confirmed that it was a wise decision to find a mentor.

> *Paul:* So, can you help me with some strategies for not allowing myself to be overwhelmed and intimidated, so that I can say in a meeting what needs to be said, even when I am being drowned out by the other person?
> *Mentor:* Well, let's start by looking at what you want to happen, in the ideal world. Let's take one of these colleagues, which should we work with first?

Paul: The doctor.

Mentor: Imagine the scenario now where you have asked him to come to see you about the complaints from colleagues and management. Imagine your ideal meeting with him. Take a minute to visualize this and let me know when you have a picture in mind.

You guide Paul in brainstorming what he ideally wants and needs from such a meeting. You prompt him to describe what he would and would not be doing, thinking and feeling, and ideally what the doctor would and would not be doing, thinking and feeling. You ask about the ideal outcome from the meeting, and encourage him to go for some wild ideas. (For more information about this technique and useful prompts to use, refer to Chapters 4 and 7.) When he completes the brainstorm, you ask him to choose which of the possibilities seem most important to him.

Paul: I saw myself standing there, staying firm while a barrage of words was being fired at me. I didn't raise my voice, but I said clearly what had to be said. That's what I want. I felt powerful then, and certainly not intimidated.

You ask him how he might turn that general aim into a specific goal. Something that is specific, measurable, achievable, relevant and in a timeframe.

 You notice that Paul is very energized and hopeful during the brainstorm. As he considers what he needs to do, he becomes more thoughtful, and he seems reluctant to specify a goal. What would you do if you noticed this? How would you remain non-directive and facilitative even though you are guiding the process of change?

Despite his initial reluctance to be specific, you help Paul to shape up this goal: 'I will meet with the doctor next week and I'll achieve my objectives for the meeting without being overwhelmed by his power and aggression'. You check with him whether this is realistic in the timeframe he has allowed himself, and how he will feel if he achieves this. He says that he will feel confident and reassured. You check with him the costs and benefits of being assertive. The personal costs almost outweigh the benefits, but Paul believes that the potential benefits for him as a leader are significant. If he can be assertive with this colleague, he will more confident in being assertive in other difficult situations, whether at meetings or with individuals.

Now that he has a specific goal you can help him to brainstorm all the possible ways he might achieve it. You encourage him to think of as many as possible, whether realistic or not. This helps him to open his mind to as many possibilities as he can. Paul begins to brainstorm strategies, which include: listening to the doctor; understanding the doctor's concerns; preparing by rehearsing for the meeting beforehand; identifying his own 'bottom line position'; deciding what is negotiable and what isn't; and trying out some arguments he might use with a friend as 'devil's advocate'. At this point you share with him some other strategies which he may not already be aware of: the C>A>N model of negotiation; using transactional analysis to examine his own reactions; doing some role-reversal to rehearse how to end a negotiation with both him and the doctor committed to the outcome. (Refer to Chapter 7 for more information on these strategies.) You also mention a couple of useful books.

 You are aware that you are halfway through the session and Paul wanted to spend the latter half discussing his 360-degree feedback, to inform his career planning. You are also concerned that this would not be a good stage to leave Paul with unfinished preparation for the meeting. You feel guilty that you have mismanaged the timing and Paul's expectations of what can realistically be achieved in this session.

What would you do? Consider the five ethical principles when making your decision: what does least harm; what does most good; what safeguards Paul's autonomy; what is fair; what is in keeping with what has been promised? Would you choose one of the options below, or do something else?

- Cut him short in his planning, saying that there are only five minutes left for this part of the session?
- Wait for a suitable moment, summarize your understanding of the session so far and mention that there is only half the session time left, asking Paul what he would like to do now?
- Do nothing and see what he says, letting him use all the time for this issue if he says nothing?

You decide to do nothing to see how things work out, but it is Paul who notices the time.

Paul: Oh! I didn't realize the time. We've only got 45 minutes left and I do need to be sure about what I am going to do at this meeting. I've brought the feedback for a discussion about my career but really that isn't the most important thing to me at the moment. Could we leave that on the back-burner until next time?

You breathe a sigh of relief! Paul has solved the problem himself. But you realize that you could have let him down if he had prepared for that part of the session and then not had the opportunity to discuss the feedback because of poor time management on your part. You have learned that whatever the problem or issue, the important thing is to have open discussion about it and to allow Paul to be involved in any decisions about how to proceed.

You want to bring the discussion back to Paul's strategies for action and so you ask him to summarize the ones he mentioned before.

 How would you now help Paul to firm up which strategy would be 'best fit' for him?

How would you help him to explore what will help or hinder that strategy?

Of all the ones mentioned Paul decides that the most useful for him would be to read the C>A>N model and then to find a friend who could act as the doctor while he rehearsed trying to express his interests clearly, communicating that he understands where the colleague is coming from and remaining calm and positive in the face of aggressive behaviour. You ask him what might help and what might hinder this strategy.

Mentor: This idea of preparing your case and then rehearsing with a friend – what will help that strategy to succeed?
Paul: The fact that I can trust my friend to be honest and supportive, and also that I really am keen on trying this out now. My friend will tell me directly what I need to change or do. Also, he knows what I'm up against!
Mentor: And what might get in the way? What might stop it from working?
Paul: If neither of us can get our diaries together. It's such a short time till the meeting. Or if I bottle out!

You have used some questions about what will help or hinder the strategy from working. These help Paul to identify untapped resources in himself or others and also anything that may sabotage his attempts at rehearsing the meeting. Now he moves to the practicalities of a manageable plan. He decides on a time when he can do his reading and preparation and he also decides that tomorrow he will approach his friend so that they can firm up a date in their diaries, within the next week.

 What would you include in discussion about a manageable action plan?

What contingency plan might be necessary?
What support might you offer ?
What about links into the next session?

You have helped Paul to firm up his action plan and now you turn to ending the session. In this second session you realize that Paul has moved from feeling stuck with his problems to the hope that came from realizing possibilities for different ways of thinking, feeling and acting. From this he, somewhat reluctantly at first, found the courage to choose a realistic goal for change. You notice that the session felt energetic and active and you used models and techniques to keep it moving. There was a hiccup halfway through when you realized about time being short, but in the end you felt it worked out OK, with Paul's objectives met. Now it is time to find out what Paul thought as you evaluate how you have worked together. You want to end the session safely, and to plan for the next session.

Mentor: I notice we have 15 minutes left. We've done quite a bit of active work together today and I'm wondering how you're feeling now?
Paul: Exhausted! I didn't realize that mentoring was such hard work! It has given me plenty to think about, and to do. My most pressing problem is the meeting but I do feel more confident after our work today. I was disappointed not to have time for the career discussion.
Mentor: Disappointed?
Paul: Yes, I think that having two things to discuss in the session is perhaps too much. Or maybe you need to make me keep more focused so that we cover more! I can ramble on a bit.
Mentor: So two ways of managing better are keeping focused or only discussing one topic in a session. Which of these would you like to do next time?
Paul: Actually, I'd like you to be a bit more challenging if I'm rambling and then we would still cover more than one topic in a session.
Mentor: That's fine by me. We can start next time by agreeing the focus at the beginning and I'll manage it in the way you say. Then we can review again at the end of the session to see if we achieved what you wanted. I've enjoyed working together today and have noticed your resourcefulness and determination. I admire your resilience in

the face of challenge and I look forward to hearing what happens in your meeting! We seem to have achieved what you wanted. But can I ask you, when we got to stating a goal did you feel I was pushing too much?

Paul: Well, actually, I didn't really want to say something so definite as 'a goal' and I did feel myself pulling back at that stage. But you did give me enough space to decide for myself so, after my initial reluctance, I went for it.

You check if there is anything else that Paul wants to say, you ask him to summarize his action plan and how he feels at the end of the session. Finally, you fix dates for the next three meetings, each two months apart. A week before the next meeting, Paul will contact you to highlight briefly what he would like to bring to the session.

 PRINCIPLES INTO PRACTICE: SESSION 2

The **context** is Paul as a leader. Firstly, he wanted strategies for a meeting with a doctor. Secondly, he wanted to explore his future career.

The **objective** was to move from the discomfort of the present situation to identifying a goal and planning realistic action. Paul took responsibility for this.

The **outcome** is that he is arranging the meeting with the doctor after doing further preparation.

The **learning relationship** is tested twice in this session. Firstly when you, the mentor, experienced 'resistance' from Paul in defining a specific goal. Secondly, when you needed to manage the time issue and negotiate about the second half of the session.

As mentor you tried to remain **facilitative** and client-centred.

The **qualities** that were needed in the mentor were: affirmation of Paul; belief in his ability to make changes; and balance of support and challenge.

Ethical practice included keeping time boundaries. As both you and Paul work in the same organization it will be essential to maintain confidentiality.

Contingency planning is necessary to support action.

ISSUES FOR MENTOR SUPPORT OR SUPERVISION: SESSION 2

You decide to reflect on the two sessions so far and to look ahead to developments in the forthcoming sessions. In particular, you want to use some supervision to reflect on your own development as a mentor, including your use of the framework and skills within the learning relationship. You want to explore how to keep the balance between support and challenge, and how to remain client-centred at the problem-solving and action stages of mentoring.

What did you do well in this case study?

What would you now like to be able to do differently?

Who will help you to develop as a mentor?

Summary

In this chapter we have:

- Developed an interactive case study with Paul, over three sessions.
- Invited you to be the mentor during each session.
- Applied key principles for effective practice and, at the end of each session, critiqued the way they have been applied.
- Used The Skilled Helper framework and given extracts of dialogue so that you, as mentor, can choose appropriate responses.
- Highlighted, for reflection at the end of each session, some ethical and professional issues which the mentor might take to supervision or to mentor support.

7 What are some useful tools and techniques?

- Introduction
- The Johari Window
- Transactional Analysis
- The Karpmann Triangle
- Career Lifeline
- Brainstorming
- Visualization
- Role-Reversal
- Cost–Benefit Analysis
- Values Clarification
- Force field Analysis
- The C>A>N model: conflict, assertiveness, negotiation
- Critical Path Analysis
- Summary

Introduction

This chapter describes some tried and tested techniques in coaching and mentoring. We have used all of these in our own work and found them to be valuable. We present them in the order in which you might use them if working with a framework which starts with helping a client to tell their story, then proceeds to ways of helping them to explore possibilities and set goals, and finally develops and manages action plans.

These tools and techniques can be powerful. The less experienced coach or mentor would be advised to familiarize themselves with the techniques in a safe and appropriate context before using them with clients. Each technique or approach is presented by addressing these questions:

- What is it?
- When should it be used?
- How does it work?
- What skills does the coach or mentor need?
- What are the advantages?
- What are the disadvantages?
- Are there any useful references?

The Johari Window

What is it?

The Johari Window (Luft 1970) is a tool for increasing a person's self-awareness and understanding of how they interact with others. Johari is an abbreviation of the first names of its inventors, Joseph Luft and Harry Ingham. The Window, which represents a person, has four panes or quadrants, as illustrated in Figure 7.1. Each quadrant represents a type of personal awareness:

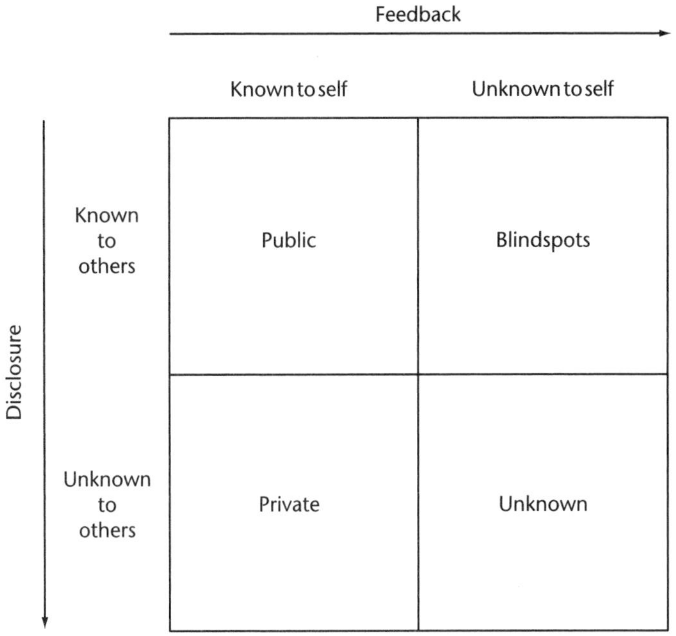

Figure 7.1 The Johari Window

- The public quadrant represents what is known by a person about themselves and which others also know about them
- The blindspots quadrant represents things a person is not aware of about themselves, although these things are known to others
- The private quadrant refers to things a person knows about themselves which they do not reveal to others
- The unknown quadrant represents things about a person that are unknown both to themselves and to others.

A person can draw their own window, reflecting the relative sizes of each panel. Quadrants can change over time and in different situations. When a person seeks information, for example by asking for feedback, the size of the public quadrant increases and the blindspot quadrant decreases. When a person discloses information about themselves, the size of the public quadrant increases and the private quadrant decreases. Notice how change in the size of one quadrant affects the others.

When should it be used?

The Johari Window can be helpful for clients in mapping how they see themselves in relation to others, and how they communicate with others. It might shed light on interpersonal conflict, or help the client to understand others' views of them. It can encourage the client to consider what sort of information, and how much, they reveal to others, and what sort of feedback, and how much, they are open to receiving. For example, someone experiencing difficulties with their boss decides to tell the boss more about work progress and how they are managing the workload. This information reduces the boss's uncertainty and concerns, and improves the working relationship. This disclosure, telling the boss more, increases the size of the public quadrant and decreases the private quadrant.

How does it work?

The client is invited to draw their window and talk in as much detail as they wish about each quadrant and the relationship between quadrants. They can discuss any changes they would like to make in the relative sizes of the quadrants.

What skills does the coach or mentor need?

The coach or mentor needs to explain the Johari Window and prompt the client to consider the relative sizes of each quadrant, and their contents. For example, looking at the private quadrant they might ask the client, either in relation to a particular context (e.g. a work team), or more generally:

- How much about your background and history do you tell others? About your personal/professional life?
- How much do you disclose about what you are thinking and feeling? About your expectations of others? About what you want?
- What might it be useful for other people to know about you?
- What kinds of information might you be comfortable/less comfortable sharing with others?

What are the advantages?

The Johari Window can help a person to re-examine and reassess their assumptions about what information they can disclose or ask for, and whether their patterns of disclosure and feedback are getting them what they want. They can gain insight into how others see them, and how their behaviour may affect the impression they make on others.

What are the disadvantages?

A client may feel that they 'ought' to disclose more about themselves or 'ought' to ask for feedback. There are risks in inappropriate disclosure and feedback, and clients should be encouraged to evaluate for themselves what might be safe and appropriate. The coach or mentor should avoid creating the impression that feedback and disclosure are always helpful, regardless of circumstances.

Are there any useful references?

Covey, S.R. (1989) *The Seven Habits of Highly Effective People*. London: Simon & Schuster.

Goleman, D. (1998) *Working With Emotional Intelligence*. London: Bloomsbury.

Luft, J. (1969) *Of Human Interaction*. Palo Alto, CA: National Press Books.

Luft, J. (1970) *Group Processes: An Introduction to Group Dynamics*. Palo Alto, CA: National Press Books.

Transactional Analysis

What is it?

It is a way of understanding a relationship by looking at the transactions between people. The idea was developed by Berne (1972). The theory states that in any communication with another person we may operate from any of three ego states: parent, adult or child. Sometimes we get stuck and can only operate from one of these. Ideally, we can flex between them as the occasion demands.

When should it be used?

The coach or mentor can use transactional analysis to help the client understand why certain relationships are not working. Either the client is stuck, or the person with whom they are having difficulty is stuck. Self-limiting patterns of relating to another person can be perpetuated. Transactional analysis can be used to highlight these and to practise different responses which make both parties feel better about each other, and about themselves. It gives the client new perspectives and resources.

How does it work?

At times, in some situations with certain people, we may have a tendency to revert to certain patterns of behaviour and ways of thinking. These tendencies can be triggered by the behaviour of the other people. In order to change our behaviour, we need insight into these patterns and we need to want to change them.

In Figure 7.2 you will notice that each person is able to operate, or indeed move between, any of the ego states in any transaction. If person A is operating from parent state it may well induce in person B the child state. In parent state, the person can be either critical or nurturing. Either way, they are not allowing for the autonomy of an 'adult' transaction in the other person. They could produce in person B a 'child' response, either overly adaptive and conforming, or rebellious. Sometimes such transactions can be useful and creative. Often, they are counterproductive.

Sometimes a comment or a situation can trigger a certain reaction. A bullying manager may trigger 'rebellious child' in a colleague. A difficult employee may trigger 'critical parent' in a manager. The task of the mentor is to help the client to be aware of what is happening and to practise some 'adult' responses.

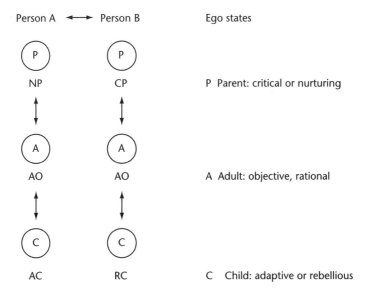

Figure 7.2   Transactions and ego states

What skills does the coach or mentor need?

These skills are all useful:

- listening to the story of the transactions
- identifying themes or patterns
- reflecting these back to the client
- explaining parent, adult and child ego states with an accompanying diagram
- giving examples of these that relate to the transaction described
- asking the client to practise from different ego states

This is how statements and responses could be reframed:

Bullying or harassment
You will finish that work by tomorrow or I will report you to the manager. (critical parent)

No, you won't. It is up to me when I finish it. (rebellious child)

I will be doing my best to get it finished. (adult)

Underperformance
These departmental meetings are a complete waste of time. Nobody ever has any good ideas. I don't want to waste my time attending any more. (rebellious child)

You don't have any choice in the matter. (critical parent)

Would you like to tell us what, specifically, would make them work better for you? (adult)

What are the advantages?

It is a quick way of helping people to make small changes in behaviour that can produce very different ways of communicating. The insights can be used in individual interactions, group work, meetings and socially. The insight can stop problem situations from escalating and improve relationships.

What are the disadvantages?

The main disadvantage is that a client may develop insight into their patterns of interaction but be unable, in the short term, to change the way they respond to others. This client may need help beyond mentoring, for example counselling.

Are there any useful references?

Berne, E. (1972) *What Do You Say After You Say Hello?* London: Corgi Books.
Berne, E. (1976) *Beyond Games and Scripts*. New York: Ballantine.
Harris, A. and Harris, T. (1985) *Staying OK*. London: Pan Books.

The Karpmann Triangle

What is it?

The Karpmann Triangle (Karpmann 1968) is another way of looking at interactions between colleagues. The coach or mentor may hear a theme or 'script' being repeated by the client. The client may not be aware of this, but when the coach or mentor reflects back what is heard, then the client will often recognize a 'script', such as 'I'm a fraud and soon someone will find out'; 'My role is

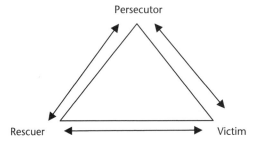

Figure 7.3   The Karpmann Triangle

to look after others'; 'Why does it always happen to me?' Some scripts are relevant to the Karpmann Triangle where a person or several people may move between the roles of persecutor, rescuer and victim (see Figure 7.3).

When should it be used?

The Karpmann Triangle should be used when it would help the client to become aware of the power of internal and external messages that limit and control their behaviour, potential and possibilities. This may enable the client to think, feel and act differently. It gives useful insight for managers and leaders trying to understand dysfunctional dynamics between colleagues.

How does it work?

The client may notice that, in a particular context which is proving trouble-some, they move between the positions of persecutor, rescuer or victim, or are stuck in one of these. They may even find that they interpret much of their experience through one of these. Some clients may notice that they always have to 'look after' others, to the detriment of having their own needs met (rescuer). Others may experience themselves as victimized, often left out of important events and decisions. They may have difficulty in stating what they want (victim). Others may find themselves being punitive or being experienced as overly critical even when they do not intend it (persecutor).

Often, a person is pushed unwittingly into one of these positions by the complementary behaviour of another. The Karpmann Triangle illustrates how, for example, the victim depends on the rescuer, the persecutor causes the victim, the rescuer and victim blame the persecutor or the persecutor may need rescuing from the victim. The dynamic can go round and round with people caught in it, not realizing how they are being influenced to behave in particular ways. The client may be able to change the dynamic by noticing it, and choosing to respond in a different way. They can, for example, change their questions from persecutor, victim or rescuer questions into 'adult' questions:

> Why does X make me feel guilty? (persecuted)
> Why do I allow myself to feel guilty with X? (adult statement)
>
> Why does Y always seem to pick on me? (victimized)
> Why do I allow Y to keep picking on me? (adult statement)
>
> Why does Z seems to think that he always needs to rescue me at meetings? (rescued)
> Why do I allow Z to continue to rescue me at meetings? (adult statement)

So, having noticed the dynamic, the client is able to consider how they wish to behave and be treated. Then they can set realistic goals and action plans in relation to these wants and needs. Instead of allowing relationships to move round the triangle, for example allowing an experience of being persecuted to produce the response of 'I'm being victimized and therefore I need rescuing', the client is breaking into the dysfunctional sequence by taking ownership, identifying the problem and producing a positive response.

What skills does the coach or mentor need?

Skills of sensitivity as well as careful timing are needed! It is quite challenging for a client to attempt to change the early decisions they made about how they view themselves, others and their place in the world. All clients are different. Some people take years to change such perceptions and some do it fairly readily. A balance of support and challenge is needed and an awareness of the impact of trying out new behaviours between sessions. Suggesting further reading could be helpful to the client.

What are the advantages?

It can be very liberating for the client to be freed from old, internalized messages. Also, it can make the client aware of ways in which colleagues, friends and family may also be 'stuck'. This can help the client to try out different strategies with them. Powerful life changes can result.

What are the disadvantages?

The realization that some parental messages were not helpful and may have held us back. Support may be needed to work with this.

Are there any useful references?

James, M. and Jongeward, D. (1971) *Born to Win*. Reading, MA: Addison-Wesley.
Karpmann, S. (1968) Fairy tales and script drama analysis, *Transactional Analysis Bulletin*, 7(26): 39–43.

Career Lifeline

What is it?

The career lifeline is a method of helping the client to look back at the development of their career in relation to other significant factors in their life. Having drawn a lifeline, they can then use this information to inform the discussion of future career plans.

When should it be used?

It can be used either as a start to a new coaching or mentoring relationship, perhaps in preparation for a first session, or as the occasion arises, for example when a client is thinking of making a significant career move. It helps clients to:

- raise awareness
- identify choicepoints
- spot external influences and internal drivers
- note themes, patterns or trends
- get a sense of 'the right time' for decisions and moves
- see the factors which influence choices and decisions
- identify threats
- clarify values
- link past to present
- link present to future
- identify resources and strategies

How does it work?

The client is asked to make a pictorial representation of their career to date. They may choose to draw a graph in a timeframe, or a picture or other visual representation. If the lifeline is drawn as a timeline on a graph, the horizontal axis represents age in years and the vertical axis represents level of satisfaction (see Figure 7.4). One line may be drawn to represent career development and another superimposed to represent significant life events which may have affected the career lifeline.

In the example shown the dotted line signifies the career journey through the years from age 15 to age 70. The solid line is the personal journey which sometimes intersects the career path, sometimes runs in parallel and sometimes overlaps. In this example the dips in levels of career and life satisfaction in the earlier years are far more marked. Some clients find the relationship between life events and career development very interesting. Others prefer to focus upon a career lifeline, without a personal one. It is interesting to look at the obvious turning points and to explore what decisions were made at those times, what resources were available to the client, what influenced decisions, and what learning there may be now, from reflecting on these events.

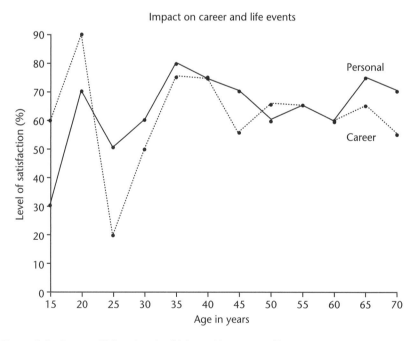

Figure 7.4   A career lifeline showing highs and lows across life stages

After the lifeline has been drawn the client is prompted to reflect on it. The coach or mentor may offer the client a list of questions, and the client can choose which they would find useful to explore:

- What do you notice about the line or about your drawing?
- Any patterns or themes about your career?
- How have you made educational and career decisions?
- Who/what has helped you in making decisions?
- Looking at high points, what inner strengths were evident?
- Looking at high points, what external conditions helped?
- Looking at low points, what would have helped?
- Looking at low points, what might you have done differently, if anything?
- What seem to be underlying values: the most important things to you?
- Identify three strengths that carry you through the hard times.
- What now are the three most important features of a job for you?
- What are your priorities for work–life balance?
- Where would you like to be in your career in X years' time?

Some people find graphs too limiting and prefer to be invited to draw a picture of the development of their career. The picture would still need to have some sense of development through time and possible linkages with significant life events.

What skills does the coach or mentor need?

This exercise needs plenty of time. It must be handled with sensitivity. Asking someone to reflect on their past may trigger memories of, for example, difficult life events. The person may get in touch with very pleasant memories, but of a life in the past, not the present! The coach or mentor needs to leave enough time for adequate debriefing. The skills of active listening, open questioning, reflecting feeling, paraphrasing and summarizing are all essential. In addition some supportive challenging may be helpful, leading to brainstorming possibilities for the future. At least one hour should be allowed for the exercise.

What are the advantages?

This can be a way of accessing strengths, resources and values. It provides a creative way of looking at career development. It also provides a useful structure for a coaching or mentoring session.

What are the disadvantages?

It may trigger memories which need careful handling. The coach should be ready to suggest further help and support if necessary.

Are there any useful references?

Bolles, R.N. (2002) *What Color is Your Parachute? A Practical Guide for Job Hunters and Career Changers.* Berkeley, CA: Ten Speed Press.
Schein, E. (1990) *Career Anchors: Discovering Your Real Values.* San Francisco: Jossey-Bass/Pfeiffer.

Brainstorming

What is it?

Brainstorming is a technique that encourages creativity and lateral thinking, by stimulating the creative right hemisphere of the brain. Hope, ideas, possibilities and optimism are encouraged, while critiquing and evaluation are discouraged. Brainstorming focuses on the future and possibilities, rather than the present situation and current facts. It has long been recognized in management as a powerful method of generating fresh ideas and creative thinking, and it can be equally powerful in coaching and mentoring

When should it be used?

Brainstorming can be useful to help the client to describe their ideal future in relation to some aspect of the current situation, to be creative in answering questions such as: 'How would you like things to be, ideally? What do you want instead of what you've got?' It can also be helpful in prompting the client to think creatively about different ways to achieve a goal: 'What are 101 ways to achieve X?'

How does it work?

The coach or mentor sets the scene and briefly explains the process, thus creating the conditions for successful brainstorming. They encourage the client to think forward in time, rather than being realistic and focusing only on the present. The coach or mentor emphasizes:

- imagining the ideal
- staying future-oriented
- focusing on 'what' not 'how'
- going for quantity of ideas
- using prompts to generate ideas
- keeping a fast pace
- having fun
- generating wild or seemingly implausible ideas.

The client is asked to imagine, in relation to the issue they have selected, what would be in place if things were much better, if they were ideal. The client is asked to paint as vivid a picture as possible of their preferred future, stimulated by a range of prompts from the coach or mentor, who writes down verbatim all responses. The aim of the brainstorming session is to generate as many ideas as possible, regardless of apparent quality, and to encourage ideas even when the client is stuck, or has 'dried up'. Some possible prompts include:

- Where are you?
- What are you doing/thinking/feeling?
- What have you achieved?
- What have you got rid of?
- What have you gained?
- In your wildest dreams . . .?
- Ideally, what might this lead to?
- If you could wave a magic wand . . .?
- Ideally, what are others saying about you?

At the end of the brainstorming session, the client reviews the ideas and is helped to identify the most important ones and to formulate realistic goals. Brainstorming can also be used to identify possible strategies for achieving a goal. It follows a similar process, with the important difference that the client is asked to think about how they might ideally achieve their goal. The responses to the brainstorm are then used to identify realistic change strategies which will work well for the client.

What skills does the coach or mentor need?

Brainstorming is a fast-paced upbeat process and the style of the coach should model hope and optimism. They must stay focused, energetic and positive, encouraging the client to produce as many responses as possible, since quantity rather than quality is what counts here. They need to encourage the client to stay future-oriented and think wild and wacky, since it is from seemingly implausible ideas that the seeds of possibility are sown.

What are the advantages?

Brainstorming can be an effective way of encouraging clients to overcome problems and blocks, to reframe their ideas and think laterally, and to access the elements of the future that are really important to them. Brainstorming is powerful in helping people to identify what they really want, rather than what others say they should have, or what they think is achievable. It can tap into the values of the client and help them to establish goals and realistic action strategies which will work for them.

What are the disadvantages?

Brainstorming is a powerful process, with potential for harm as well as good. The client should not be left 'high and dry' in the face of a gap between their ideal and their reality, because this might leave them feeling hopeless or help-less. If this is likely, time must be allowed to help the client to identify realistic or feasible elements or actions from the brainstorming output. In this way, they can link the future with the present. In addition, clients can be surprised by their unexpected responses to brainstorming prompts, and it is important to explain clearly the brainstorming process in advance and check that they are ready to 'have a go'. They may need time after the brainstorm to discuss their reactions to what they have produced and any surprises. Also, some people find brainstorming difficult. The sensitive coach or mentor will 'stretch' the client without becoming too challenging or insisting on using a technique which is not helpful for that client.

Are there any useful references?

De Bono, E. (1992) *Serious Creativity*. New York: Harper Business.
Rawlinson J.G. (1986) *Creative Thinking and Brainstorming*. Aldershot: Gower.
Rich, J.R. (2003) *Brainstorm: Tap into your Creativity to Generate Awesome Ideas and Tremendous Results*. Franklin Lakes, NJ: Career Press.
Rickards, T. (1997) *Creativity and Problem Solving at Work*. Aldershot: Gower.

Visualization

What is it?

Visualization is a way of helping a client to imagine an ideal future. This could be an aspect of a current job that they want to improve, a new job, career, or any plan into the future.

When should it be used?

Whenever seems appropriate in trying to envisage a different or better future. It can be used as an alternative to brainstorming to develop wants and needs in a preferred scenario. It can be used whenever the client seems to be stuck and needs help in opening up possibilities. It can also be used to compare and contrast two or more different scenarios if each is visualized and debriefed in turn.

How does it work?

1   Explain the process to the client and ask if they would find it helpful.
2   Invite the client to make sure that they are comfortable and then to close their eyes and relax. They are then guided into relaxation, reminding them not to fall asleep! You can slowly remind them to relax their facial muscles, jaw, neck, shoulders, arms, hands and fingers. Then remind them to breathe slowly and deeply and gradually to relax their chest, abdomen, hips, legs, feet and toes.
3   Invite them to imagine their ideal. Let us take as an example a future job opportunity. The coach or mentor would ask them to imagine their ideal job, perhaps imagine that it is now X months ahead and they have been in the job for a while. Ask them to spend a few moments just getting into that picture, imagining what they are doing, whom they are with, where this ideal job is, how they are feeling.
4   When they have built up a full picture, ask them to keep their eyes closed and, when they are ready, ask what they see. Prompt, if necessary, to get details.
5   When they have given you the picture, the full picture, you can then gently bring them out of that visualization by saying: 'Now you are going to leave that picture and slowly and gradually you can open your eyes and come back to this room, with me, on X date, in X location.'

6   When the client has opened their eyes check they are OK.
7   Now debrief the visualization by helping the client to summarize what they found in their ideal picture that they want in their future job. They will also have probably clarified what they don't want!
8   Finally, the visualization exercise should lead to a critique of what will be realistic now to shape into some sort of goal.

What skills does the coach or mentor need?

This exercise can be a creative way of accessing ideas. The coach or mentor needs to appear relaxed and calm. It is best used by the experienced coach or mentor who has familiarized themselves with the technique in a safe and appropriate context before using it with clients. The process should be explained clearly and the client asked whether they would like to do this. While the client is visualizing, the coach or mentor needs to observe the client to check that they are relaxed. If there are any non-verbal signs of discomfort the exercise should be reviewed immediately to see if the client wishes to stop. Appropriate prompts are used to guide the visualization (see the brainstorming section earlier in this chapter for examples). Careful timing and debriefing are essential for safe practice.

What are the advantages?

Visualization frees up the imagination. It can feel very positive for the client. It helps them to access new and exciting possibilities. It can be a powerful way of comparing different scenarios.

What are the disadvantages?

Some clients may not like relaxation exercises or may find imaginative work difficult. It is important to check. It is possible that the gap between current reality and future dreams is so great as to make a client despondent. This would need to be addressed and time allowed for good debriefing. However, most clients are likely to find the exercise energizing and motivating. The coach or mentor needs to ensure that the client is well 'grounded' after the visualization experience and so it should take place well in advance of the ending of a session.

Are there any useful references?

McKay, M., Davis M. and Fanning, P. (1981) *Thoughts and Feelings*. Richmond, CA: New Harbinger Publications.
Vickers, A. and Bavister, S. (2005) *Teach Yourself Coaching*. London: Hodder Arnold.
Whitworth, L., Kimsey-House, H. and Sandahl, P. (1998) *Co-active Coaching*. Mountain View, CA: Davies Black Publishing.

Role-Reversal

What is it?

Role-Reversal is an opportunity for the client to develop new perspectives on a problem by role-playing. It developed from the 'empty chair' technique used in Gestalt therapy.

When should it be used?

It is useful when the client is telling their story, in order to develop new perspectives and to challenge blindspots. It can also be useful when testing out new ways of negotiating or being assertive.

How does it work?

1 The coach or mentor asks the client to describe a typical scenario with person X, where there has been some difficulty or where the client wants to rehearse an interview or a meeting. They are asked to say exactly what X is like, what they might say, how they might feel and what they might do.
2 The coach or mentor then role-plays the scenario, with the client as themselves and with the coach or mentor playing the difficult person X. The scenario can be quite short, but enough time needs to be given for typical responses to be voiced.
3 There is then a debrief of what happened, asking the client to say whether X was portrayed accurately and, if so, what the client learned about both parties in the role play.
4 It may be appropriate to then re-run that same scenario with the client trying out some different responses.

5   Now get the client to play X while the coach or mentor plays the typical responses of the client. This helps the client to empathize with X.
6   At the end of the exercise the debriefing should make clear what is role play and what is reality. The client is reminded that they are who they are, not X.

What skills does the coach or mentor need?

The skills of role-playing. This requires clear instructions and the ability to flex between roles as the occasion demands. The skills of debriefing are needed to ensure that the client does not end up confused. Sensitivity is required because role play can be a way of accessing previously unacknowledged ideas, feelings and actions.

What are the advantages?

It can bring a session alive. It is a quick way of finding out exactly what goes on in a difficult interaction. Skills of empathy, assertion and negotiation can be practised in a safe setting.

What are the disadvantages?

None, if it is done carefully, allowing enough time for debriefing. However, the coach or mentor should not assume that a client will want to use role play. Some people do not like it at all. Some find it difficult to engage in a way that may seem artificial to them. Others engage readily but then find out that the exercise touches a raw nerve. The wise and safe coach or mentor goes carefully and is ready to adapt at any stage in the process.

Are there any useful references?

Blatner, A. (1996). *Acting-In: Practical Applications of Psychodramatic Methods*, 3rd edn. New York: Springer.
Fritchie, R. and Leary, M. (1998) *Resolving Conflicts in Organisations*. London: Lemos & Crane.
www.mindtools.com has a section on role-playing.

Cost–Benefit Analysis

What is it?

Cost–benefit analysis is a technique for comparing the expected costs with the expected benefits of a course of action, in order to decide whether to proceed. It can also be used to compare several possible options in order to chose the best one. As a business technique, cost–benefit analysis may involve financial measures of cost and benefit. A simplified version of cost–beneft analysis can help the client to evaluate their goal and decide whether to proceed, or whether the goal needs to be reconsidered.

When should it be used?

When the client needs to test their commitment to a goal or evaluate a proposed course of action.

How does it work?

The client clarifies their goal statement, and is then asked to list all the potential advantages of achieving their goal: for themselves, for other people and for their wider context, for example department, organization or family. They then list all the disadvantages for themselves and others and the wider context. The two lists can be thought of as balances on a set of weighing scales, and the client assesses whether the benefits outweigh the costs (see Figure 7.5).

What skills does the coach or mentor need?

The coach or mentor needs to use prompting questions to help the client identify all costs and benefits, some of which may have been overlooked.

What are the advantages?

The technique identifies the advantages of the chosen goal and thereby strengthens commitment to it. It also identifies disadvantages and can help the client to consider whether the gain is worth the pain, or whether any disadvantages could be minimized. It ensures that the client is really committed to a goal or course of action that is realistic for them.

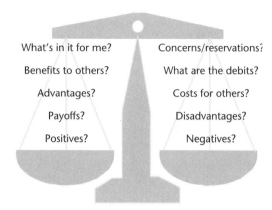

What's in it for me?   Concerns/reservations?

Benefits to others?   What are the debits?

Advantages?   Costs for others?

Payoffs?   Disadvantages?

Positives?   Negatives?

Figure 7.5 Cost–benefit analysis

What are the disadvantages?

The client may discover that the goal or action is unrealistic or not right for them. They may need to pause and reflect on how to proceed, or whether there is more exploration of issues needed. This may be seen as failure, and the client may become disheartened. If this is the case, the coach or mentor needs to be appropriately supportive

Are there any useful references?

Egan, G. (forthcoming) *The Skilled Helper*, 8th edn. Belmont, CA: Brooks/Cole. www.mindtools.com describes this and other evaluation techniques.

Values Clarification

What is it?

Values Clarification is a way of helping the client to articulate the things that are really important to them in choosing a job, in being satisfied at work and in achieving potential. There are several exercises which are used by coaches and mentors. The wheel of work and wheel of life pinpoint life and work activities and allow for exploration of areas of satisfaction and dissatisfaction. Career drivers affect motivation and commitment and so they are linked to satisfaction, release of potential and delivery of results.

When should it be used?

Whenever the client is trying to prioritize and make decisions about work, career or work–life balance. It can also be used to help to understand why a client is feeling too stressed, demotivated or demoralized at work. If faced with exciting opportunities where it is difficult to choose between two equally good prospective jobs, values clarification can help to distinguish what is really important to the person.

How does it work?

This tool is widely used by coaches and mentors. They provide a blank template of the wheel of work, showing ten possible hubs. Figure 7.6 gives an example of the ten aspects identified by a client showing the least valued (1) as 'writing reports' and the most valued (10) as 'leading'.

1   Clients are invited to make a list of ten aspects of their work. They write these on a blank template of the wheel of work, below.
2   They are then given ten stickers each with a number 1–10.

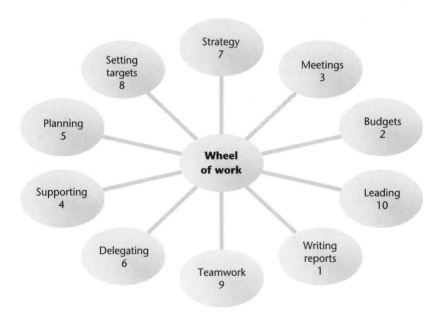

Figure 7.6   A wheel of work

3   They are invited to place one of these on each spoke of the wheel according to how much they value that part of their work at present: 1 would indicate the lowest area of satisfaction and 10 would indicate the highest.

4   They are then asked to think about the proportion of time spent on each activity. For example, the client may put the '10' sticker on leading, indicating the highest value for that aspect of work, but the percentage of time given to leading is only 20 per cent of total work time.

They can instantly see where the areas of satisfaction and dissatisfaction are. They may become clearer about what they value in work. They can also see the difference between what they may want and need and what they have actually got. If this is the current situation with their job they can then be invited to repeat the same exercise for their ideal job, and to compare and contrast the two wheels.

Another version of this is a wheel of life. This helps clients who have problems with work–life balance. The client can be invited to suggest their own categories for what they value in life. They may include areas such as partner, money, health, leisure, personal growth, spirituality, family, friends and career.

When areas on either of these wheels have been identified and prioritized, the client can move to goal-setting around, for example, delegation, time management, career development or work–life balance. These exercises help clients to become clearer about what they value in work and life.

Francis (1994) talks about career drivers and how motivation and satisfaction at work are affected by these. They relate to values. The client can be asked to put the list of career drivers in their order of priority and the coach or mentor can help the client to become aware of how each driver is connected to a fundamental concern. A person who puts 'affiliation' at the bottom of the list of drivers will not be looking for 'closeness' at work and may prefer working in a virtual organization. A person who puts 'challenge' at the top of the list will soon get frustrated in a repetitive working environment and may be surprised to learn that 'competition' is the main concern linked with the driver for challenge. Discussion with the coach or mentor will establish how far the need for challenge is for self-challenge or how far it is concerned with competing against others.

Some career drivers which relate to values are shown in Table 7.1.

Table 7.1   Career drivers

Driver	Concern
Autonomy	Being able to choose
Power and influence	Dominance – making an impact
Material rewards	Wealth
Affiliation	Closeness
Challenge	Competition
Creativity	Originality
Expertise	Mastery
Security	Being assured that . . .
Status	Position – respect and recognition
Lifestyle	Integration and holism

What skills does the coach or mentor need?

The skills of eliciting information from the client about the important categories in their life and work. The skills of open questioning and clarifying, as well as clearly presenting the techniques and instructing the client how to use them.

What are the advantages?

A very visible way of accessing important priorities and of noticing imbalances. Something that can be done either wholly in a coaching or mentoring session, or partly done between sessions.

What are the disadvantages?

The awareness of gaps between what the person wants and what they have got may require further support from the coach or mentor. This may not be a disadvantage, but is certainly something to consider.

Are there any useful references?

Francis, D. (1994) *Managing Your Own Career*. London: HarperCollins.
Robbins, A. (2004) *Awaken the Giant Within*. Riverside, NJ: Simon & Schuster.

Schein, E. (1990) *Career Anchors: Discovering Your Real Values*. San Francisco: Josey-Bass/Pfeiffer.

Vickers, A. and Bavister, S. (2005) *Teach Yourself Coaching*. London: Hodder Arnold.

Zeus, P. and Skiffington, S. (2000) *The Complete Guide to Coaching At Work*. North Ryde, NSW: McGraw-Hill.

Force Field Analysis

What is it?

Force Field Analysis is a technique derived from the ideas of the psychologist Kurt Lewin (1951). He said that all the forces and influences on a situation needed to be taken into account in understanding that situation. If a person wants to change their behaviour, or change a situation, they need to look at the forces which might help move things in the desired direction, and the forces that are holding back change.

When should it be used?

Force field analysis can be useful at different stages in coaching or mentoring to:

- Look at the forces which are holding a problem in place and those pushing for change. This analysis can help the client to identify blindspots, new perspectives and a point of leverage.
- Test the realism of a goal and commitment to it. This analysis can help to identify the forces which support goal achievement and those that are restraining it.
- Test the feasibility of an action plan.

How does it work?

The following example illustrates how force field analysis can be applied to identify what will help or hinder goal achievement. In this example the client's goal is physical fitness.

1   The client is asked to write down their goal statement with a vertical line drawn beneath it, as in Figure 7.7. Next, they draw horizontal arrows showing all the factors or forces which will support and assist the goal achievement, i.e. the *helping forces*.

Force Field Analysis

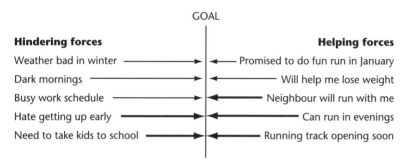

By 31 December I will run three miles in 20 minutes
at least twice a week

GOAL

Hindering forces	Helping forces
Weather bad in winter	Promised to do fun run in January
Dark mornings	Will help me lose weight
Busy work schedule	Neighbour will run with me
Hate getting up early	Can run in evenings
Need to take kids to school	Running track opening soon

Figure 7.7   Force Field Analysis

2   The client is prompted to think about: forces under *their* control: things about themselves; forces dependent upon *others*: colleagues/ friends/family; forces *within the organization and wider context*: events, policies, norms.
3   The forces can be drawn in graphically, ideally in green, with bold arrows for large forces, and smaller, finer ones for less powerful forces.
4   The client then draws, ideally in red, all the *hindering forces* that will prevent them achieving the goal. As in step 2, they consider forces under their control, forces dependent upon others and forces in the organization or wider context.
5   The final step is to consider which forces can be increased, diminished or diverted, to increase the likelihood of success.

This method could also be used to map the enabling and restraining forces impacting on a proposed action strategy. The action strategy would be drawn as the vertical line and the forces enabling or restraining successful implementation would be mapped.

What skills does the coach or mentor need?

The coach or mentor needs to prompt the client to identify the key helping or hindering forces. They then need to offer support and challenge to encourage the client to consider ways of shifting the balance of forces to increase the overall helping effect. The coach or mentor can use prompts, for example:

Can you reduce/divert any hindering forces?
Can you find new helping forces?
Will reducing any enabling forces also reduce resistance?
Can you increase any helping forces?

What are the advantages?

Force Field Analysis can make visible the positive and negative forces which have been previously overlooked. It can help the client reflect on their motivation, strengths and weaknesses, and also to reflect on the factors in their situation or context which will help or hinder them. Having identified these factors, the client selects manageable ones to work on and thus increases their probability of success.

What are the disadvantages?

No obvious ones, except to notice that Force Field Analysis is a visual representation, but not a science. A client may choose, even in the face of large restraining forces, to pursue a goal that is important to them.

Are there any useful references?

Lewin, K. (1951) *Field Theory in Social Science: Selected Theoretical Papers*. New York: Harper & Row.
Pedler, M., Burgoyne, J. and Boydell, T. (1994) *A Manager's Guide to Self Development*. Maidenhead: McGraw-Hill.

The C>A>N model: Conflict, Assertiveness, Negotiation

What is it?

There are many situations at work which require skilled negotiation in order to prevent or resolve conflict. C>A>N is a three-stage model which we have developed for understanding the processes of conflict management and for developing the skills of assertiveness and negotiation.

When should it be used?

Whenever the need arises. It can improve performance with individuals, groups or teams. It can help clients tackle difficult situations in meetings. It can be used as part of action planning.

How is it used?

Box 7.1 demonstrates the process in full.

Box 7.1 The C>A>N model

CONFLICT

Conflict occurs when two or more parties want different things.

1   Understand the differences: ideas, values, power, processes, outcomes.
2   Listen carefully to the other party to find out where they are coming from.
3   Show that you empathize with their point of view or their expectations.

ASSERTIVENESS

Assertiveness means clearly, positively and realistically stating what you want.

1   Prepare your own case. Consider how the other party will approach things.
2   Present yourself carefully: appearance, posture, facial expression.
3   Know what you want and be prepared to state it clearly and positively.

NEGOTIATION

Negotiation involves movement between different interests.

1   Be clear about what you want and need. List in order of priority what you could give to the other party without too much cost to yourself or to your organization and what you may not be able to give under any circumstances.
2   Negotiate. Acknowledge others' wants and needs alongside your own. Separate the person from the issue. Ask questions, find out what is behind the stated position. Be flexible to offers and creative alternatives.
3   Aim for win–win, but accept that compromise can also be a successful outcome. In many negotiations the relationship as well as the outcome is important.

Note: negotiation will work only if both parties are prepared to adjust to different interests.

Connor and Pokora 2007

What skills does the coach or mentor need?

The coach or mentor will need to model skills of empathy, assertiveness and negotiation. The ability to role-play will also be required. Alongside this, the coach or mentor needs to inspire the client with the confidence to 'have a go' at role-playing a conflict situation.

The coach or mentor can offer the model when a client experiences a conflict situation at work. It could be useful to go through all the stages of the model, rehearsing some of the skills and behaviours involved. This would involve the coach or mentor doing some role play in which they are the 'other party' in the negotiation. This would give the client invaluable practice and insight into ways in which the other party might experience them. It may be useful to reverse roles. The client is invited to get 'under the skin' of the other party by taking on their role, and the coach or mentor plays the role of the client. The debriefing of this exercise is important, in order to identify the learning points and to set goals for practising new ways of being assertive, and negotiating desired outcomes.

What are the advantages?

If the model is rehearsed within a coaching or mentoring session, it is an excellent opportunity for the coach or mentor to observe how the client might behave in a negotiation. Direct feedback can then be given and goals set for practice of assertiveness and bargaining skills.

What are the disadvantages?

Real life can never be completely replicated in a coaching or mentoring session. It is important to have a follow-up session with the client to check how the negotiation went in real life and the learning from this. Forewarned is forearmed. Some of the recommended reading deals in more depth with reasons why all the best skills won't always work!

Are there any useful references?

Fisher, R. and Ury, W. (1987) *Getting to Yes*. London: Arrow.
Kennedy, G. (1992) *The Perfect Negotiation*. London: Century.
Stone, D., Patton, B. and Heen, S. (1999) *Difficult Conversations: How to Discuss What Matters Most*. London: Michael Joseph.

Critical Path Analysis

What is it?

Critical path analysis is a technique frequently used when planning large, complex projects with interdependent activities and timescales. A much simplified version can be used in coaching and mentoring to help the client to identify the action sequence necessary to achieve their goal.

When should it be used?

Critical path analysis is used in action planning when the client is considering the details of how they will implement their strategy and achieve their goal.

How does it work?

The client is asked to draw a horizontal line and mark their goal, with a date for completion at the extreme right. Working backwards from that date, they are then asked what needs to be done *before* that date in order to meet the goal deadline, and what needs to be done before that, and so on. The key actions and dates are plotted on the line, from right to left, eventually reaching the current date, i.e. the start point. The resulting line represents key actions and milestones along the path to achieving the goal. So, assuming today's date is 1 September, an example of using this technique might look like Figure 7.8 where a client is planning a team awayday.

What skills does the coach or mentor need?

The coach or mentor may need patience and persistence in helping the client to stay focused on this task. Some may find it laborious, or over-detailed, and it may prove challenging for those, whether helping or being helped, who get bored easily or dislike detail.

1 Sept	10 Sept	15 Sept	8 Oct	15 Oct	23 Oct
Book venue	Meet facilitator	Circulate draft programme	Discuss with department	Circulate final programme	Team awayday

Figure 7.8   Critical path analysis

What are the advantages?

A skilful coach or mentor helps the client to ensure the best possible chance of success when they act, and this technique can be a powerful aid. It identifies all the tasks which need to be completed, any which are interdependent and timeframes associated with each. So, it enables the client to check the feasibility of goals and deadlines and helps them to clarify whether goals are achievable. The client may discover that their timescales need adjusting, or the goal refining, or that a critical step in the process needs more detailed consideration. Alternatively, it may confirm that the goal is achievable, and give the client a clear set of action steps. For longer-term goals, the technique is helpful in defining interim milestones.

What are the disadvantages?

The client may become disheartened or discouraged if the goal proves unachievable, and will need to be supported in redefining their goal or time-frame. It is important that they do not see this as a failure, but rather as a smart piece of advance planning.

Action planning does not always mean the end of a coaching or mentoring journey. In many cases the client will return to the next coaching or mentoring session to tell the story of what happened when they implemented their action plans. It is important that they feel adequately supported to return, even if plans have not gone entirely as anticipated, without feeling that they have 'failed'.

Are there any useful references?

www.mindtools.com describes critical path analysis and other planning techniques.

Summary

In this chapter we have:

- Evaluated 12 tools and techniques which are used by coaches and mentors.
- Used a series of questions to evaluate each tool or technique.
- Explained the skills which would be needed by the coach or mentor

and indicated where each tool or technique might be used within the mentoring process.

- Outlined the advantages and disadvantages of each, using the experience of coaches and mentors to identify what works well and what needs to be used with care.

8 How can I train and develop?

- Introduction
- Assessing your training needs
- Selecting a training programme
- Training standards
- Developing skills
- Developing yourself
- Developing a learning climate
- Ethical and professional training
- Evaluating training
- Summary

Introduction

In our experience, well-designed training is helpful for those involved in coaching and mentoring, and should be regarded as essential by those considering a full-time coaching or mentoring role.

Currently, anyone may call themselves a coach or mentor, without any training or qualification. Both purchasers and providers of coaching and mentoring services have raised concerns that coaches and mentors who are not trained may do more harm than good. Moreover, individuals who are asked to take on a coaching or mentoring role without formal preparation and training can feel ill-equipped. The CIPD annual survey of learning and development (2006: 11) included a question on the extent to which in-depth coaching training was provided to coaches in organizations. The total of responses in the categories 'to a small extent' and 'not at all' was 70 per cent. On the other hand, it could be argued that the trend towards accreditation will place increasing emphasis on formal training, and may run the risk of undervaluing experience.

This chapter describes the principles and practice of effective coach and mentor training and offers guidelines for choosing a training programme and for developing coach and mentor training. Using material drawn from a variety of sources, including an established programme, the key components of training are described. This chapter will be of particular relevance if you want to:

- understand more about training
- select the right training course
- get the best out of a course you are on already
- commission coach or mentor training for your organization or professional body
- design or develop coach or mentor training for your organization or professional body

Throughout the chapter, case examples illustrate key topics, and practical exercises will help you to design or choose the right training programme for you, and get the most out of training.

Assessing your training needs

In assessing your training needs, a good place to start is to ask yourself why you are interested in training at this time in your life and work. It may be that external factors are steering you; perhaps you have been asked or required to work as a coach or mentor in your organization. It may be that personal interest is the major factor. Becoming a coach or mentor, whether full- or part-time, may be part of your personal development plan. For many people, it is a mixture of motivations. When participants are asked about their reasons for attending training programmes, typical replies include:

- I've been doing mentoring for several years . . . it's about time I found out if I was doing it right!
- Many junior staff approach me for help, and I want to feel more confident in having a framework and the right skills for working with them.
- I do coaching in my organization, but I think I'm often quite prescriptive and give people advice . . . I wonder if there is a better way.
- I want to set up a mentoring scheme in my company and need to find out what it's all about.
- I've been asked to take on a mentoring/coaching role, which I see as an opportunity, but also daunting. I've experienced it being done badly and I want to do it better.

- I don't think we get the best out of our managers at work, and I think coaching could support them and help to deliver better results.

 What is happening in your organization or professional environment that makes training important at this time?

A **review of personal development planning** in a large organization showed that many employees would benefit from individual support in addressing their training and development needs. The organization commissioned a coaching skills programme for managers, designed to increase their confidence and skill in supporting their staff, whether high flyers or those with performance problems.

 What is happening for you in your career or at work that makes training important at this time?

Examples of reasons why training might be important include a new or changed job role, increased responsibility for staff, an experience of handling a 'difficult' person, or a requirement to take on a formal coaching or mentoring role.

Kim, a manager says: I've just joined an organization where staff development is a high priority, and I will have a large number of people reporting directly to me. I'm used to troubleshooting problems myself, but I'm not so experienced at delegating and developing others. I need some training to help me find out how to build good relationships and support staff while at the same time getting the work done.

In assessing your training needs, it is also helpful to think about your preferences in leading, working and learning. In previous chapters, the usefulness of inventories and questionnaires is described. You can use insight from these to consider your training needs.

Diane is outgoing and decisive and prefers to learn by doing, with the opportunity for experimentation and trial and error. She wants a coach training programme which will allow her to capitalize on this strength, with plenty of practice, but also challenge her to work in other ways. She has a tendency to 'act first, think later', and knows that she may miss opportunities for learning. She wants to develop the capacity to be reflective, which will be important both while being trained and also while being a coach.

Another exercise that may help to clarify your training needs is to focus, either on your own or with colleagues, on what you hope to achieve from coach or mentor training. Clarifying your ideal can highlight what is important to you. Here is an example:

> **A group of doctors** decided to set up a mentoring scheme for all staff working in health centres, and asked for volunteers to be trained as mentors. The trainee mentors brainstormed their ideal for the mentoring scheme, and shared ideas about what it would be like if it were working really well. The brainstorming session created a sense of excitement and possibility among the would-be mentors about what they could achieve. Using the results of brainstorming, they set up specific goals for their training and for establishing the mentoring scheme.

 Thinking ahead, imagine that you have successfully completed or implemented a coach or mentor training programme, and it has gone very well, better than you could have hoped for.

What would be different in your organization?
What would be different for you personally?
What would you have achieved?

A final approach to exploring your training needs is based on a typology of learning. Pedler and Aspinwall describe four types of learning:

1   *about* things (or *knowledge*).
2   to *do* things (or *skills, abilities, competences*).
3   to *become ourselves, to achieve our full potential* (or *personal development*).
4   to *achieve things together* (or *collaborative enquiry*).

(1996: 25)

The first involves acquiring information or knowledge, for example:

* I learn that coaching requires the key skill of active listening.

The second is knowing how to do something:

* I learn to listen actively in coaching practice and coaching situations.

The third, the way you are as a person, happens when the first two are integrated into your personal development, often involving your values and beliefs:

- I find myself listening in this different way in many aspects of my life, which changes the nature of my interactions with others.

The fourth, achieving things together, includes the learning between people as they work together:

- We reflect, in my leadership team, on the way in which we listen to each other, and hear, and check understanding. This has an impact on us, and on the decisions we make together.

 Which of these four kinds of learning are important to you in coach or mentor training? In what way are they important? Completing the following sentences may help you to answer these questions:

- I want to know more about/find out about . . .
- I want to be able to . . .
- I'd like to become a person who . . .
- In our organization, I'd like us to . . .

Don't underestimate the power of mini self-analyses such as these. On training programmes we ask participants similar questions, and have never ceased to be surprised at how perceptive and accurate individuals' self-assessments are.

Selecting a training programme

Objectives

Your assessment of training needs will influence your choice of coach or mentor training programme. The previous section helped you to clarify your training requirements. The next step is to choose the right programme for you. An obvious starting place is the training programme objectives. Are they clear and explicit? Is the programme flexible or fixed? Can it be tailored to your requirements or is it 'off the shelf'? How close is the match between your needs and the programme objectives?

Whatever your objectives, a training programme should describe in simple language the aims and learning outcomes. A training provider should be clear about what they are offering, and also indicate any important topics not covered. If your aim is to find out more about coaching and mentoring, a short programme of a day or thereabouts may be sufficient. Such a programme is best considered as an introduction, and will probably include topics such as:

- definitions of coaching and mentoring
- the benefits of coaching and mentoring – individual and organizational
- approaches, frameworks and skills
- implementing coaching or mentoring schemes
- future trends in coaching and mentoring

The training objectives of knowledge focused programmes such as this one are characterized by words such as: understand, be introduced to, ideas, frameworks, research, trends, concepts, evidence.

If you want to develop coaching and mentoring skills then a longer programme is essential. Training objectives for skills programmes are likely to include phrases such as: be able to, practise, get feedback, try out, develop skills.

A mentor development programme which targeted both knowledge and skills included these outcomes:

By the end of the programme participants will have:
- understood what mentoring is and how it differs from counselling or patronage
- been introduced to a framework for mentoring
- practised each stage of the framework and the associated skills, received feedback and reviewed their skills development
- considered the ethical and practical issues involved in being mentors and setting up mentoring schemes

Timescale

Our experience is that four days' training are needed, and five days are preferable, for those who are developing skills as coaches or mentors. These days are best spaced out over time to enable participants to assimilate learning and to practise skills. However, we agree with Jarvis (2004: 15): 'In the past, the reputation of the coaching industry has been weakened by training providers who claim to produce professional coaches from five-day training courses'. Training is the start, not the end, of the coaching or mentoring journey. Completing a training programme is an important step in developing as a coach or mentor, but it is only the beginning.

Structure

When considering potential programmes, find out how the training time is structured. Will there be formal inputs on models, theories and approaches? Will there be practical demonstrations of skills being taught, either live or on video? Will there be the opportunity to practise skills and get feedback? When skills development is a key objective, our recommendation is that at least 50 per cent of the course time should be spent on skills practice and review of learning. Will there be the opportunity to discuss how the skills have been used at work, and of ethical and practical issues arising? A mixture of activities and learning methods is preferable.

A learning design might include:

- a variety of learning and teaching methods, including input, large-group discussion, demonstration of a framework and skills, small-group skills practice, and small-group activity
- a balance between learner-centred activity (e.g. discussing experiences of practising the skills at work) and theory-centred activity (e.g. taught input)
- a breadth of content, including a framework for coaching or mentoring, the skills, ethical and professional considerations, and coach or mentor self-development
- a time gap between the programme days, to allow for assimilation of skills and practice in everyday settings
- discussion of life after training, including ongoing support and supervision
- opportunities for networking during and after the programme

Trainers

A key resource on a training programme is the trainer or trainers. How many will there be and what is the ratio of staff to participants? For skills development, small-group work is essential and a workable ratio is one experienced facilitator or tutor for every three participants. What is the background and experience of the trainers? Do they have coaching or mentoring experience and relevant qualifications? Another important indicator of training quality is how the prospective participant or purchaser is dealt with when making enquiries. Do the staff of the training organization deal with you in a manner which reflects the values of coaching and mentoring? What does the organization literature and procedures tell you about their values and approach?

Participants

The participants themselves are another key learning resource. A training programme needs sufficient numbers for breadth and variety of style and experience, but not so many people as to make large-group dialogue difficult. If skills development is a priority, the ratio of tutors to participants is important. In addition, consider what other resources are available. These might include course materials, books, online materials, case studies, training follow-up days and trainer support back at work.

Ethical considerations

A discussion of ethical and professional issues is an important aspect of coach and mentor training. A training programme is frequently part of an organization's initiative to develop a coaching or mentoring scheme, or to create an organizational culture which fosters coaching and mentoring. It is therefore important to consider how a coaching or mentoring scheme would work in practice within the organizational culture and existing systems. Participants need to think about how their coaching or mentoring role will work in their organization or professional body, how it will fit in with their other roles and the ethical and professional dilemmas that might arise from coaching and mentoring in practice. In addition, participants need to plan how their support and supervision needs will be met. Ethical issues are discussed in greater depth in Chapter 9.

Having introduced in overview the assessment of training needs and training programme selection, the remainder of this chapter explores in greater depth several aspects of training. Consideration of these will contribute to the selection and design of a training programme.

Training standards

There are a large number of coaching and mentoring training programmes available, ranging from one-day workshops through to master's-level programmes and even doctorates. Providers include private organizations, professional bodies and universities. Whether you are an individual purchaser or acting on behalf of your organization, you will need to consider whether formal qualifications or accreditation are important to you.

Some programmes are accredited by universities, and some recognized by professional bodies and other organizations. Coaching and mentoring professional bodies offering accreditation of training programmes include the ICF and EMCC. In addition, purchasers may wish to know whether trainers are members of a professional body, and whether they adhere to a code of ethics and ethical guidelines.

Evidence of completion of approved training may be part of the requirement for individual accreditation as a coach or mentor. Several professional bodies offer individual accreditation, and details of accreditation requirements and procedures can be obtained from their websites.

The Appendix to this book contains a list of useful website addresses for those wishing to find out more about these topics.

Developing skills

However much you 'know about' coaching and mentoring, to be an effective practitioner you must 'be able to'. Figure 8.1 shows how skills may be acquired during training.

Figure 8.1 Acquiring new skills

An effective training programme should address each of these levels, so that participants have the opportunity to:

- *learn* about skills
- *recognize* them when they are used
- *practise* them in training conditions, with appropriate feedback

- *use* the skills outside of the training environment
- *integrate* skills into their personal and professional development

A mentoring training programme addressed each of these five levels in developing mentoring skills, which included:
- Active listening
- Challenging
- Focusing and prioritizing
- Goal setting
- Commitment testing
- Action planning

Skill development followed this pattern:

Learning about skills
An input on a mentoring framework in overview, followed by an in-depth look at each stage of the framework and the mentoring skills associated with that stage.

Recognizing skills
A real-time demonstration by trainers of a selected stage of the framework and the associated skills. One trainer was the client, the other was the mentor. The demonstration was 'warts and all' and not rehearsed, and the trainer client brought a real issue (see below) to the session. Participants were encouraged to identify skills they saw, and raise any questions. The participants critiqued and explored the trainer's mentoring skills.

Practising skills
Participants worked in threes, taking turns to be mentor, client and observer. Each trio was supported by a facilitator. In the client role, participants brought their real-life issues, both problems and opportunities, to the programme. Typical issues included handling a difficult work relationship, making a career choice, and balancing work and home. Working with real issues helped to give participants first-hand experience of managing appropriate boundaries and using the skills in a time-limited context. It also gave them a direct personal experience of helping and being helped.

Trying out and using skills
Participants were encouraged to identify skills to practise, and appropriate situations in which to practise, and report back on their experience of trying out the skills in everyday situations.

Using naturally

At a follow-up day, several months after the programme, participants were asked about the impact of the training programme on their approach at work. What were they now doing differently? Had skills and knowledge from the training programme been integrated into new ways of working?

This skills development sequence, with the emphasis on *doing* rather than *talking about*, does lead to skill development. It has been described as rather like learning to ride a bike. At first, you are unaware of your lack of skill, because it is not something you have tried (this has been called unconscious incompetence). Then you try, and fall off (conscious incompetence). Then, if you concentrate, you can stay upright, at first only for a few seconds, then for minutes (conscious competence). Finally, you just get on the bike and ride it, without thinking about it. The skill has become automatic (unconscious competence). On a training programme, you should expect to reach the level of conscious competence in basic skills, and if you are lucky you may reflect on moments of unconscious competence! Of course it is not always comfortable to move through this learning curve, which is why a supportive learning climate is so important.

> **Luke:** When I first tried to practise active listening, it was hopeless. I'm so used to asking closed questions in my job that it felt impossible not to try to solve the client's problem. I knew I wasn't supposed to do that, but I couldn't remember what to do instead. However, the trio I was working with were great, and they helped me out. We pressed an imaginary 'pause' button when I got stuck. Gradually, I found I could use the skills and was amazed at their impact. It has made me think about how I do my job. I still need my expert knowledge but I see a need for these skills as well.

> **Jenna is used to giving advice** in her job as tax accountant. She tends to use this approach when managing her staff and coaching trainees, and realizes it isn't always helpful. She wants to practise asking open questions when staff come to her with problems, rather than always giving her advice and solutions. Helped by a learning partner on the training programme, she highlights a few key phrases that she is going to practise back at work:
>
> . . . tell me some more about that?
> . . . let me check I've understood you . . .
> . . . it's a problem for you because . . . ?

Developing yourself

As you develop skills, you develop yourself. As noted earlier, skills development often goes hand in hand with personal development. An evaluation of mentor training found that 87 per cent of participants reported that 'personal development is important if I want to be a mentor' (Connor 1997: 45).

An effective training programme creates opportunities for self-insight and self-development, and there are many different ways to do this. Below, we list some that we have found valuable through our direct experience. Each of these methods might also be used in coaching or mentoring. So, experiencing them on a training programme has an added advantage for the trainee coach or mentor, who can reflect on their experience of the method and its potential advantages and disadvantages.

Learning journal

This is a private record, in your own words, of your experiences and learning. It might include new ideas, reflections on experiences in a training programme or at work, skills that you have tried out and their impact, interesting conversations, your aims – anything that seems significant. Being on a programme may confirm some views and beliefs and challenge others. You may want to record feelings, questions, insights and issues to be explored further. Learning journals, while usually private, may form the basis for conversations with a learning partner.

> **Bruce:** I was pretty sceptical about keeping a journal and it took some doing at first! However, when I reread it and talked with my learning partner, it underlined some key learning moments for me, and highlighted how I'd changed in my views, and also my skill development.

Career lifeline

This technique is described in detail in Chapter 7. It involves drawing a line or visual representation of career, past, present and future, to illustrate the highs and lows and significant events. It is an opportunity to reflect on the development of a career in relation to other factors in life, and to consider future direction. On a training programme, you will usually reflect on your lifeline in a small group of participants, who will help you to notice themes, influences and important factors in your career. The career lifeline is a powerful technique in coaching and mentoring and so its inclusion on a training programme is useful in giving participants first-hand experience of using it themselves and facilitating other participants.

> **Ali:** On my training course we drew our own career lifelines and talked in small groups about ourselves, past, present and hopes for the future. It was a powerful exercise, which highlighted the high points and low points in my career to date and got me thinking about what I really wanted for the future. I would consider offering this activity to a client, but only when we'd got to know each other and if I thought it would be helpful. It needs a supportive atmosphere and plenty of time to debrief it.

Psychometric instruments and questionnaires

These include instruments such as the Myers-Briggs Type Indicator questionnaire and can provide helpful insights into preferences in working with others, and your strengths and preferred style, either as coach or mentor or as client. This approach values the differences between people, and sees an appreciation of individual strengths as the start point for personal development. These values are congruent with coaching and mentoring values.

> **Krysia:** I'm quite easy-going and relaxed. I like exploring options and gathering more information, rather than closing down options. I do sometimes find it hard to meet deadlines and finish things on time. Understanding this made me think about how I will work as a mentor, and the advantages of my preferences as well as possible disadvantages.

The Learning Styles questionnaire, described in Chapter 3 (Honey and Mumford 1992), can help you to understand how you prefer to learn, and which elements of a training programme you might find easier and more enjoyable, and which more difficult. It is also useful for thinking about client learning preferences, and your role as coach or mentor in working with these preferences.

> **Phil:** My learning style is quite reflective and I need time to mull things over. I found the skills practice, where I just had to get on with it, quite difficult. I didn't feel as if I'd had enough time to prepare. I noticed too that as a coach I'm quite happy with silences, but some clients aren't!

Another relevant questionnaire is the Career Anchors Inventory (Schein 1990). It is a self-scored questionnaire which helps clarify the important values and drivers that underpin career decisions and choices.

When using psychometrics, care should be taken to establish that instruments are reputable and are administered in accordance with professional protocols.

Developing a learning climate

The training journey parallels the coaching or mentoring journey. In a safe and effective coaching or mentoring relationship, a working agreement and ground rules are agreed at the outset, in order to establish the right conditions for learning – the leaning climate. Similarly, in a safe and effective training programme, ground rules and working agreements are clearly established and agreed at the beginning. This enables participants to learn. They feel safe enough to take the risk of letting go of old behaviours and old assumptions, and trying out new ones. They know that confidences will be respected, and understand the appropriate boundaries for disclosure. They feel confident enough to challenge respectfully and be challenged. And, more prosaically, they arrive on time, and cancel only if absolutely unavoidable. Trainers should be explicit about these issues from day one, ensure that they themselves adhere to ground rules and, by giving plenty of opportunity for review, catch any difficulties as they arise. When this is done well, a positive learning climate is created.

Here is a description of a learning climate, taken from the profile of a 'Learning Company':

- If something goes wrong around here, you can expect help, support and interest in learning lessons from it
- People make time to question their own practice, to analyse, discuss and learn from what happens
- There is a general attitude of continuous improvement – always trying to learn and do better
- When you don't know something, it's normal to ask around until you get the required help or information
- Differences of all sorts, between young and old, women and men, black and white etc. are recognized and positively valued as essential to learning and creativity.

(Pedler *et al.* 1991: 27)

On a training programme with a positive learning climate, you might expect to see some of the characteristics described in Box 8.1.

Box 8.1 A learning climate in coach and mentor training

- Participants are supported in trying out new skills and expanding their knowledge
- Participants receive constructive feedback
- Trainers get feedback from participants if something goes awry
- Trainers and participants are flexible and open to new ideas
- There is time to discuss and make explicit both individual and group learning
- People learn from each other, not just the trainers
- Training and development goals are appropriate and challenging
- Differences between people are valued
- No one is marginalized on account of difference, for example gender, age, race

---

Another way to describe learning climate is to look at the balance of support and challenge. These can be plotted on axes, as shown in Figure 8.2, which presents a version of this method. If there is too much challenge and

HIGH CHALLENGE

Defensive and wary	Constructive feedback
Play cards close	Safe to share problems
Watch your back	OK to say what you want
Fix blame and dodge blame	Reflective
Point-scoring	Questioning – makes you think
Winners/losers	Respect for individual views
Aggressive	Differences encourage dialogue

LOW   HIGH
SUPPORT   SUPPORT

Tentative	Cosy
See the way the land lies	Groupthink
Non-committal	Going along with
Polite and platitudes	Boring
Collusion to avoid tricky topics	No apparent conflict but ...
Keep on safe territory	Disagreement may go
Ritual conversations	underground
	Safe to share problems

LOW CHALLENGE

Figure 8.2 Learning climate: the balance of support and challenge

not enough support, participants become wary and defensive, and learning will not occur. The opposite situation, with high support and low challenge, can lead to a safe but too 'cosy' group climate, which stifles feedback and learning. The climate most conducive to learning has a balance of healthy amounts of support and challenge.

Thinking back to a training programme that you have organized or attended, how would you describe the learning climate? Which of the four boxes in Figure 8.2 best describes it? What helped individual and group learning? What hindered it?

Thinking forward to coach or mentor training, what would be important for you in a training environment? What would you want to avoid? What could you do to help create the best learning climate?

A healthy learning climate doesn't happen by chance, and below are some of the factors which can help to create a positive learning climate. The trainers are potential role models, and their behaviour is important.

Behaviour

- Do the trainers behave in a way which demonstrates what you might expect from a good coach or mentor?
- Do they show respect, empathy and genuineness?
- Do they listen carefully? Do they acknowledge others' views?
- Do they explore differences without becoming defensive?
- Do they seem clear about what is important to them?
- If they don't know something, do they say so?
- Are participants encouraged to do likewise?

Context

- Are the rooms large enough and sufficiently private?
- Are there comfortable chairs and natural daylight?
- Are there adequate comfort breaks, refreshment breaks, food options?
- Is the timetable clear and agreed?
- Are materials (handouts, presentations etc.) clear and timely?
- Does the programme start and finish on time?

Ethical and professional training

As we have stated, the training experience parallels the coaching or mentoring experience. An effective training programme is based on a clear understanding about what is offered and required to make it successful. Ethical and professional standards are important in the training programme, and it is vital that trainers act with integrity, impartiality and respect (Connor 1994). These values are closely linked with the moral principles described in Chapter 8. The questions in Box 8.2, adapted from Connor, are prompts for assessing a training programme.

Box 8.2 Ethical and professional training

- Are the trainers open about their qualifications and experience?
- Do the trainers model the behaviour they expect from participants?
- Are training policies clearly communicated?
- Do the trainers adhere to a code of practice or ethics?
- Do the trainers treat all participants fairly?
- Is it clear what is/is not confidential to the programme?
- Are the methods of assessment, if any, made clear to participants?
- Are the trainers sensitive to issues of race, gender etc.?
- Do the trainers deliver the training programme as agreed?
- Are the trainers clear about any support offered outside the programme?
- Is it clear how the programme is evaluated?

Just as successful coaching and mentoring are based on voluntary commitment from both parties and on mutual responsibility, so successful training requires voluntary commitment and mutual responsibility. Often, the responsibilities of participants are overlooked, but in this example they were made clear:

> **Participants attended a half-day taster session** to enable them to decide whether to commit to a full six-day coach training programme. The commitment to the six-day programme was explained. Participants would be expected to:
> - Commit to attend all training days
> - Practise skills between sessions
> - Offer/ask for constructive feedback
> - Complete a learning journal
> - Become a coach in the organization's coaching scheme, subject to their progress on the course

Evaluating training

In this chapter, we have emphasized the importance of clarity of objectives and learning outcomes in coach and mentor training. Evaluation, whether ongoing (formative) or at the end of a programme (summative) is important in understanding whether training objectives have been met and how they have been achieved.

Kirkpatrick (1994) identified four levels of training evaluation, and his model can be applied to assess:

- trainee reaction to the training;
- change in trainee knowledge;
- change in trainee behaviour;
- impact on business/work context.

Evidence for each of these levels may be both quantitative and qualitative, and examples of qualitative questions include:

- What has been your main learning on the programme?
- What has helped you to learn?
- What would you do to improve the programme?
- What support do you need now in order to develop as a coach?

These questions invite participants to describe in their own words not only what they have learned but also how they have learned it, and what will support their ongoing development. However, follow-up evaluation would be needed to investigate whether participants' behaviour at work had changed as a result of the training, and the impact of any changes on their organizations.

Of course the outcomes of training are not always as trainers or partici-pants expect. The unanticipated outcomes of training programmes may be as interesting as those that are planned. In a follow-up evaluation of mentoring training for doctors (Connor *et al.* 2000: 749), respondents reported that while their highest priority prior to attending training was 'developing mentoring skills', after the training they assessed the most important outcome as 'being part of a network of senior doctors'. Frequently, training has impacts beyond those specified in the formal statement of training objectives.

> **Milos, a lawyer,** finds that the skills he learned on a recent coach training programme are impacting on other aspects of his life. He has noticed that the way he communicates with legal clients and colleagues is changing, and he finds himself trying to listen more attentively to their underlying concerns. This, in turn, has a positive effect on their response to him.

Summary

In this chapter we have:

- Used interactive prompts to help you to assess individual and organizational training needs.
- Highlighted some important aspects to consider when selecting and developing a training programme.
- Outlined one training approach to developing coaching and mentoring skills, and listed some tools for trainee self-development.
- Described how you might recognize a positive learning climate and assess ethical and professional aspects of training.
- Referred to one framework for evaluating training outcomes.

9 What are the ethical issues in coaching and mentoring?

- Introduction

- How are ethics relevant?

- What are the responsibilities of the coach or mentor?

- Establishing a practical, ethical working agreement

- The working agreement: confidentiality

- The working agreement: boundaries and role conflict

- The working agreement: time and place

- The working agreement: ways of working and ongoing review

- Support and supervision

- Making ethical decisions

- Ethics and diversity

- Ethics and endings

- Ethics – a final word

- Summary

Introduction

This chapter explores the issues and dilemmas which might arise in coaching and mentoring. It sets out to answer the following questions. As a coach or mentor, what dilemmas might you face? As a client, what practical and professional issues should you clarify? How can coach, mentor and client address ethical, practical and professional questions? It illustrates, with case examples, the ways in which coaches and mentors might work with their clients in managing such issues.

How are ethics relevant?

Ethics can be defined as a set of moral values or principles. 'Moral' relates to the difference between right and wrong and what is considered good or bad behaviour. Questions of ethical practice may be familiar territory to the lawyer in relation to clients or the medical practitioner in relation to patients. However, 'ethical practice' might not seem relevant to the manager asked by their organization to mentor several staff as part of a corporate management development programme, or provide some one-to-one coaching sessions.

Nevertheless, our experience is that consideration of ethical principles forms an important keystone which supports safe and effective coaching and mentoring. If coaching or mentoring were new to you at the start of this book, you might have wondered what differentiated them from everyday conversations, and required such attention to ethics. Reading the preceding chapters may have given some indication, and the example below provides further illustration.

> **Louise, a partner in a consultancy**, is approached by Raoul, a promising young executive in the firm, and asked for some mentoring sessions. After working together for several months, it has become clear that Raoul, while successful at work, is just about coping, and is struggling with a demanding workload and the domestic pressures of a young family. At a partners' meeting it emerges that Raoul is being considered for promotion to a challenging new role, and Louise is unexpectedly asked to comment: 'You know him quite well, what do you think? Fortunately, the phone rings at that moment, and she has a chance to reflect.

> Louise wonders about the right thing to do. Here are some of her thoughts:

> •   What would be best for Raoul? Surely more stress wouldn't help him at the moment?
> •   What have I agreed with Raoul about confidentiality? Can I say anything at all about the pressure he's under? Maybe I should make a general remark without going into specifics?
> •   Perhaps I'm taking too much responsibility here – it's Raoul who has to decide whether he wants the job. But what if he felt he had to accept a promotion and then couldn't cope, wouldn't I be to blame?

How do you think Louise should respond?

It may be useful for Louise to consider the moral perspective. Below are some moral principles that she might refer to.

- Beneficence: what achieves the greatest good?
- Non-maleficence: what avoids or minimizes any harm?
- Autonomy: what gives the best opportunity for each person to implement their own choices?
- Fidelity: what keeps promises made?
- Justice: what is the fairest?

Each principle is worthy in its own right. The difficulty comes, however, in real life, when one principle may conflict with another. This can leave the coach or mentor struggling to decide the best course of action.

> Louise has reflected on the potential conflict between:
> - Keeping promises (what did we agree was confidential?) and avoiding harm (but if I say nothing, he may be pressured to accept a job that he can't cope with)
> - Doing good (maybe a discreet word in the right ear . . .) and autonomy (isn't it really up to Raoul to decide?) and justice (what about other candidates who don't happen to have their mentor in the room?)
>
> Louise is a wise mentor who is aware that she sometimes has a tendency to take too much responsibility for others. She decides that she shouldn't assume responsibility for Raoul, or for how he might react to this offer. Moreover, it would be inappropriate for her to break mentoring confidences. She thinks that it is important to be seen by her colleagues as someone who is clear about mentoring boundaries. So, when the phone interruption finishes, she says, 'I do know Raoul quite well, but he knows himself best, so why don't you sound him out informally about this promotion?'

This example illustrates the special quality of relationship that develops in effective coaching and mentoring. A coaching or mentoring conversation is more than a strictly business conversation. It is often about emotions and personal issues. However, coaching and mentoring are neither counselling nor therapy. Clarity about boundaries, and about how moral principles might apply, will help the coach or mentor and client to stay on track. It will help to create learning relationships that will be productive and robust enough to cope with any difficulties that may arise, and proactive enough to anticipate tricky issues and plan ahead.

There is much discussion about professional regulation and ethical standards within coaching and mentoring. Many of the organizations involved publish their own codes of ethics and conduct, and there is a list of some useful websites in the Appendix. These codes are of general interest, and may be particularly helpful for the full-time coach or mentor setting up their own practice. In addition, purchasers of coaching and mentoring services would be advised to consider the ethical frameworks of prospective providers.

What are the responsibilities of the coach or mentor?

The effective coach or mentor is responsible for considering their ethical perspective, and agreeing with the client how they will work together. It is the responsibility of the coach or mentor to create the climate where ways of working can be discussed. It is their responsibility to monitor their own standards of practice and reflect on how they are working with clients. It is also their responsibility to be aware of other sources of help which they or their client might call upon if needed.

Being clear about ethical principles when working as a coach or mentor is important for several reasons. Firstly, clarity guides the coach or mentor to work safely, without doing any harm (either intentional or otherwise) to the client.

> **Marco, an experienced coach:** I have a responsibility to be clear about the commitments I make, and to honour them. For example, confidentiality is very important. If I promise confidentiality and then let slip something that a client has told me, they will feel confused and let down and possibly even betrayed. When I am clear about what issues I might not be able to keep confidential, then the client understands this from the start and can take informed responsibility for what they tell me. Clarity applies to other areas too. I cannot normally undertake telephone coaching, and I say this early on, so that a client will not ring me up 'on the off chance', and feel hurt or rejected if I cannot speak to them. I've learned to be clear about what I can realistically offer, and not to make promises which I can't keep.

Secondly, when the coach or mentor is clear about their principles and preferred ways of working, they express themselves clearly to the client, and in so doing they encourage the client to do likewise.

Marco: Occasionally a coaching relationship hits a bumpy patch – it's not unusual and it can be a real learning opportunity for me and the client. I used to worry about this, but nowadays I'm upfront with clients and say that if either of us is having difficulties with the way things are going, we'll talk to each other first, before we talk to anyone else. I think it's been really helpful to say this, because it's made it OK, and given both of us permission to raise issues and learn from them.

Thirdly, clarity encourages the coach or mentor to work effectively, in the best way, to help clients achieve results. Time with clients is precious and needs to be used well.

Marco: If I talk about autonomy, but stray into giving my advice and opinion, then I limit the opportunities for my client to grow. I encourage dependency, which, by the way, normally backfires when plans go awry and the client says resentfully, 'But I just did as you suggested!' If I can supportively challenge the client to generate their own ideas, then I am helping them to develop their resources and abilities.

Fourthly, it encourages the coach or mentor to be aware of and sensitive to issues of difference and diversity, and how these may impact on the relationship with the client, as well as the fair provision of services. An effective coach or mentor monitors their own potential blindspots.

Marco: I worked with a client whose cultural perspective was very different from mine. This was challenging, for us both, and made me think hard about some of the ideas and beliefs that I had assumed were 'givens'.

Finally, clarity about ethical principles serves as a reference point to inform any decisions a coach or mentor might make and actions they might take.

Marco: There have been some situations which were difficult. I've found it useful to reflect on the principles, sometimes in co-supervision, and it's helped me to steer a path and create some clarity for myself.

However, a coaching or mentoring relationship is usually approached with a mixture of hope, anticipation, concerns and questions, not a list of moral or ethical principles! Important as the principles are, they are not the most natural start point for clients, coaches or mentors. Principles may seem to be rather tricky issues, best left unspoken, and yet paradoxically conversation about them is often an excellent start point for clarifying the working relationship.

Establishing a practical, ethical working agreement

The client's issue

A natural place to start a coaching or mentoring conversation is to ask the client about what is on their mind, and what they want to talk about. The coach or mentor asks this for several reasons. It encourages the client to clarify for themselves the issue and to begin to explore it. It communicates the coach or mentor's respect for the client and their agenda, and puts the client 'centre stage'. It checks that the issue is appropriate. The context of coaching and mentoring is work. Warning bells might ring if a client wants, for example, to unpack long-standing relationship difficulties, albeit that these are affecting their work. Coaches and mentors are not relationship counsellors and to accept this kind of assignment may risk the coach or mentor and the client getting out of their depth.

The working relationship

In addition to asking what issues are on the client's mind, the initial conversation should always include a discussion of how the coach or mentor and client are going to work together. Talking about 'how' gives the coach or mentor a chance to clarify any ethical and professional issues, to understand more about the client's concerns and perspective, and to agree jointly a way of working. The 'what' conversation is, for most people, the more natural one. The 'how' conversation may be less natural and even a little strange or uncomfortable at first. However, one way in which mentors and coaches are helpful is to make the undiscussable a little more discussable. Talking about 'how' helps to answer questions and resolve uncertainties in both parties. It frees up emotional and intellectual energy to focus on the learning journey, rather than being distracted by unanswered questions or concerns.

Getting started: coach, mentor and client questions

We have asked participants on training courses to describe from their own experience the questions and concerns that they might have, and that clients might have. In a real-life coaching or mentoring situation, some of these questions would be freely shared and others might remain unspoken. Box 9.1 lists some typical questions that clients might have, and Box 9.2 lists questions that a coach or mentor might have.

Box 9.1 Getting started: some client questions

- What if coaching or mentoring doesn't seem to be useful for me?
- How confidential is confidential?
- Will the coach or mentor tell other people that we're working together?
- Should I tell other people?
- Will the coach or mentor judge me?
- How competent are they? Have they had any training?
- Will they take notes?
- Will there be conflicts of interest with the coach or mentor?
- Do I really want to do this? What will be involved?
- Is it some kind of therapy?
- What if I don't want to discuss something?

Box 9.2 Getting started: some coach and mentor questions

- What if I don't seem to be able to help the person?
- What if they don't turn up for a session/stop coming?
- What if they tell me something I can't keep confidential?
- Realistically, what can I offer?
- What happens if it gets emotional and there's distress or aggression?
- What if the values of the other person, or their actions, conflict with mine?
- What is my duty of care to this person?
- Do I need professional indemnity?
- How will I manage the ending?
- What if the person needs therapy rather than coaching or mentoring?
- What if there is a conflict of interests, or I need to whistle-blow?
- What if the person talks about someone I know well?
- Can I be a coach/mentor and manager at the same time?

Hidden concerns or questions which stay hidden may interfere with the coaching or mentoring process. The following example illustrates how one coach addressed an unspoken question and established one aspect of a working agreement.

> **Brian** has agreed, with some encouragement from his boss, to some coaching sessions with an external coach, but he has doubts about the process and whether working with the coach will have any real benefits. At their first meeting, Brian is surprised and relieved when the coach says, 'I imagine you may be wondering whether coaching is right for you. I suggest that we take stock after three sessions to see how we're doing, and decide at that point whether we want to continue. How does that sound to you?' Brian responds positively, and they then start to talk about what would constitute benefits of coaching, how they would assess 'how we're doing', and what 'progress' would look like from Brian's perspective.

Here the coach has taken the initiative, perhaps picking up some cues from Brian. In discussing 'how', the coach has helped to bring a hidden question to the surface and make it discussable. He has also demonstrated openness and shared accountability for the coaching process.

In the next example, the original agreement seems unclear, and has led to difficulties.

> **Adeola** has agreed to offer mentoring to a newly-promoted colleague, Tim, and at their initial session they establish that they will meet for an hour every fortnight. Tim frequently arrives rushed and late, with the result that sessions start late and overrun the hour. Adeola has begun to feel irritated and resentful and is concerned that mentoring is taking time from her other work commitments. She finds herself being rather short with Tim and looking meaningfully at her watch! In a review session she shares her concerns with Tim. He is finding the mentoring very useful and has been unaware of the knock-on effect of late finishes. Adeola explains that while she is happy to set aside an hour a fortnight, she cannot overrun the finish time. They agree that, in future, regardless of when Tim arrives, they will finish on time. This establishes the principle of autonomy on both sides. Tim is responsible for arriving on time or, if not, having a shorter session. Adeola is responsible for keeping the agreed timeslot free, but not for providing an hour's mentoring regardless of start time. Both are relieved to clarify their arrangement.

A clear working agreement

There are, as these examples illustrate, several advantages to a clear working agreement. In particular:

- it establishes a joint basis for ongoing review

- it demonstrates the coach or mentor's willingness to share responsibility
- it clarifies what each party can expect from the other
- it creates the opportunity to discuss questions that might otherwise remain hidden
- it establishes a precedent and a ground rule of openness and collaboration in the relationship
- it pre-empts confusion and unnecessary ambiguity

While it may be useful to have the working agreement written down (and professional coaches and mentors would normally include this as part of a formal contract), a written document is no substitute for a conversation. A robust working agreement will usually address the following issues:

- confidentiality
- boundaries and role conflict
- place, time and timescales
- ways of working
- ongoing review
- expectations and limitations

The working agreement is explored in Chapters 2 and 3, together with some practical exercises.

The working agreement: confidentiality

Limitations

Confidentiality is perhaps an obvious issue. Both client and coach or mentor need to be clear about what confidentiality is being offered and being sought. They should be aware of obligations and constraints imposed upon them by the law of the land or by their profession or organization. Members of professional organizations may be required to adhere to codes of ethics and standards. Most sizeable organizations have policies and procedures which may impact on coaching and mentoring.

It is unwise and unrealistic in coaching and mentoring to offer or accept an assurance of total confidentiality. Rather, the coach or mentor should consider carefully what limits of confidentiality they can offer and sustain. The client should consider what confidentiality they want and be prepared to explore this with their coach or mentor. In addition, both parties should consider how they would work in a situation where the limits were tested.

In what circumstances, and how, might confidentiality agreements need to be reviewed?

> **Mari works within the HR function** of a large consultancy firm and offers confidential coaching for senior managers and partners, with the understanding that there is no feedback to the organization. In the course of a coaching session, it emerges that her client is struggling with an alcohol problem and work is suffering. The client asks Mari to keep this information 'strictly confidential'. Mari believes that her first duty of care is to the client, but she is also concerned about the client's staff and colleagues, and the firm's reputation. Mari and the client together clarify the corporate policy on alcohol misuse, which is not, as the client had imagined, punitive. Mari and the client explore the possibility of involving the local HR manager to help the client to get treatment. Reassured, the client contacts the HR manager.

Organization feedback

Where coaching or mentoring are sponsored by an organization, or are part of a change process or development initiative, the organization may ask for feedback. What information will be given, to whom, and in what format, needs to be agreed at the outset. Here is an example of how one coach responded to such a request.

> **Simon was asked to provide coaching for several senior executives** in a large financial institution. This was intended to support a leadership development and culture change programme which the chief executive had initiated. Simon saw each executive for eight sessions over the course of a year. The chief executive was interested in any themes emerging which might impact on the overall development programme. She understood the need to respect individual confidentiality. Simon agreed that at the end of the year he would feed-back to the chief executive his perception of any broad general themes emerging from coaching sessions, but in a way that protected individual confidentiality.

Public or private?

Another aspect of confidentiality concerns how public or private the coaching or mentoring relationship is within the organization. Confidentiality is often easier for external coaches or mentors to manage, since they will usually hold meetings on their own premises away from the client's offices. It is important that the coach or mentor and client share the same understanding of who knows about the relationship. This will be different in differing contexts. For example, MBA students will frequently be provided with a coach or mentor as a part of their study arrangements, and this is common knowledge in the university context. In contrast, in a different organization, a mentoring scheme was aimed at those in difficulty at work. A person experiencing difficulty could request a mentor, and the relationship was kept confidential unless the person wished to disclose it.

Confidentiality applies to smaller as well as more substantial issues, as this example illustrates.

> **A mentor happened to meet a client in a workplace setting** a few days after a mentoring session where work difficulties had been discussed. In a misguided attempt to show that he had been fully attentive in the previous session, the mentor asked the client about the difficulties. The client looked embarrassed, and the mentor learned the lesson that he could not assume that it was appropriate to discuss mentoring issues anywhere other than within mentoring sessions.

Note-taking

Confidentiality also applies to any notes made during coaching or mentoring sessions. It is advisable that the coach or mentor and the client agree who will make notes, if any, and who will keep them between sessions. If the coach or mentor is keeping the notes, it is best practice to store them securely. The two parties should also agree what will happen to the notes at the end of the coaching or mentoring relationship.

Supervision

In supervision, the identity of the client is not normally disclosed, and the focus is on the coach or mentor, not the client. When clients understand this, they can be reassured that their coach or mentor is paying attention to professional development and maintaining standards.

Box 9.3 lists questions about confidentiality that a coach or mentor, and client, may wish to consider.

Box 9.3 Confidentiality checklist for coaching and mentoring

- Are there any legal, professional or organizational constraints or obligations which affect confidentiality?
- What will be confidential? What will not be?
- Under what circumstances might this need to be reviewed?
- How would we do this?
- Is the relationship confidential?
- What about any notes? Who takes them? What for? Where are they kept? Disposed of?
- What feedback, if any, is there to the organization? By whom? For what purpose?
- Does the coach or mentor have supervision? How is client anonymity preserved?

The working agreement: boundaries and role conflict

There can be potential or actual conflicts between the role of coach or mentor and other relationships they have with the client. Even if confidentiality boundaries have been agreed, the coach or mentor cannot 'unknow' something that has been shared in a coaching or mentoring conversation. For example:

- A mentor is asked to give a reference for a client, and knows that, while apparently performing well at work, the client is struggling to manage.
- A client attends an internal selection panel and finds that their coach is on the panel.
- Mentor and client find themselves both attending the same work meeting. A previous mentoring conversation has focused on the client's difficulties with a colleague who is at the same meeting.
- Coach and client meet unexpectedly in a social setting.

 If you were the coach or mentor in the above situations, what would you do? If you were the client, what would you want?

While it is obviously impossible to anticipate every contingency, it is worth considering possible conflict or boundary issues and agreeing in advance how these might be handled. Below are two case examples, the first where this was done and the second where it wasn't.

> **Jaime is mentor to Alice.** While he is not her line manager, he does have indirect management responsibility for some of her work. He is likely to be asked to comment on her work for her annual performance appraisal. They agree, together with Alice's boss, that Jaime will limit any comments he makes to Alice's work performance and results achieved.

> **Chris is a coach** and his client Mike has talked quite a bit in coaching sessions about his family, in relation to career and personal development issues. Chris and Mike live in the same city. They meet unexpectedly in a cafe, both with their families. Both are uncomfortable, and Chris makes polite conversation and leaves as early as he can. He reflects afterwards that he had not anticipated such an eventuality, or discussed it with Mike. In future, Chris decides, he will discuss with each new client 'what if we meet socially?'

The working agreement: time and place

Time

It is important to agree where and how often meetings will take place, both the number and frequency of meetings, and overall timescale. This might be a formal contract: 'We will meet for two hours every six weeks, initially for five meetings. At our fifth meeting we will review the work we have done, and decide whether more sessions would be useful.' It may be more informal: 'Feel free to drop in whenever you want', although experience suggests that this can be an unsatisfactory arrangement on both sides. Here is an example of a very informal arrangement which did not work well.

> **Sheena has offered to mentor two new employees,** and has suggested that they can 'feel free to drop in for a chat any time'. One employee frequently pops into her office, rarely takes up more than ten minutes of her time and finds the sessions valuable. He uses Sheena as a sounding-board to think through work decisions. Sheena is pleased to offer her support, but notices that his visits are becoming more frequent and wonders whether he may rely on her too much.

> The other employee has never been to see Sheena. In fact, he is struggling in his new job and is he is concerned about appearing to

be unable to cope. He notices that Sheena hasn't called him to ask how work is going, and assumes she is busy. Sheena meanwhile is puzzled. She had tried to be encouraging to both individuals, but one has yet to contact her. She doesn't want to put pressure on him to see her, so she is reluctant to contact him.

The moral principles described earlier in the chapter include: doing most good, avoiding harm, fairness, faithfulness to promises, and autonomy. Thinking back over these principles, it is clear that there are some dilemmas in this situation for the mentor.

 Imagine you are Sheena. What dilemmas do you see?

Here are some that you might have noticed:

- Should Sheena leave each employee to make their own choices about if/how often they see her? What is equally fair to both employees? Should she contact the employee who hasn't been to see her?
- Should she have a discussion with the employee whom she sees frequently? Should she share her concerns that he may be becoming over-reliant? How can she do this in a way that is not too challenging?
- What does each person understand has been agreed by 'feel free to drop in for a chat any time'? How clear is this agreement?
- Is there any agreement about confidentiality?

 Imagine that you are each of the employees. What would you want Sheena to do? Anything you'd prefer her not do?

Finally, if you were Sheena, what would you do? What actions are possible? Which are preferable? Are there any other dilemmas you can see?

Place

The meeting-place is important. The least satisfactory venue is the client's office, where interruptions are inevitable and job demands intrude. Many external coaches and mentors have their own premises where privacy and quiet are guaranteed. Some internal coaches and mentors use their own offices, but this may emphasize any hierarchy/power difference between coach or mentor and client. Here too, everyday work pressures can interrupt. A quiet meeting room can be a satisfactory alternative.

In addition to agreeing where and for how long meetings will take place, it is useful to clarify whether there will be contact between meetings, either by phone or e-mail. E-coaching and e-mentoring are becoming increasingly popular and may form part of the relationship. In agreeing time and place, it is important that both parties honour commitments and do not cancel meetings or phone calls except in extreme circumstances. It is useful, however, to agree in advance how they will handle a situation where this becomes unavoidable. Box 9.4 lists some helpful questions for both parties.

Box 9.4 Time and place checklist

- Where will we meet?
- For how long?
- How many sessions will we have?
- What happens if one of us cannot make the meeting?
- What happens if the client doesn't turn up? Is late?
- Is contact between sessions part of the way we will work?
- If not, what if an urgent matter arises between sessions?

The working agreement: ways of working and ongoing review

Setting the scene

Clients want to know, and coaches and mentors need to be clear about, what coaching and mentoring will involve. The skilled coach or mentor will be able simply and briefly to explain how they work, what they expect and offer, and any models or frameworks they might use. Box 9.5 contains an extract from a mentor's description of mentoring during an introductory session with a client.

Professional background

The coach or mentor should be open about their own experience and training. This does not necessarily mean presenting a list of academic achievements, but it does mean being prepared to offer a brief description of your background, experience and qualifications and responding to client questions about these.

Box 9.5 Extract from an introduction to mentoring

Let me tell you how I usually work, and then we can decide together what would suit us. These sessions are an opportunity to explore the career issues you've outlined, and to develop goals and plans in relation to these. Rather than give advice, I will try to help you to reflect on problems or opportunities, and clarify your goals and what you can do to achieve them. Mentoring works best if you come to each session with your ideas of what you want to discuss, and we'll start each session by agreeing how we use the time. Towards the end of the session, I'll ask about any action or plans, because doing things between meetings is important. It's helpful if you make notes of these plans, and bring them to the following meeting. It's also helpful to review the way we've worked together and anything we want to change for the next time. How does that sound to you?

Action

It is important to encourage clients to identify action that they will take between sessions, otherwise the risk is that the sessions become a talking shop and nothing changes in the client's life. If talking becomes a substitute for action, rather than stimulating and supporting it, then the coach or mentor is not being fully effective. Of course, action takes many forms. For example, for some clients, taking time for reflection may be a useful action.

The questions in Box 9.6 can help to identify themes emerging from coaching or mentoring sessions, and possible actions. Some clients find that

---

Box 9.6 Questions for action

- What has happened since the last time we met?
- What have you done? What impact have your actions had? What helped or hindered your actions?
- How do you feel about what you have achieved?
- What has emerged for you from this session (e.g. questions, themes, issues, insights, ideas, answers)?
- What has been most important for you in what we've discussed?
- What do you intend to do between now and next time we meet?
- Who/what might help/hinder this? Anything you can do to increase the probability of success? Who/what could help you?
- How will you know if you've been successful?

taking notes in their own words of the key themes, goals, action plans or learning points is a powerful aid to action.

Way of working

Regular review of coaching and mentoring work is a cornerstone of safe and effective coaching and mentoring. We cannot emphasize enough the power of joint review with the client. This may involve a conversation about the working session, or other arrangements, for example frequency of meetings or satisfactoriness of venue. Box 9.7 lists some questions which might encourage a constructive and open review, so that responsibility is shared and any difficulties can be raised in a problem-solving rather than blaming fashion.

In the following example a mentor and client review, after three sessions, how they are working together.

> *Mentor:* It seems as though the sessions have helped you to get focused. I notice you are always ready to challenge yourself and open to thinking afresh, and that seems to help you clarify what's important to you. A few times I've interrupted you and wondered if that was unhelpful. I'd appreciate some feedback on that.
>
> *Client:* It has been useful having this time to focus on me, and really think about where I'm going in my career. You haven't judged me or given advice, but you have helped me to question myself and some of my ideas. I didn't always want to bother to write things down at the end of sessions, but I can see that it's been powerful in keeping me focused. Perhaps I should take time to prepare before sessions as well. I like the way that you sometimes give me space and sometimes interrupt me. At first the space was a bit scary and I realize now that it is challenging – it makes me think. Your interruptions are helpful in keeping me on track. I'd like more of them if you think that I'm starting to ramble!

Box 9.7 Questions for review of a session

- What's been helpful (e.g. things I've done/you've done, use of time, structure of the session, pace, venue)?
- Anything that's been less/unhelpful?
- Anything you'd like me to do differently next time?
- Anything you'd like to do differently next time?
- Any other reflections?

These comments illustrate how the review process creates the basis for dialogue, as perceptions and perspectives are shared. Notice that the mentor is concerned that they might be interrupting too much and the client is asking for more!

Referral

A skilled coach or mentor considers with the client the scope and nature of the work they will do, and the possibility that at some point referral elsewhere may be appropriate. As a coach or mentor it is important to be aware of other referral resources, which might include occupational health, counselling, special careers advice, training or development programmes. In our experience, clarifying areas which are not your expertise, should they arise, enhances, not diminishes, your credibility as a coach or mentor.

> **Clare is coaching an able young chemist**, Hugh, who has just been appointed to lead a large project, with high corporate visibility. Hugh comes to the coaching session asking for help with thinking through the business strategy relating to this project. Strategy is not Clare's forte, and she says so. However, she is able to help Hugh create a list of potentially useful resources. On the list are names of several people in the organization, and he selects two who are particularly experienced in strategy, and agrees to contact them before the next coaching session. The list also identifies other resources, including online educational material, which might help him.

Support and supervision

To work safely and effectively the coach or mentor must ensure they have adequate personal and professional support. Supervision is one way of obtaining this support and many professional organizations offer guidelines on supervision. Chapter 2 contains additional information.

Managing yourself

This involves monitoring your own well-being and ensuring that you have adequate emotional, physical and personal resources to work effectively. Coaches and mentors do not do their best work, and indeed may risk doing harm, when they are stressed, suffering from fatigue, or overwhelmed by personal or work crises. Anyone who does a reasonable amount of coaching or mentoring work will at some time find themselves needing to take a break and gather and replenish their personal resources. Sometimes the break may be enough, at other times additional support or supervision may be required. Box 9.8 provides a checklist of questions for assessing your well-being as a coach or mentor.

Box 9.8 A checklist for assessing well-being

- Am I too tired to concentrate during the session?
- Am I hoping the client will cancel the session?
- Are my own concerns intruding on the sessions?
- Am I finding it difficult to give my full attention during a session?
- Am I worrying continuously before/after a session?
- Have I cancelled a session for non-urgent reasons?
- Am I avoiding supervision or support?
- Have I got a healthy work-life balance?

Managing your practice

This means paying attention on an ongoing basis to how you are working as a coach or mentor. Regular review of the working agreement with the client is important. Supervision or other support is equally important. Those who work as coaches or mentors can use supervision or support to reflect on how they are working, on any problems or difficulties and on any ethical or professional dilemmas. The focus of supervision or support is the coach or mentor, not the client. If you work as a full-time coach or mentor, your supervision arrangements should involve regular planned meetings. If you offer occasional coaching or mentoring, it may be sufficient to be part of a network you can call on from time to time. However, all coaches and mentors should know one person who can provide support or supervision at short notice, and have agreed with that person that help might be requested if urgently needed.

Making ethical decisions

In ideal circumstances, the coach or mentor has time and space to consider without undue pressure the best ethical decision to make. They have time to involve the client and to consult with a supervisor or support resources. The client has time to reflect on what they want and need, and what they expect from their coach or mentor.

Bond (1993) describes a framework used in ethical decision-making. Adapting and reworking this framework, the coach or mentor might ask the following questions:

- How do moral principles inform this decision? What does most good, least harm, is faithful to any promises made, gives maximum autonomy and is fair?
- How does the law impact on this situation? What must I do? What am I entitled to do? What am I prohibited from doing? What are the laws of the land, or rules of my professional body or organization, and how might these define or limit my actions?
- What resources do I have at this point which might limit or enable me? How much time and energy do I have? How much capacity, mental or physical? Am I working within my competence, or at the edge? How much support am I receiving from supervisory or other sources? Am I overlooking potential resources or overestimating any?
- My personal view of the situation. What do I want to do? What is my 'gut feel?'

Figure 9.1 shows that each of these aspects interlock and all may contribute to making a sound ethical decision.

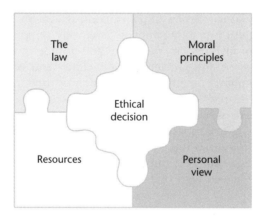

Figure 9.1   Ethical decision-making in coaching and mentoring

Sometimes the coach or mentor is faced with a decision which requires a rapid response. The following guidelines may help when making decisions under pressure.

- Don't panic. If you have just been told something difficult or troubling, that thing already exists, and the telling of it has not caused it to happen. If you have been told of something that might happen, it hasn't happened yet.

- Keep listening. It is all too easy, when anxious or concerned, to stop listening to the client and hear only our own inner voices 'Oh heavens, what shall I do, what if?' Try to keep listening!
- Take time. In almost all cases, you do not have to respond instantly. Check what you have heard.
- Listening is not necessarily agreeing or colluding. It is accepting the story of the other person and trying to understand it.
- Keep the focus on the client and give them space to arrive at their own answer.
- You have valuable perspectives to share but not to impose.
- Sometimes no action is better than the wrong action. If you decide to act, review your decision, even if only for a few minutes. If unsure, it may be best to reflect rather than act hastily.
- Create 'time out' if necessary. Having a break can give both you and the client the time to gather thoughts and consider resources.
- Get help. If you can, take the issue to supervision or support.

 Which of these tactics might be easy for you? Which might you find harder to do? Are there any examples from your own experience where you have used these approaches? What was the result?

Will and his mentor have been working together for several months, helping Will make the transition into a senior management role at work, which seems to be going well. The mentor is surprised when Will starts a regular session by blurting out that family problems have been getting him down and this morning he felt like 'giving up'. Will is clearly upset, and says that everything seems hopeless. The mentor is concerned, and in addition he knows that Will is facing a long drive that day followed by an important meeting.

 Imagine you are the mentor. How might you be feeling? What might you be thinking? Which moral principles and ethical considerations might be relevant here? What courses of action might you consider?

Imagine you are Will. What might you be thinking? Feeling? What might you want your mentor to do? Not do? What might help you?

The mentor allows Will to talk about his feelings and the family upset. Will has space to 'let off steam' and becomes visibly calmer as the session progresses. The mentor wonders whether Will is temporarily upset or if there is something more than that, and so asks Will if he thinks he needs help from anyone else, for example a doctor. The mentor does not get drawn too deeply into the family matters but helps Will to work through some strategies for coping with them. Finally, the mentor checks with Will how today's events may affect him at the meeting. Towards the end of the session, he checks with Will whether he is safe to drive and they discuss how Will could make contact with the mentor before the next session if necessary.

Ethics and diversity

The effective coach or mentor is sensitive to issues of difference and diversity, for example race, religion, status, gender, age or disability. These issues are important and may impact not only on an individual coaching or mentoring relationship but also on fair provision of coaching or mentoring services, on supervision (Hawkins and Shohet 2000) and on the use of coaching and mentoring as tools for promoting equal opportunity (Clutterbuck and Ragins 2002).

For example, if the coach or mentor is acting fairly and justly, they will want all clients to be able to access the benefits of coaching and mentoring. They will consider whether the approaches and frameworks used are equally applicable to all clients, whatever their background, ability, ethnicity or cultural expectations. Such awareness can lead to expanding and diversifying the ways in which coaching and mentoring are offered, for example using e-coaching to reach more clients.

In addition, the ethical coach or mentor will respect the individuality and autonomy of clients. They will constantly seek to increase their awareness with regard to their practice. Ongoing supervision, training and support are all important in helping them to monitor and review their own ethical practice.

Clutterbuck and Megginson (2005: 42) identify coaching and mentoring as positive opportunities for developing diverse talent: 'Developmental dyads between people of different race and gender, or between able and disabled people, help to identify hidden causes of discrimination. They also provide a safe environment where people can discuss and develop tactics for dealing with cultural barriers to advancement'.

Ethics and endings

Who decides?

There are many reasons why coaching and mentoring relationships come to an end. Sometimes it is a planned ending, bringing to a close a productive working relationship. At other times, it may be more abrupt. An unforeseen event means that the relationship has to be cut short. Reasons may range from family emergencies to sudden job transfers. Sometimes the relationship is not working and the client needs to move on. Sometimes changes in job roles produce a conflict of interest. Sometimes a referral to another helper has been arranged. The circumstances will obviously impact on the nature of the ending.

Most endings involve a mixture of loss and gain on both sides. The skilful coach or mentor involves the client in managing the ending. This is particularly important if the coach or mentor has the greater initiative in the ending. This minimizes the risk of the client feeling rejected. Of course, it may be that the coach or mentor experiences some feelings of rejection, especially if it is the client who has decided to move on. However, endings can be celebrations and a time to acknowledge the relationship, work well done and goals achieved, as in this example.

> **The client of a coach** suggested going out for lunch at the end of their last session, as a way of marking the transition from coach–client to work colleagues.

 Think of the ending of a coaching or mentoring relationship that you were part of. Was it planned or sudden? What thoughts and feelings did you have at the time? What helped you to manage the ending? Did anything make it more difficult for you?

Endings from the beginning

Ideally, plans for endings will have been agreed at the beginning of the coaching or mentoring relationship, and be included in the working agreement. When this happens, and ongoing review is built into the relationship, the path for a good ending is smoothed. Allowing space for ongoing review will ensure that if these plans change, it will be mutually agreed and there will be no surprises. If the coach or mentor has worked in a way that encourages the client to be proactive, then the client will be resourceful in planning their future and, if appropriate, identifying alternative resources, coaches or mentors.

The final session

The final session is an opportunity to affirm what has been achieved and celebrate the working relationship. Wherever possible, there will be time put aside for this review. It will include a conversation about what next for the client, so that they are adequately supported. It will also include clarification of 'what if we meet in the street/office/at a social event?'

Ethics – a final word

One of us, a bit of a worrier, has a cartoon pinned on the kitchen notice-board depicting an anxious person anticipating the possible disasters which might occur during the day, and deciding therefore to stay huddled in bed. The final caption shows the worrisome thought entering their head : 'But . . . even so . . . there is always . . . death by mattress!' The topic of ethics can seem a bit like death by mattress! The array of ethical, moral and professional considerations to bear in mind, the potential moral and legal dilemmas which might arise – these could lead us to conclude that we might be better off staying in bed and not taking any risks! We are only too aware of this reaction, especially among trainee coaches and mentors, who may feel quite overwhelmed by 'what if . . .?'

In reality, many of the ethical decisions we face are not overwhelming: they are commonplace and, for a trained and reflective coach or mentor, they are manageable. Only occasionally are we faced with very difficult and complex decisions. Nevertheless, ethical practice pervades all aspects of coaching and mentoring. The more thoughtfully we consider in advance our own boundaries, the more we help the client to consider and manage theirs. When we work in this way, we are more likely to prevent ethical dilemmas occurring, or handle them wisely if they do.

Summary

In this chapter we have:

- Listed some ways in which consideration of their own ethical perspective can help the coach or mentor to work effectively.

- Described the importance of a clear working agreement in ethical practice.
- Offered checklists to help you to develop a working agreement and use it for ongoing review in the coaching or mentoring relationship.
- Referred to a framework for ethical decision-making and suggested some pointers for decision-making under pressure.
- Discussed the links between ethical practice and diversity issues, ethical practice and effective endings, and ethical practice and coach or mentor support.

10 How can a coaching and mentoring culture be developed?

- Introduction
- Developing the culture: why bother?
- What is a coaching or mentoring culture?
- How do you develop a mentoring culture?
- How do you develop a coaching culture?
- What helps or hinders?
- What are the links with other aspects of learning and performance?
- What difference does it make?
- How do you assess your organization?
- Summary

Introduction

In this final chapter we share with you the voices of people involved in coaching and mentoring initiatives in organizations. We hear from them the possibilities and problems; the costs and benefits; the highs and lows; the resistances and the rewards. Between them, their experience encompasses both coaching and mentoring, delivered both internally and externally. They are:

Wendy Briner   Leadership Coach and Researcher, Ashridge Management College

Malcolm Hurrell   Vice-President HR, AstraZeneca UK

Shaun Lincoln   Programme Director for Coaching and Mentoring, Centre for Excellence in Leadership

Nancy Redfern   Specialty Dean Director, Northern Postgraduate Medical and Dental Deanery, and Consultant Anaesthetist, Newcastle upon Tyne Foundation Trust

Wendy Briner works as a coach and researcher on the Ashridge Leadership Process. She describes the results of research into how different organizational cultures respond to leaders who have coaching as part of their leadership development. Malcolm Hurrell tells how AstraZeneca has developed both coaching and mentoring as complementary learning and development methodologies within an organization which constantly seeks to achieve both individual and organizational learning. Shaun Lincoln shares his experience from the learning and skills sector, providing evidence that a programme called Leaders as Coaches is influencing culture change. Dr Nancy Redfern shares a journey of culture change in a large city hospital where consultants trained as mentors. They supported one another and gradually influenced key stakeholders to recognize the need for mentoring and to give resources for a hospital-wide mentoring scheme for doctors.

Developing the culture: why bother?

Coaching and mentoring are increasingly being recognized as powerful learning and development tools. Carole Gaskell, who worked with a building society which decided to use a positive coaching approach alongside internal performance review, reports that:

> Coaching can have a dramatic impact on an organisation's culture, people and bottom-line. When woven into the fabric of a business, the benefits of coaching are there for all to see. It can accelerate the development of talent, improve staff retention and create a high-performance culture that offers a company a real competitive advantage.
>
> (Eglin 2006: 6)

The climate is changing. It is only a few years since our research into the effects of mentoring training on 71 senior doctors who had attended mentoring training programmes. We also surveyed stakeholders in the 49 National Health Service (NHS) organizations where they worked (Connor *et al.* 2000: 747–53). The objectives of the training were to: develop mentoring skills; to provide a forum for personal and professional development for senior doctors; and to develop a mentoring network for junior and senior doctors. We found that the training was highly valued and that the skills learned were transferred to everyday work situations. However, two problems emerged. Firstly, the most difficult task for the doctors was trying to deliver mentoring in a culture where junior doctors did not readily seek help. Secondly, the stakeholders surveyed, including medical directors and HR directors, agreed that time would be needed for doctors to mentor their juniors but they were not hopeful that resources would be made available for this.

The 2006 CIPD learning and development survey notes a new trend. While the level of coaching usage in organizations remains similar to 2004, the trend towards the development of a coaching culture is now apparent: '80% of respondents using coaching claim that their organisation aspires to develop a coaching culture, and 75% report investing time, resources and effort into achieving this aim'. Ninety-three per cent of those using coaching 'believe that a coaching culture is either "very important" or "important" to the success of their organisation', with individual and business performance cited as the main objectives for developing such a culture (CIPD 2006: 10).

Two factors which seem to support the development of coaching and mentoring in organizations are:

1   A culture of openness, learning and development within the organization.
2   A culture which acknowledges that resources are needed for coaching and mentoring, not just externally, but also internally. These include time, training, development and rewards.

Shaun Lincoln is realistic about what organizations want. He says:

Organizations come to us typically asking for help to:

• Develop a coaching leadership style in their managers
• Develop an internal coaching capability of formal internal coaches, who will coach colleagues they do not line manage

They often have a clear idea of what this will look like. However, they will also often then talk about the desire to develop a 'coaching culture' that underpins this. When asked to describe this and how they will know when they have achieved it, there is much less consensus and, if useful, we will spend time to work on what this would look like. What emerges is that our clients are not interested in developing a coaching culture for its own sake, but are looking for a way to change existing behaviour and attitudes between managers and staff at all levels in a way that impacts bottom-line performance. Organizations often find that introducing strong leadership, compliance processes and 'fear of failure' can improve performance in the short term, but they need to look to something else to take performance to the next level and on a more sustainable basis. This is what often drives their interest in coaching and coaching culture.

Some organizations encourage coaching and mentoring as part of learning and development for all; some embed this type of learning in the everyday processes and activities of the organization; some view coaching and mentoring as something for those with remedial problems; others see coaching and mentoring as a perk for high-flyers. Increasingly, organizations are moving towards developing internal coaches and mentors with selective use of external resources.

What is a coaching or mentoring culture?

Clutterbuck and Megginson (2005: 19) define a coaching culture as one where 'coaching is the predominant style of managing and working together, and where a commitment to grow the organisation is embedded in a parallel commitment to grow the people in the organisation'. We would include mentoring in that definition. They view coaching and mentoring as complementary learning and development opportunities. They refer to Alison Hardingham's (Hardingham *et al.* 2004: 187–8) characteristics of a coaching culture in which there is an emphasis on teams, not just on individuals. She highlights: cross-company teams; rotating leadership of teams according to specific purpose; and an atmosphere of openness, trust and respect. She also highlights frequent goal-setting in all aspects of the life of the organization. Clutterbuck and Megginson list six areas which they identify with a coaching culture. These are listed in Table 10.1.

Table 10.1 Characteristics of coaching and mentoring cultures

Coaching culture (Clutterbuck and Megginson 2005: 28)	Mentoring culture (Megginson et al. 2006: 7)
1 Coaching linked to business drivers	1 Clear link to a business issue, where outcome is measured
2 Being a client is supported and encouraged	2 Part of a culture change process
3 Provide coach training	3 Senior management involved as clients and mentors
4 Reward and recognize coaching	4 Link to long-term talent management established
5 Systemic perspective	5 Clients in the driving seat
6 The move to coaching is managed	6 Light-touch development of individuals and scheme
	7 Clear framework, publicized, with stories
	8 Scheme design-focused on business issues and change agenda

Megginson *et al.* (2006:4) define mentoring as 'off-line help by one person to another in making significant transitions in knowledge, work or thinking'. They distinguish between sponsorship mentoring and developmental mentoring. In the former, the mentor champions the mentee, is more influential and more senior. In the latter, the mentor is more experienced but the exchange emphasizes learning. In organizations there is room for both. The mentoring culture would: value people; value learning from others; value learning by discovery rather than telling; respect personal as well as organizational development; encourage talent; and actively promote career planning.

Megginson *et al.* report findings from three organizations with a mentoring approach: Janssen Pharmaceuticals (J&J Europe), Walsall Council and the Scottish Executive. These organizations had eight characteristics in common which are shown in Table 10.1. The table presents information from two different sources: six common coaching characteristics (Clutterbuck and Megginson) and eight common mentoring characteristics (Megginson *et al.*).

Malcolm Hurrell talks about the coaching and mentoring culture at AstraZeneca and there are links with some of the cultural factors shown in Table 10.1.

> Optimizing the performance of our people in every position in the company is a strategic priority, owned and sponsored by our senior executive team. We have a long history of supporting both coaching and mentoring in the organization, seeing each as being distinctly different in approach and accountability of those involved, but being highly complementary.
>
> ### Coaching
> A tutorial process carried out by the line manager or project manager in order to enhance the performance and development of an employee in their existing role. Seeks to transfer skills and understanding from a more practical point of view drawing on the skills and experience of the coach.
>
> ### Mentoring
> A relationship involving two people, one having more experience of the issue and able to provide organization-wide thinking and context with the development being usually broader and longer-term. We recommend it is carried out by someone outside the line or function relationship and it is often linked to future capability or to people beginning new and challenging positions, possibly in a new environment (e.g. international assignee).

In simple terms we seek to use the coaching process to build capability in role whereas the mentoring process facilitates reflective learning to enhance awareness, understanding and wisdom that can be applied to a broader perspective. Both processes are essential if we are to achieve our aim of being a learning organization able to constantly reinvent itself.

AstraZeneca sees coaching as a core process, expected to be engaged with by all employees, whereas mentoring is taken up on a voluntary basis, both by mentee and mentor. As a learning organization we position acquiring the skills of mentoring as a critical capability of high-performing experienced professionals across the organization. The process provides the opportunity for people to learn from each other, mutual benefit being afforded to both parties and to organizational and team performance.

Wendy Briner cautions against a 'one size fits all' view of culture.

Organizations need to work it out for themselves in a conscious way what coaching culture they want. They need to make the implicit explicit. They should ask themselves, 'What do we want and what difference would it make to us?' rather than thinking that there is one definition of a coaching culture.

How do you develop a mentoring culture?

The previous example illustrates how coaching and mentoring develop as a result of corporate strategy aimed at optimizing the performance of the organization by continually developing the talents and strengths of its people. However, cultural change can develop from the bottom up as well as the top down. It can evolve through the initiative of employees. The next example highlights how volunteer mentors are changing a medical culture in a large inner-city acute hospital trust.

Dr Nancy Redfern describes an employee-driven mentoring initiative which illustrates that developing a mentoring culture takes time.

Newcastle upon Tyne Foundation Trust is a large NHS acute hospital providing care to the population of Newcastle, with tertiary referrals from the North East and beyond. It employs 550 consultants, many of whom are academics at Newcastle Medical and Dental Schools.

Being a consultant in the NHS has always been a responsible job. But doing the job well and meeting the expectations of an increasingly well-informed public while achieving the targets and throughput expected by the NHS was taking its toll. This pressure was even more challenging for our junior staff, who did not yet have the security of a permanent consultant post. We were aware that many trainees looked to their consultants as role models, and thought we should be better prepared than we were for the role. Thus, when an opportunity to attend a mentor development programme presented itself in 1995, several of us were keen to take this up.

The course was a great success. We spent six days (a day a month) learning the skills of mentoring and we used The Skilled Helper framework to guide discussions. Spending time working together, using as our material the challenges and opportunities we faced at work, made us realize the power of mentoring for ourselves. So, having come on the course with the aim of providing mentoring for our trainees, many of us left thinking that we might do better to use our skills among our colleagues.

The next move was to set up a mentoring scheme within the Trust. Offering mentoring to all of the consultants seemed overwhelming, and rather beyond our still nascent skill set. We retreated from this, choosing to use our skills between ourselves while we built up our numbers.

We realized that mentoring is of most use at a time of change, and decided our first focus should be a scheme for newly-appointed consultants. The aims were to provide an opportunity for consultants to have a confidential conversation with someone from outside their area of work, to help them settle into the role of consultant, to manage their work most effectively and achieve their full potential. In the longer term, we hoped that building up the numbers of trained mentors and mentees would create a learning culture in which people would make time to question their own practice, where it would be normal to ask when you don't know something, and where giving and receiving support from colleagues is seen as a sign of strength.

What was achieved?
Each newly-appointed consultant is offered the opportunity of having a mentor, and nearly all meet one of the mentors who introduce them to the scheme and describe how others use mentorship.

Mentoring is described on the consultant induction programme, and some of the experienced mentors explain how we use the scheme among ourselves. Examples of common topics discussed with mentors are outlined and include influencing, managing difficult situations or working with colleagues, team-building, change management, and organizing and prioritizing work or work–life balance.

As the scheme has become more established, the Trust offers a mentor to doctors facing difficult professional situations, or those who are struggling. Thus we are developing some expertise in supporting colleagues in difficulty. Mentoring appears to help people become engaged in making changes in their practice and developing skills to prevent further difficulties, rather than feeling isolated and looking over their shoulder.

The number of consultant mentors has grown gradually, and now 10 per cent of consultants in the Trust are trained mentors. Mentors now also include nurses, midwives, pharmacists, university academics and managers.

Some reflections

By nature, doctors and senior NHS managers prioritize patient care over their own professional and personal development. They have professional values and training based on taking individual responsibility, and a tradition of 'coping' rather than asking for help. For those who do not have a burning issue to discuss, there can be a reluctance to prioritize mentoring for themselves over a busy clinical workload.

So, it takes time for a scheme to become established. Informal feedback from people who have used the mentoring scheme or trained as mentors, about what they gained personally, seems to be the most effective publicity.

In earlier years, a few senior consultants expressed the view that 'mentoring was for the needy, weaker characters, and not something they would entertain'. Either this view has died out as personnel have changed, or the culture is now one in which such opinions are rarely heard. However, for some, there may always be a perception that asking for help is regarded as weakness.

How do you develop a coaching culture?

In the mentoring example above, the culture change happened through training a critical mass of volunteer mentors over a period of several years. In the
example which follows, the driver for change was that a new type of leadership
development was needed to improve performance and deliver results. This
culture change had strong commitment from leaders in the organization.

Shaun Lincoln delivered the Leaders as Coaches (LAC) programme and
worked with Sean Mileusnic, Head of Leadership and Development at Greater
Manchester Police (GMP). They explain how they work together and how a
coaching culture is developing (adapted from Hilpern 2006: 42–5).

> 'The chief benefit of leadership coaching at GMP is that it is not
> task-oriented. It's not about the mechanics of doing things, but about
> looking at yourself as a whole and how you perform. Surely that is the
> most fundamental thing you can change, and that's why I think it's
> working' (Alan Weeks, Coachee, GMP).
>
> There is an ever-increasing need for leadership within the organiza-
> tion to meet rising performance targets, and to enable people to
> develop and reach their potential. GMP therefore took the decision
> to develop a positive culture change around leadership that would
> have an impact on everyone – not just those in supervisory positions.
> A new leadership charter was developed to manage expectations,
> while coaching, mentoring and buddy schemes were introduced
> alongside leadership programmes aimed at staff with high potential.
> 'It's an initiative that represents a radically new way of how the police
> view and nurture leadership,' says Sean Mileusnic. 'Traditionally we
> have been a problem-focused culture, but we are trying to shift to a
> solutions-based way of doing things that gets results quickly.'
>
> Each person on the Leaders as Coaches programme goes on to coach
> three people at any one time. The idea is to bring about a funda-
> mental culture change whereby coaching eventually becomes part of
> the ethos of the organization, and all police officers – and indeed all
> police staff – feel confident in their leadership skills as a result.
>
> The Centre for Excellence in Leadership encourages coachees to state
> individual goals and suggests they rate on a scale of 1 to 10 how well
> they think they are doing in reaching them. But while a more
> problem-based approach might require the coach to focus on the gap

between their rating and 10 – in other words, what's stopping them getting there – the LAC solutions-based model says: 'Wow, you're at 4. Well done. Now, let's look at what got you to 4 and find ways of helping you do more of it so you can reach 10.' It is also significant that LAC is aimed specifically at shifting organizations from a command and control leadership style and focuses heavily on challenging individuals' ingrained ways of thinking.

Some employees already report feeling more competent, confident and in control of their own development. Meanwhile, the general public is happier because they feel GMP staff are more able to make the kind of decisions required to manage crime effectively. Sean Mileusnic stresses that leadership coaching is enabling GMP to implement the philosophy of 'leadership for all' while staying clear of implying that 'one size fits all'.

'In a perfect world, we'd like to have coaches professionally trained right across the organization, but that's impossible in terms of resources,' admits Sean. 'In fact, that was one of our earliest lessons – not to be unrealistic about what we can do.' The aim is to have 36 professionally qualified coaches within the senior ranks, who will follow up their work with accreditation, and a smaller pool of internally trained coaches in each division and branch. 'Not every individual will be a coach or coachee, but we hope that indirectly they will benefit from the coaching culture,' Sean says.

Shaun Lincoln believes the programme is working well largely because leadership coaches within GMP aren't necessarily line managers. 'Sometimes it's actually better that coaches aren't line managers because individuals can usually be open with their coach in a way that perhaps they couldn't be with a line manager,' he says. Coaching at GMP even cuts across ranks. 'Like many organizations, GMP is quite hierarchical, yet you have people coaching people higher up the ranks than them,' he says. 'The great thing about this is that to create a real coaching culture, you need to have coaching working in four ways: the ability to coach each other and yourself, and to coach upwards and downwards.'

What helps or hinders?

The CIPD survey found several reasons why, despite positive attitudes to coaching and mentoring, a successful culture may not develop: 'competing business pressure (66%) forms the main barrier to developing a coaching culture. This is followed by some of the more usual suspects – lack of expertise (52%), lack of investment (48%) and poor senior management commitment (48%)' (CIPD 2006: 12).

Where there is senior management commitment to leadership development across the organization there is a strong possibility that a coaching and mentoring culture will develop.

Wendy Briner has carried out research into what happens to participants of the Ashridge Leadership Process who have ongoing coaching as part of the programme. She finds that coaching is a vital component in leadership development but that the sustainability of behaviour change in leaders back at work varies according to their leadership culture.

> By the late 1990s the Leadership Development Programme was still a popular offering at Ashridge Management College but its shelf-life was ageing. Developing its successor involved asking past participants what they valued about the programme and what suggestions they had for improvement. Their message was clear. The workshop is great, we go away with enthusiastic intentions, but the impact in practice is diluted, nothing sustains us.
>
> Ashridge Leadership Process was so christened because development takes place over six months. Coaching is integrated into this process, starting with a telephone conversation prior to the workshop, with two meetings during the workshop and two meetings in the subsequent six months. We set up a developmental network of coaches whose aim was to enable participants to make sense of the self-awareness, ideas and aspirations that the workshop provided, so that they could become self-sustaining in developing their leadership in practice.
>
> The coaching approach we use is primarily solutions-focused, complemented by appreciative enquiry. Coaches value and have confidence in their client capacities. They encourage clients to identify and elaborate what is constructive in them and their situations. They ask clients to consider who they are, what they have and what they want. They aim to help them to focus on what they can do and want to do in their context.
>
> **What leaders value most in their development process**
> They tell us there are four interactive and integrative learning processes that make most difference to their development in practice.

These are shown in Figure 10.1.

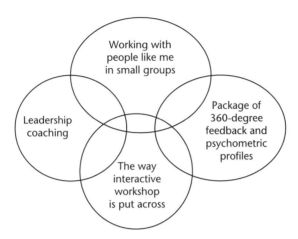

Figure 10.1   Four interactive and integrative learning processes

Development is a social and practical process so the opportunities to discuss, reflect and try out alternatives, while focusing on a future that is seen as in some way better, generates tangible benefits. Leadership coaching is one of those processes and leaders value its unique contribution.

Leaders say they value coaching because:

- It is one-to-one, confidential and a period of time that is separate from the frantic activity of everyday work. They can stop the clock and step outside to reflect on what they're doing and the impact they're having
- Your coach is a professional in listening, asking the right provoking questions, summarizing and running developmental discussions. The coach is interested in you but impartial and not implicated in other aspects of your life
- It provides a focus and brings clarity around your own agenda and you find your own solutions that do make a difference
- It is affirming and enables you to use your capabilities to make more effective contributions

Culture can help or hinder coaching

Coaching is popular; most participants take the coaching opportunities offered and report significant benefits. They work out rapidly how they can make good use of what is, for many, a new experience.

Being coached and finding it useful, they say, enables them to incorporate coaching into their way of relating.

We compared four organizations and the impact of coaching, and, where the organization culture is seen to value relational leadership, coaching is seen to be useful and compatible. By relational leadership we mean doing things with people in a participatory way to deliver results, i.e. meetings which are participatory, bouncing ideas off one another, using awaydays. In these organizations, change is in tune with the culture and is more acknowledged, valued and sustained.

Among leadership cultures where delivery is based on structure and consistent processes, coaching is seen to be relevant, but less durable. Likewise, in cultures where professional autonomy, rather than teamwork, is emphasized, coaching is personally useful but has little impact on the culture. In these cultures, there were changes in individuals' leadership style as a result of coaching, but there was less appreciation by, for example, colleagues, of its relevance. A colleague might wonder, 'Shouldn't she or he be tougher?' or, 'This more participatory approach may be OK for today's problem but will it work in the future?'

Reflections for leadership development

- Coaching enables leaders to construct a bridge from having good intentions to putting them into practice in their complex context. Having some time to do this in a personalized and bespoke way recognizes how necessary this apparently simple step is in bringing about significant positive development and impact
- Many developers underestimate the impact that coaching has with the individual and the organization. They see workshops, content and exercises as most important in fostering development. Feedback from leaders suggests that workshop and group sessions have a part to play in orienting, stimulating and supporting leaders in their development but leadership coaching is much more valued. It is a vital component in a leadership development process.

Shaun Lincoln develops coaching with further education colleges as well as with police organizations. He recognizes some helpful and unhelpful factors in organizational cultures.

What helps?

1 Agreement on the need for culture change and for senior management to actively support this.

2   For senior management to understand what coaching is and the benefits it can bring. In the organizations where we have had most success this has often been where the leader had already experienced coaching.

3   Senior management team commitment to achieving this and being trained as coaches themselves so they are part of the change they want to see.

4   Time and space for the coaching to happen.

5   A clear need for culture change to happen as the result of feedback such as the outcome of an external inspection, or external drivers to improve performance, distribute leadership and help people realize their full potential and thus improve organizational performance.

6   A request for coaching from potential coachees themselves – typically via staff surveys.

7   After an initial coaching cohort, coaching is reported to make a clear difference, and even better if it is seen to deliver to the bottom line (and thus represent a return on investment), which in turn results in a second and third cohort going ahead and coaching becoming more widespread and sustainable.

8   Our work at creating coaching cultures has worked best where the initial training has been high impact and created a 'wow' factor, and where this was immediately followed up by participants formally coaching people they do not line manage for four to six months, even if their long-term goal was to coach their own teams. This has the twin benefits of building their confidence to use these new skills while also keeping the momentum. Equally important is to then have a group supervision session six weeks after to share and celebrate coaching success stories ('quick wins'), and iron out any questions and concerns. Finally it is important that the college principal hears the progress made in a final review day so that they decide how to develop and sustain this.

9   Not taking a deficit approach to coaching – for this reason we use a solutions-focused coaching model. This builds on what managers already have, rather than working with deficits.

What hinders?

1   A lack of all the above.

2   The cost of using external coaches.

3   Coaching being seen as imposed, with little buy-in or consensus.

4   Lack of understanding of what coaching is by senior management team.

5 Lack of buy-in from coachees if there has been no prior consultation with them, and fear that coaching is remedial: 'If you are being coached you have a problem'.

6 After the training, just relying on managers to then use these new skills informally with their own teams, without then developing confidence and expertise via formally coaching two or three people they do not line manage. Where little or no formalization has been in place to sustain initial enthusiasm for the coaching training, impact has been less, there have been no follow-up cohorts and the organization has not moved so significantly towards creating a coaching culture.

7 Lack of resources.

What are the links with other aspects of learning and performance?

In recent years there has been rapid development in the areas of talent management, appraisal, personal development plans (PDPs) and continuing professional development. Those who have been trained in coaching and mentoring skills have found these transferable to activities such as appraisal interviewing. While there is a difference in purpose between these activities, people are finding that one can lead to the other. For example, a problem identified in an appraisal interview may lead to referral for coaching on a specific issue. An action stated in a PDP may lead to some mentoring within the organization, or externally, with regard to career planning.

Malcolm Hurrell explains the interface between learning, coaching and mentoring in AstraZeneca (AZ).

Coaching and mentoring are used within performance management alongside other supporting processes and materials (e.g. executive coaching or action learning groups). They are used within a philosophy that effective learning takes place not on formal training courses but 'in real time': predominantly 'on the job' (70 per cent); supported by 'off the job' manager support and 360-degree feedback (20 per cent); and through appropriate training interventions (10 per cent). This philosophy therefore relies fundamentally on the ability of managers and experienced colleagues to engage in active coaching and, for some individuals, to complement this with a mentoring relationship. Key supporting factors are:

1 Clear accountability between manager and employee in terms of

performance management and supporting performance. Mentoring must not confuse or substitute this core process.

2   Skills workshops are provided on coaching and mentoring, with e-learning modules for both sides of the relationship.

3   Coaching is available for performance, skills, management, strategy and executive leadership.

4   The manager is constantly looking for different situations where coaching and learning can take place: projects; deputizing; representing the team; analysing a problem and recommending change; expanding responsibilities. We would also expect the employee to be contributing to this by: defining individual learning objectives; suggesting learning opportunities and actions; and taking responsibility for their own development.

5   External coaches traditionally used to support senior-level executives in areas of on-boarding, expanded responsibilities and integration, development, performance, managing vision and purpose, and strategy. External coaches offer an expertise in the challenges inherent in senior management positions, unique insights, objective feedback and independent confidentiality. External coaches can often probe and challenge more than an internal coach can. All AZ external coaches are validated to ensure consistency of outcomes given that the focus here is predominantly on executive high impact leadership.

In the very different organizational culture of senior doctors who had been trained as mentors and who were trying to develop a mentoring scheme for themselves and for their junior colleagues, what were the links with other learning initiatives? **Dr Nancy Redfern** continues her story.

Our real breakthrough came with the advent of consultant appraisal. This became mandatory in 2001, and linked to revalidation and clinical excellence awards. But the notion of discussing progress and potential, revealing strengths and weaknesses to a colleague, was very different from the culture of the doctor as expert, with which the majority of consultants had grown up. How was the organization going to introduce appraisal for all and make it a genuinely valuable exercise rather than just a 'tick box'? The mentors decided to offer to be appraisers. We thought that the best way forward would be a peer appraisal system which at least reduced the threat of disclosing uncertainties to a manager. This system would then feed to the clinical director. Peers needed the skills for a confidential conversation and the ability to draw out the key points to feed into management. They needed the ability to separate these out from the things that the client wanted to work on personally. Our 'mentor' skill set also proved to be very useful for appraisal, so we offered to help in the training of appraisers and in the development of the appraisal system. Having trained mentors as appraisers meant that when more complex issues were raised at appraisal, the appraiser could put the client in touch with a mentor.

This led to visible support from the medical director, both for appraisal and for mentoring. From this came the opportunity to raise awareness at the consultant induction, giving new people the clear impression that mentoring is 'normal' or 'what's expected' in the organization. Informal sessions in which clients describe their experiences to their peers raise awareness and expectation, which influences the culture.

At this time, mentoring was becoming more popular in both the public and private sector. The Trust gradually realized that having a mentoring scheme would be a selling point when attracting new staff. Once the organization had 'bought into' mentoring being a good thing to offer, we obtained secretarial support from the HR department to manage the practicalities of the scheme. A scheme will only work if you know who has been appointed, and introduce them to the trained mentors.

In the early years, momentum was largely sustained by one 'champion', who was spurred on by the value everyone got from the course and its relevance to everyday practice. People used their skills with trainees, with patients, in meetings, in managing change and developing services. They described themselves as better at taking hold of personal and professional development, taking on new roles, capitalizing on success and dealing with severe difficulties. Many felt increased confidence and job satisfaction, from better working relationships and teamwork, enhanced abilities at problem-solving and an increased sense of collegiality. So, although there wasn't yet a visible mentoring network, mentoring skills were making an impact on everyday work.

Having one and now several champions who have gradually gained more senior positions in the organization has increased the visibility and acceptability of the scheme.

What difference does it make?

In the case example above, Nancy Redfern explains the link between using mentoring skills and using appraisal skills. She also shows how these skills were transferable and made a difference to the way doctors worked in a range of situations. In this section there are more examples of some of the observable differences in organizations when coaching and mentoring cultures develop.

Shaun Lincoln quotes leaders in the further education sector to illustrate some outcomes of the Leaders as Coaches (LAC) programme.

> The examples below focus specifically on how we have worked with organizations to develop a coaching leadership style and in some cases a coaching culture. The programme can be used in two ways:
>
> 1 Manager-coach version – helping managers in the organization develop an informal coaching leadership style with the staff they manage
> 2 Internal coach version – developing individuals to act as a formal pool of coaches available to colleagues on a no-line manager basis
>
> One key aspect of creating a coaching culture via the LAC programme is the team-building between the coaches themselves, as well as between coach and coachee: 'We undertook the LAC programme so that the senior management team could offer coaching support to middle managers. This proved to be extremely powerful in terms of both self-awareness and team awareness, and it generated a terrific "wow" factor and a buzz. Even experienced managers learned from this experience and carried it into their teams. We've seen positive development right across the piece, an impact right across the board. Coaching can certainly be a catalyst to trigger step change. The team awareness aspect has been particularly interesting. Managers are learning about themselves and appreciating that they have their own roles to play in the team, and that they may in fact be part of the problem, which previously they would have sought to externalize' (David Pomfret, Principal, Boston College).
>
> Another outcome is that several of the senior management teams now use coaching techniques in their meetings. Some structure their meetings around such techniques. The solutions-focused approach has led to culture change, to greater sharing of problems, focusing on what works and finding solutions

'The main impact I would describe is that firstly it has had an impact on management behaviour in terms of how they have approached managing their staff. Secondly it has changed the language of dialogue about issues in the organization. People are recognizing that as culture is beginning to change, people are expected not only to present problems but also to present solutions as well. This does not mean that the solutions identified are "soft", they are often addressing very difficult issues that require the effective use of performance management tools, for example capability and discipline. Middle managers are more challenging in a positive solutions-orientated approach. This has been challenging, in a positive way, to the senior management team' (Paul Head, Principal and Chief Executive, College of North East London).

Another difference is that coaching has often been most successful where a pool of internal coaches has been developed. This enables staff to discuss with coaches aspects or concerns about their work that they would be less likely to discuss with their line manager. In this way they can obtain many of the benefits of external coaching in a way that the organization can afford. It also increases the likelihood that this organizational learning is retained and acted on. Key to this has been using a non-directive coaching approach, as in the example earlier in the chapter from GMP.

Malcolm Hurrell shares some learning from initiatives taken at AstraZeneca where the GROW model is used for internal coaching by all core staff.

The core approach to coaching in AZ is the GROW model.

Goal
Here the coach engages the employee in identifying the overriding goal – what is the longer-term change in performance/development we are seeking to achieve?

Reality
Here the coach helps the employee tell the story of what is not going well or missed opportunities to be more effective. This phase can be of enormous help in itself by helping the employee appreciate the issues. The coach can challenge beliefs and misconceptions of the employee and help break down the tasks and focus on those that will leverage greatest impact on performance.

Options
Here the coach helps the employee to see what good performance would look like and to explore different ways to achieve this. It is an

opportunity to share personal experience and insight and to establish clear outcomes to be achieved. Finally the coach guides the employee to a clear choice of what to work on and gets a commitment to action.

Will
Here the coach helps the employee move to action by exploring ways to deliver the desired performance. Once decided this helps form a detailed plan of action alongside agreed ways to monitor and evaluate improved performance.

A senior director in finance talks about some of the outcomes of a coaching programme: 'I am more curious, more questioning, more demanding and stretching in my questions. I have seen a real difference in my team and in their approach to learning. We are embedding coaching in performance management targets. The performance of my direct reports is increasing. We are using a common language around capability and learning. I have now taken up an executive coach as ongoing complementary learning.'

A coaching intervention was implemented in AZ Information Systems (IS). It was a passion for value leadership programme based on the material 'From Good to Great' and used three key statements, namely that the IS organization should focus on:

- What it is passionate about
- What it is best at
- Delivering recognizable value

Aside from the leadership capability interventions, the programme introduced coaching based on applying these key statements at a personal level:

- Providing coaching to individuals using the 'Now Discover Your Strengths' approach devised by Gallop, which provides insights on your 'natural talents' which you will therefore be passionate about and can turn into strengths.
- Providing coaching to individuals using 360-degree feedback which helps individuals understand what they are 'best at' in other people's eyes.
- Requiring individuals to present back to groups of people on the 'value they had delivered'.

External coaches led groups of leaders over three days, followed by one-to-one external coaching sessions, wrapped up by re-forming the leaders' groups for a two-day session, nine months later. What was the impact on individuals and on the business?

From a business perspective, 77 per cent of line managers stated that they had seen an improvement in leadership contribution. From an individual perspective, both the principles and the results from 'Now Discover Your Strengths' resulted in some significant changes. These were either to the approach that leaders took to their roles or to their decisions in changing roles – sometimes quite radically. Some IS leaders left the organization while others applied for, and got, more senior posts.

Two important lessons were learned. Firstly, that there is power in the simple message that we should be 'developing our talents into strengths' rather than trying to become 'fully rounded people by always focusing on our weaknesses'. This message breathes new life into individual development and the approach it can take. Secondly, that the organization needs to be ready for the amount of internal people movement and sometimes turnover that occurs as a result of deep-searching individual coaching.

How do you assess your organization?

If the benefits of coaching and mentoring at work are to be fully effective, then the culture of the organization will encourage, sustain, support and reward those who lead and manage these forms of learning and development. Clutterbuck and Megginson (2005: 96) identify four progressive stages on this journey: nascent, where there is little commitment in evidence; tactical, where the organization recognizes a need but does not show understanding about what will be necessary; strategic, where managers are involved in coaching as part of everyday work and where this is rewarded; and embedded, where coaching and mentoring are an integral part of learning and development and where all levels are involved in both the delivery and the receipt of coaching and mentoring.

The questions below have been developed from the material provided in this chapter by the four contributors. They reflect some of the factors which have been highlighted as significant, in practice, when developing a coaching or mentoring culture. They may help you to reflect upon the development of a coaching and mentoring culture in your organization.

Box 10.1 Assessing the coaching and mentoring culture of your organization

1   Are performance and development a strategic priority?
2   Does your organization link individual development to business performance?
3   Does senior management actively sponsor individual development? How?
4   What systems, procedures or processes support individual development? How well do these operate?
5   Are coaching and mentoring viewed as learning and development in your organization? If not, how are they viewed?
6   Are coaching and mentoring encouraged throughout the organization? If so, in what ways are they encouraged?
7   Do senior managers talk about using coaches and mentors themselves?
8   Do leaders and managers coach and mentor staff?
9   How would you describe the style of leadership in your organization? How does it fit with coaching and mentoring values?
10 In what ways are teamwork, participation and interdependence encouraged and rewarded?
11 Is there a 'blame' culture at any level in the organization?
12 Is there a culture where 'everything is a learning opportunity' operating at any level in the organization?
13 What complementary forms of learning are provided to support coaching and mentoring, for example action learning and e-learning?
14 Is coaching and mentoring non-hierarchical: downwards, upwards, peers, self?
15 Do managers embed coaching and mentoring in the way they work? How?
16 What resources are available for training and support of coaches and mentors?
17 Can you access both internal and external coaching and mentoring?
18 Is coaching and mentoring seen as developing potential, or for remedying deficits?
19 How are the outcomes of coaching and mentoring reported?
20 What would be your main recommendations for your organization now that you have completed this questionnaire?

Summary

In this chapter we have:

- Argued that in order for coaching and mentoring to be effective they must be integrated into the whole learning and development culture of the organization.
- Reported the experience of four contributors who have been involved in coaching or mentoring in public and private sector organizations.
- Identified key features of coaching and mentoring cultures and highlighted factors which help and hinder the development of coaching and mentoring at work.
- Used the experience of the contributors to illustrate how coaching and mentoring are linked to other aspects of learning, development and performance at work.
- Concluded with a self-assessment questionnaire, based upon the experience of the contributors, to help you identify the coaching and mentoring culture in your organization.

Appendix: useful contacts and websites

AC: The Association for Coaching
www.associationforcoaching.com

APECS: Association for Professional Executive Coaching and Supervision
www.apecs.org

BPS: British Psychological Society (see Special Group in Coaching Psychology)
www.bps.org.uk

CIPD: Chartered Institute of Personnel and Development
www.cipd.co.uk

Coaching and Mentoring Network
www.coachingnetwork.org.uk

EMCC: European Mentoring and Coaching Council
www.emccouncil.org

ENTO: Employment National Training Organization
www.ento.co.uk

ICF: International Coaching Federation
www.coachfederation.org

Mindtools
www.mindtools.com

Bibliography

Adair, J. (1986) *Effective Teambuilding*. London: Pan.

Bandura, A. (1969) *Principles of Behaviour Modification*. New York: Holt, Rinehart & Winston.

Barden, S. (2006) The team: the heart of executive coaching, *Coach and Mentor: The Journal of the Oxford School of Coaching and Mentoring*, 6: 6–7.

Belbin, M. (2000) *Beyond the Team*. London: Butterworth-Heinemann.

Belbin, M. (2003) *Team Roles at Work*, 2nd edn. London: Butterworth-Heinemann.

Berglas, S. (2002) The very real dangers of executive coaching, *Harvard Business Review*, 80(6): 86–92.

Berne, E. (1972) *What Do You Say After You Say Hello?* London: Corgi.

Berne, E. (1976) *Beyond Games and Scripts*. New York: Ballantine.

Bion, W.R. (1961) *Experiences in Groups*. London: Tavistock.

Blanchard, K. (1994) *Leadership and the One-Minute Manager*. London: Harper-Collins Business.

Blatner, A. (1996) *Acting-In: Practical Applications of Psychodramatic Methods*, 3rd edn. New York: Springer.

Bluckert, P. (2006) *Psychological Dimensions to Coaching*. Maidenhead: Open University Press.

Bolles, R.N. (2002) *What Color is Your Parachute? A Practical Guide for Job Hunters and Career Changers*. Berkeley, CA: Ten Speed Press.

Bond, T. (1993) *Standards and Ethics for Counselling in Action*. London: Sage.

Burgoyne, J. (1990) Doubts about competence, in M. Devine (ed.) *The Photofit Manager*. London: Unwin Hyman.

CIPD (2006) *Learning and Development: Annual Survey Report*. London: CIPD.

Clutterbuck, D. (2001) *Everyone Needs a Mentor*. London: CIPD.

Clutterbuck, D. and Megginson, D. (2005) *Making Coaching Work*. London: CIPD.

Clutterbuck, D. and Ragins, B.R. (2002) *Mentoring for Diversity*. London: Butterworth-Heinemann.

Connor, M. (1994) *Training the Counsellor*. London: Routledge.

Connor, M. (1997) *Mentoring for Medics*. York: University College of Ripon and York St John.

Connor, M., Bynoe A.G., Redfern N., Pokora, J. and Clarke J. (2000) Developing senior doctors as mentors: a form of continuing professional development. Report of an initiative to develop a network of senior doctors as mentors, 1994–99, *Medical Education*, 34: 747–53.

Covey, S.R. (1989) *The Seven Habits of Highly Effective People*. London: Simon & Schuster.

De Bono, E. (1992) *Serious Creativity*. New York: Harper Business.

Downey, M. (2003) *Effective Coaching: Lessons from the Coaches' Coach*, 2nd edn. London: Texere.

Easterby-Smith, M., Burgoyne, J. and Araujo, L. (eds) (1999) *Organisational Learning and the Learning Organisation*. London: Sage.

Eaton, J. and Johnson, R. (2001) *Coaching Successfully*. London: Dorling Kindersley.

Egan, G. (2002) *The Skilled Helper*, 7th edn. Belmont, CA: Thomson Brooks/Cole.

Egan, G. (2006) *Essentials of Skilled Helping*. Belmont, CA: Thomson Wadsworth.

Egan, G. (forthcoming) *The Skilled Helper*, 8th edn. Belmont, CA: Thomson Brooks/ Cole.

Eglin, R. (2006) Building a more efficient society, *The Sunday Times*, 14 May, p. 6.

European Mentoring and Coaching Council (2004) *Guidelines on Supervision: An Interim Statement*, www.emccouncil.org.

European Mentoring and Coaching Council (2005) *Press Release EMCC19*, December, www.emccouncil.org.

Fisher, R. and Ury, W. (1987) *Getting to Yes*. London: Arrow.

Flood, R.L. (1999) *Rethinking the Fifth Discipline*. London: Routledge.

Francis, D. (1994) *Managing Your Own Career*. London: HarperCollins.

Fraser, S. and Greenhalgh, T. (2001) Complexity science: coping with complexity, educating for capability, *British Medical Journal*, 323: 799–803.

Fritchie, R. and Leary, M. (1998) *Resolving Conflicts in Organisations*. London: Lemos & Crane.

Fritts, P.J. (1998) *The New Managerial Mentor*. Palo Alto, CA: Davies Black.

Gallwey, T. (2000) *The Inner Game of Work*. London: Orion.

Garret-Harris, R. and Garvey, B. (2005) *Towards a Framework for Mentoring in the NHS*, Evaluation Report on behalf of the NHS. Sheffield: Sheffield Hallam University.

Garvey, B. and Garret-Harris, R. (2005) *The Benefits of Mentoring: A Literature Review*, report for East Mentors Forum. Sheffield: Mentoring and Coaching Research Unit, Sheffield Hallam University.

Goldsmith, M., Lyons, L. and Freas, A. (eds) (2000) *Coaching for Leadership: How the World's Greatest Coaches Help Leaders Learn*. San Francisco, CA: Pfeiffer.

Goleman, D. (1998) *Working With Emotional Intelligence*. London: Bloomsbury.

Greene, J. (2003) *Solution Focused Coaching*. Ashland, OR: Momentum.

Hardingham, A., Brearley, M., Moorhouse, A. and Ventner, B.(2004) *The Coach's Coach: Personal Development for Personal Developers*. London: Chartered Institute of Personnel Development.

Harris, A. and Harris, T. (1985) *Staying OK*. London: Pan.

Hawkins, P. and Shohet, R. (2000) *Supervision in the Helping Professions*. Buckingham: Open University Press.

Hilpern, K. (2006) Bringing law to order, *Coaching at Work*, 1(2): 42–5.

Hofstede, G. (1994) *Cultures and Organisations*. London: HarperCollins Business.

Honey, P. and Mumford, A. (1992) *A Manual of Learning Styles*. Maidenhead: P. Honey Publications.

Honey, P. and Mumford, A. (2006) *The Learning Styles Questionnaire: 80 Item*. Maidenhead: P. Honey Publications.

Inskipp, F. and Proctor, P. (1989) *Skills for Supervising and being Supervised*. St Leonards on Sea: Alexia Publications.

Jackson, P.Z. (2002) *The Solutions Focus*. London: Nicholas Brealey.

James, M. and Jongeward, D. (1971) *Born to Win*. Reading, MA: Addison-Wesley.

Jarvis, J. (2004) *Coaching and Buying Coaching Services – a CIPD Guide*. London: CIPD.

Karpmann, S. (1968) Fairy tales and script drama analysis, *Transactional Analysis Bulletin*, 7(26): 39–43.

Katzenbach, J.R. and Smith, D.K. (1993) *The Wisdom of Teams: Creating the High-performance Organization*. Boston, MA: Harvard University Press.

Kelly, G. (1963) *A Theory of Personality*. New York: W.W. Norton.

Kennedy, G. (1992) *The Perfect Negotiation*. London: Century.

Kirkpatrick, D.L. (1994) *Evaluating Training Programs: The Four Levels*. San Francisco: Berrett-Koehler.

Kolb, D. (1984) *Experiential Learning*. Englewood Cliffs, NJ: Prentice Hall.

Kolb, D. and Fry, R. (1975) Towards an applied theory of experiential learning, in C.L. Cooper (ed.) *Theories of Group Processes*. London: Wiley.

Korzybski, A. (1994) *Science and Sanity: An Introduction to Non-Aristotelian Systems and General Semantics*, 5th edn. Brooklyn, NY: Institute of General Semantics.

Kotter, J.P. (1998) *What Leaders Really Do*. Boston, MA: Harvard Business School Press.

Lewin, K. (1951) *Field Theory in Social Science: Selected Theoretical Papers*, ed. D. Cartwright. New York: Harper & Row.

Luft, J. (1969) *Of Human Interaction*. Palo Alto, CA: National Press.

Luft, J. (1970) *Group Processes: An Introduction to group Dynamics*. Palo Alto, CA: National Press Books.

McKay, M., Davis, M. and Fanning, P. (1981) *Thoughts and Feelings*. Richmond, CA: New Harbinger Publicaitons.

Megginson, D., Clutterbuck, D., Garvey, B., Stokes, P. and Garret-Harris, R. (2006) *Mentoring in Action: A Practical Guide for Managers*. London: Kogan Page.

Neenan, M. and Dryden, W. (2002) *Life Coaching: A Cognitive Behavioural Approach*. London: Routledge.

Parsloe, E. (1999) *The Manager as Coach and Mentor*. London: Institute of Personnel and Development.

Parsloe, E. and Wray, M. (2000) *Coaching and Mentoring: Practical Methods to Improve Learning*. London: Kogan Page.

Pedler, M. and Aspinwall, K. (1996) *Perfect PLC?* Maidenhead: McGraw-Hill.

Pedler, M., Burgoyne, J. and Boydell T. (1991) *The Learning Company: A Strategy for Sustainable Development.* Maidenhead: McGraw-Hill.

Pedler, M., Burgoyne, J. and Boydell, T. (1994) *A Manager's Guide to Self Development.* Maidenhead: McGraw-Hill.

Phillips, A. and Pokora, J. (2004) Diagnostic versus active listening, unpublished presentation to GP Leadership Programme, Northern Deanery.

Pokora, J. and Briner, W. (1999) Teams and the learning organisation, in R. Stewart (ed.) *Gower Handbook of Teamworking.* Aldershot: Gower.

Rawlinson, J.G. (1986) *Creative Thinking and Brainstorming.* Aldershot: Gower.

Revans, R. (1983) *ABC of Action Learning.* Bromley: Chartwell-Bratt.

Rich, J.R. (2003) *Brainstorm: Tap into Your Creativity to Generate Awesome Ideas and Tremendous Results.* Franklin Lakes, NJ: Career Press.

Rickards, T. (1997) *Creativity and Problem Solving at Work.* Aldershot: Gower.

Robbins, A. (1992) *Awaken the Giant Within.* Riverside, NJ: Simon & Schuster.

Rogers, C.R. (1961) *On Becoming a Person.* London: Constable.

Rogers, C.R. (1983) *Freedom to Learn in the 80s.* Columbus, OH: Charles Merrill.

Rogers, J. (2004) *Coaching Skills: A Handbook.* Maidenhead: Open University Press.

Schein, E. (1990) *Career Anchors: Discovering Your Real Values.* San Francisco, CA: Jossey-Bass/Pfeiffer.

Senge, P.M. (1992) The Fifth Discipline. London: Century Business.

Starr, J. (2003) *The Coaching Manual.* London: Pearson Education.

Stone, F.M. (1999) *Coaching, Counselling and Mentoring.* New York: American Management Association.

Stone, D., Patton, B. and Heen, S. (1999) *Difficult Conversations: How to Discuss What Matters Most.* London: Michael Joseph.

Sulaiman, T. (2006) How to mentor: it's a shared experience, *The Times,* 11 May.

Tuckman, R.W. (1965) Developmental sequences in small groups, *Psychological Bulletin,* 63: 384–99.

Vickers, A. and Bavister, S. (2005) *Teach Yourself Coaching.* London: Hodder Arnold.

Whitmore, J. (2002) *Coaching for Performance: GROWing People, Performance and Purpose,* 3rd edn. London: Nicholas Brealey.

Whitworth, L., Kimsey-House H. and Sandahl P. (1998) *Co-Active Coaching: New Skills for Coaching People Toward Success in Work and Life.* Mountain View, CA: Davies Black.

Zdenek, M. (1983) *The Right Brain Experience.* London: Corgi Books.

Zeus, P. and Skiffington, S. (2000) *The Complete Guide to Coaching at Work.* North Ryde, NSW. McGraw-Hill.

Index

Related books from Open University Press
Purchase from www.openup.co.uk or order through your local bookseller

---

DEVELOPING A COACHING BUSINESS

Jenny Rogers

- How do I set up a coaching business?
- How do I find clients?
- How do I market myself successfully?

If you are considering these questions, then this is the book for you.

The coaching market is thriving but many coaches need practical help on how to develop and grow their businesses. Being a good coach is never enough. This book gives practical help based on many years of successful experience. Many coaches make the mistake of starting too broadly when the secret is to find a niche – but how do you do this? How do you find your natural clients? How do they find you? What should you charge? Should you have an office or can you work from home? Start-up costs are never as minimal as they might look, so how do you sustain yourself while you are building the business?

It is essential to promote your fledgling business but which methods work and which are just a waste of time and money? You must have a web site but what should it contain to carry the right message about you and your coaching practice? Then there is the whole question of selling – a process many coaches dread but which has to be done because word of mouth on its own will never generate enough clients to earn a decent living. Finally, how big do you ultimately want your business to be? What are the plusses and minuses of growth?

This book explains step by step how to build a successful new coaching business using an innovative method of selling with integrity. Using helpful case studies, Jenny Rogers clearly analyses the practical issues that can make or break a new venture. This book is the first step in running a successful coaching business.

Contents
Series Preface – Introduction – Coaching as a business – Positioning: Identifying your niche – Promoting your offer: Foundations – Presenting yourself to clients – Selling – Up and running: Managing your brand – The future – Bibliography – Useful websites – Acknowledgements – Index.

2006 160pp

ISBN-13: 978 0 335 22049 6 (ISBN-10: 0 335 22049 5) Paperback
ISBN-13: 978 0 335 22050 2 (ISBN-10: 0 335 22050 9) Hardback

COACHING, MENTORING AND ORGANIZATIONAL CONSULTANCY
SUPERVISION AND DEVELOPMENT

Peter Hawkins and Nick Smith

- What are the key skills needed to be a successful coach, mentor or supervisor?
- How can personal development be effectively facilitated?
- What are the ethical guidelines for practicing as a coach, mentor or organizational consultant?

In the last ten years, there has been an enormous growth in the fields of coaching, mentoring and consultancy. These professions, like psychotherapy and counselling before them, are going through a phase of professionalization, with the establishment of formal standards, European bodies and standard requirements for supervision.

This book provides a response to these growing demands with sections that examine:

- Differences and similarities between coaching, mentoring and organizational consultancy
- Personal and professional development that leads to sustainable change
- Qualities, capabilities, skills and values necessary for effective coaching, mentoring and supervision
- Guidelines for practice

Divided into three parts the book first discusses the practice of coaching, mentoring and consultancy. A second section goes on to look at development and supervision of these roles whilst a third section addresses the wider issues of training, skills and capacities required in these roles. Throughout, information is presented in an accessible and user-friendly way which, whether they have previous knowledge of these areas or not, should enable readers to fully understand the benefits of the methods discussed.

Contents
*Acknowledgements – Preface – Golden threads of practice – **Section one: Coaching, mentoring and organizational consultancy** – Introduction to section one – Coaching – Mentoring – Team coaching – Organisational coaching and consultancy – Creating a coaching culture – **Section two: Development and supervision** – Introduction to section two – The development of coaches, mentors and consultants – Coaching, Mentoring and consultancy: why, what and how – Seven-eyed process model of supervision – Supervising in groups and peer groups – Shadow consultancy of consultant teams – **Section three: The skills and capacities for coaches, mentors, consultants and supervisors** – Introduction to section three – Developing key skills for coaches, mentors and consultants and supervisors – The key qualities or capacities – Ethical capacity – Supervision across the difference: transcultural supervision – Conclusion: Polishing the professional mirror – Appendix one: APECS ethical guidelines – Appendix two: EMCC guidelines on supervision – Appendix three: AFS code of ethics and good practice – Appendix four: International coach federation code of ethics – Appendix five: Deference threshold – Resources – Bibliography – Feedback request – Index.*

2006 368pp

ISBN-13: 978 0 335 21815 8 (ISBN-10: 0 335 21815 6) Paperback
ISBN-13: 978 0 335 21816 5 (ISBN-10: 0 335 21816 4) Hardback

REALLY MANAGING HEALTH CARE
Valerie Iles

Valerie Iles has such a sensitive no-nonsense style that she easily succeeds in seducing the reader to accept her arguments about what is going so badly wrong with management in health care ... The case studies can only be described as 'gems' ... But perhaps the greatest message this book can give to the NHS, and health care managers in particular, is that change is unstoppable. All organisms must adapt with their environment or die.

Health Service Journal

Yes! This is a book that draws heavily on real-life observations with an appropriate balance of theory and pragmatism. It tackles the challenges we all face in our everday work – managing people, change, money, ourselves and organisations.

Nursing Times

... anyone who has a part to play in managing health services would benefit from reading it.

British Medical Journal

Much has been made of the distinction between management and leadership, but in health care this separation is unhelpful. Like the first edition, this completely revised edition of *Really Managing Health Care* describes a model, real management that brings the two elements together and demonstrates its application in health care settings. Drawing on theory across a wide range of management disciplines and illustrating these with practical examples, Valerie Iles succinctly answers three crucial questions:

- How can I manage clinical professionals?
- How can I increase the influence of my service?
- What changes do I need to introduce to improve the quality of care my service is offering?

Written specifically for people suspicious of management jargon, *Really Managing Health Care* is designed for service leaders from across health and social care, and introduces ways of approaching the management task which recognize the particular dynamics of this field.

Contents
Acknowledgements – Introduction – Really managing people: working through others – Really managing people: working with others – Really managing people: working for others – Really managing resources – Really managing change – Really managing yourself – Really managing organizations – Case studies – Concluding thoughts – Appendix 1: How not to be 'nice' – Appendix 2: Clinical practice and real management – Appendix 3: Further reading – Index.

2005 296pp

ISBN-13: 978 0 335 21009 1 (ISBN-10: 0 335 21009 0) Paperback
ISBN-13: 978 0 335 21010 7 (ISBN-10: 0 335 21010 4) Hardback